A Century In A Small Town

One Family's Stories

Evelyn Sangster Benson

Evelyn Sangster Benson

Enjoy!

Westminster Publishing

New Westminster, British Columbia, Canada

2013

Dedicated to the memory of

JAMES LEWIS "Lewie" SANGSTER,

1891 - 1968

my father and my inspiration.

Book design by H. Mueller Design
Edited by Don Benson
Cover art by Kim Benson
Photos:
The Sangster Collection
New Westminster Museum & Archives
New Westminster Public Library
City Hall Collection

Canadian Cataloguing in Publication Data
Benson, Evelyn 1934 –
      A Century In A Small Town, One Family's Stories, 1st ed.
      ISBN 978-1-895493-02-3

      1. History—New Westminster—British Columbia
      2. New Westminster—History
      3. Oral History
      971.133

Westminster Publishing
Unit 116
707 Eighth Street
New Westminster, B.C. V3M 3S6
Canada

Foreword

History books, in their quest for accuracy, often can be quite boring exactly because the human elements of the characters are always missing.

By contrast, in this wonderful collection of short stories, Evelyn Benson succeeds in capturing the history of a small town in the Pacific Northwest in full colour, warts and all. Through the use of oral tradition, Benson paints what life was like through stories about the everyday of real-life characters. With her, we share their humour, their successes and their disappointments. And for older readers like myself, there is a healthy dose of nostalgia to enjoy.

Evelyn Benson (nee Sangster) comes from a family with deep roots in British Columbia for many generations. She has arranged the stories in three eras: 1895 – 1938, 1939 – 1947, and 1948 – 1993. Benson has deliberately kept the stories short and easy to read. Yet she still pays attention to detail such as the names of everyday household products that were used, and the songs that were in vogue. The stories are so enjoyable that one hardly notices the passage of time, both while reading and when the stories take place.

As mayor of New Westminster where many of these stories are set, I do have a soft spot for the people of the Royal City and our history. If you are from here, you would certainly recognize many of the characters. However, the stories, while real, are generic enough that the book will be enjoyed by all, no matter where you are from. I grew up in a town a thousand miles from New Westminster, and yet life was pretty much the same there as here. I highly recommend this work to all readers with an interest in our fellow human beings no matter where they have come from.

Mayor Wayne Wright
New Westminster, British Columbia

About Oral History

Oral history is the preservation of historical information based on the personal experience and observations of the people who lived the events. While it takes the form of eye-witness accounts of past events, oral history can include stories passed down over the years.

Oral history provides an opportunity to explore the past and "experience" history firsthand. It helps to bridge the generations by capturing detailed and meaningful characteristics from the past that might otherwise be lost forever. It is a way of exploring the past that has the power to surprise, delight and enrich the reader.

The history that makes its way into history books is too often the stories of people with influence and power. But common folk have stories to tell just as much as those famous enough to have their names written down in archives. For history is not only to be found in documents and old newspapers, but also in the memories of the people who experienced the events.

Their real-life experiences and insights offer us a first-hand glimpse into the way things really were. They help to fill in the information gaps that are commonly part of documented history. Through the first-hand accounts of the people who were there, we get not only the outline of history, but the living colours.

The people quoted in this book, myself included, tell their stories as they remember them–warts and all. Some of the anecdotes reflect the prejudices of the times, for some of those prejudices were actually the law of the day! **Nevertheless, it was the way it was**. We can't change history.

This book is four generations of real-life experiences.

Author's Preface

Raconteur: a person who is skilled in relating stories and anecdotes in an interesting way.

I come from a family of *raconteurs*. My father, Lewie Sangster, was a masterful story-teller who could keep any audience enthralled as he recounted adventures he and his brothers had growing up in the early days of New Westminster. The stories he told me of his service in World War I France were indelibly imprinted on my young mind.

After Dad's passing in 1968, I began taping the stories of his youngest brother, George Sangster, whose recollections were just as vivid as Dad's. George added details to Dad's adventures and had many of his own stories to relate.

It wasn't until I had children of my own that I realized that I, too, had had adventures worth passing on. And during twenty-seven years as a substitute teacher at the local high school, whenever I discovered an absent teacher had not left me a lesson plan, my skill as a *raconteur* came in useful by keeping a restless class of teenagers fascinated with stories of days gone by. The students' questions and comments about my tales of yesteryear made me realize how much things have changed, and yet how many things remain the same.

Over the years, my husband and I came to realize that we both have very retentive memories. Sometimes, when talking with people we had gone to school with, they would give us puzzled looks and say, "I don't remember that!" That encouraged Don and me to submit historical articles to local newspapers. Three of those articles won provincial honours for community history.

Over the years, many people, including students I have taught, urged me to put my stories into a book, and I would reply, "One of these days." Well, one of those days has arrived.

~ Evelyn Sangster Benson

Acknowledgements

My heartfelt thanks go firstly to all the old-timers who shared their memories with me, particularly my pioneer kinfolk whose voices I can still clearly hear within my head and my heart.

Gratefully, I acknowledge those who took their time to proof-read my manuscript and catch my errors: Jane Kupfer, Candice James, Gavin Hainsworth, Katherine Freund-Hainsworth and Ray Pigeau. Janet Benson for her talent with computers and social media. Also Barry Dyke at the New Westminster Museum & Archives, Jay Benson for his research on "This Old House", Kim Benson for her talented artwork and literary contributions and my layout artist Heidi Mueller, for her skill and talent, her patience with my many indecisions and changes, and whose friendship I cherish.

My deepest thanks go to my husband Don, not only for his gifted literary contributions, but for his encouragement and unwavering belief that this book will be an important contribution to the history of the times. He is my most honest critic and devoted fan and has been my beloved helpmate for more than sixty years.

Table of Contents

Part II ~ 1939 - 1947

Part III ~ 1948 - 1993

Appendix

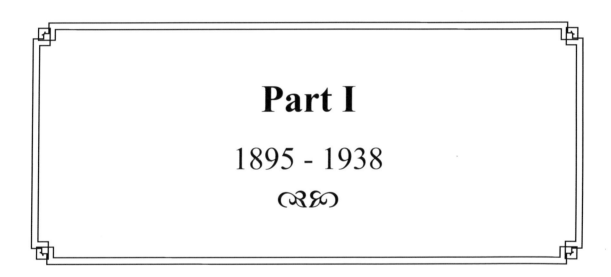

Part I

1895 - 1938

൝ඞ

Boy With A Camera

There was a time when the concept of giving a child a weekly allowance was almost unheard of. In fact, it used to be the other way around. Children who earned money after school or on weekend jobs turned their earnings over to their parents to help with the family finances.

In the 1890s, even though my grandfather, Alex Sangster, had a secure, middle-class job as foreman for Brackman-Ker Milling Company on Front Street, the economy of the times required that large families like his (2 adults and 7 children) budget very carefully. Most families kept chickens for meat and eggs, grew and preserved fruit and vegetables and baked their own bread. My grandfather cobbled his family's shoes, and much of their clothing was handmade by the females in the family.

Besides doing their fair share of household chores, the boys of the family were expected to work at after-school and week-end jobs. Beginning at age seven, my father sold newspapers, delivered telegrams, picked fruit and shined shoes during his youth. In his later teens, when the weather was cold enough to freeze Burnaby Lake*, Dad set up a tent where skaters could pay a small fee to "check" their shoes, purses and extra clothing. He would build a campfire and make hot cocoa which he sold to the skaters.

All the money he earned from these enterprises was turned over to his mother to help meet the costs of raising seven children. In turn, his mother gave him back 25 to 50 cents a month for his own use. The amount increased over the years, but this practice continued until Lewis became a clerk at City Hall. He then paid room and board until he left home to be married at age twenty-three!

15-year old Lewie Sangster. Note camera case attached to bicycle cross-bar. - Sangster Collection

One year at the 1st of July celebration in Queen's Park, they held foot races in the oval. First prize in each race was a silver dollar! At school, Dad was hailed as a fast runner, so his chums urged him to enter. They held his coat and cheered him on. Dad entered and won FIVE races. Flushed with victory, he spent his winnings on food and entertainment for himself and his friends. When he got home, he proudly informed his mother that he had won five silver dollars! She held out her hands, expecting Lewie to hand over the money. Five dollars was a large portion of a week's salary for her husband. When dad explained he had spent it frivolously on himself and his chums, he got the licking of his life.

Dad was a "go-getter". He squirreled away coins until, by 1905, he had saved enough to buy a Kodak postcard camera. Although only 14 years old, he realized that his new hobby would have to pay for itself. So beginning that spring, he photographed the May Day parade and the crowning of the May Queen along with other festivities, then rushed home to his little cellar darkroom to develop the prints. That evening, he was at the May Day Ball selling his postcards at a small profit. This kind of enterprise kept him in film,

The young lad with the pork pie hat on the extreme right is Province carrier 10-year old Lewie Sangster ~ Photographer unknown.

paper stock and chemicals without putting a strain on the family's finances. If you study the photo on the opposite page you will see Dad's postcard camera strapped to the bar of his bike.

Although Dad was an amateur at photography, he had a keen understanding of this fledgling science, and his love of New Westminster is reflected in his work. He understood the "candid" snapshot in an era when almost all photographs were posed and stiff. And he seemed to have an uncanny instinct for subjects that would fascinate later generations.

He left our family a legacy of hundreds of photos and negatives that are still being catalogued. The *Sangster Collection* has been turned over to the civic archives to share this photographic legacy with the community. Most of the photographs in this book are his. Thanks, Dad.

* Sometime in the Twenties or Thirties, the Municipality of Burnaby drained enough water out of Burnaby lake to expose more industrial land on its shoreline. Unfortunately for skaters and boaters, the lower water level allowed the sun to reach the bottom and soon water-lilies and other water plants took over the lake to the detriment of skaters and swimmers. In 1973, funds for the Canada Summer Games were used to dredge an area to allow for boat races. Once the Games were over, the water plants once again choked the lake.

ℂỹ

Paddlewheeler Adventures

The Sangster family came to New Westminster from Victoria in 1895.

Elizabeth and Alexander had five sons and two daughters. Two of the boys were twins – Lewis my father, and Philip, his non-identical twin. During the voyage from Victoria on the side-wheeler, *Yosemite*, Philip, age 4, went missing! Panic ensued as passengers and crew searched the ship from stem to stern. Finally a deckhand spotted him high atop the wooden housing that covered one of the great side-paddle wheels. The four-year-old was face-down on the very edge of the housing with his head over the side watching in fascination as the great wheel propelled the ship through the waters of Georgia Straight! A deckhand climbed up the housing, retrieved Philip, and returned him to his frantic mother.

Three years later, when her youngest child, George, was five, Elizabeth took him with her when she made an overnight trip back to Victoria to visit old friends. You can bet that she kept him close to her side as she sat in the ladies salon, a richly appointed area of the ship where ladies could go to avoid the riff-raff sometimes aboard, and the perpetual shower of hot cinders and flying soot that poured out of the smokestacks.

Ordinarily, Native Indians and Chinese were allowed only on the open decks, whatever the weather, but on this particular trip an exception had been made. A richly dressed Chinese woman, who had been carried aboard by servants in a sedan-chair, was allowed to stay in the ladies salon. She was obviously the wife of a very important Chinese merchant, and somehow strings had been pulled and palms had been greased in order to allow this non-Caucasian woman into the salon.

My grandmother discovered that the young Asian woman, although only recently arrived from China, understood a fair amount of English. Eventually, as the two women gained a rapport, the young woman shyly lifted the hem of her beautifully embroidered garments and showed Elizabeth her feet.

Uncle George, who witnessed this, told me that although he was only five, he knew that what he was viewing was something out of the ordinary. He knew that no grown woman should have feet that small. Not small – tiny! She had the feet of an infant! They had been bound at birth. Foot-binding was a sign of nobility, because a woman with bound feet had to be carried everywhere, and only the very rich nobility had the servant-power to accommodate this kind of infirmity over a lifetime. It also prevented concubines from running away.

Uncle George sensed that revealing her feet to a non-Chinese person was somehow embarrassing for the lovely Chinese lady, and he realized that his mother, my grandmother, must have sensed this too, for then Elizabeth raised the hem of her gown, and showed the young woman HER infirmity – a high-laced boot that had a four-inch sole because Elizabeth had been born with one short leg and always used a cane whenever she traveled outside her home.

Uncle George said he would never forget the image of those tiny feet, and in hindsight, he often speculated on the suffering that young woman must have endured as a child.

The paddle wheeler Yosemite docked at New Westminster. Note the huge wooden housing over the paddle wheel. Photo - New Westminster Archives.

CR

The Great Fire Of 1898: One Family's Story

For the Sangster family, the Fire of 1898 hit close to home, literally.

Alexander Sangster was foreman at Brackman-Ker Milling on the waterfront where the fire began. By the time the alarms awakened him on that fateful Saturday night, he knew it was already too late to help save his workplace, so he rushed to the Baptist Church on Agnes Street where he served as a Deacon. He and another man managed to save two high-backed chairs, some church records, an oak lectern and the big Bible before flames drove them out of the building. These historic relics are proudly displayed in today's Olivet Baptist Church at Seventh Street and Queens Avenue which was built to replace the original burned out church. The Agnes Street lot was later sold to the Masonic Order.

Meanwhile, at the Sangster home on Seventh Street, my grandmother Elizabeth awakened her seven children and the family began packing – poised to flee up the hill if the flames reached their house. The youngest child, George, was only four, yet at his 100th birthday party, he recalled the impressions that were etched into his memory that night, of a steady stream of families struggling past the Sangster house carrying, pushing, pulling and wheeling buggies, barrows or wagons loaded high with cherished household effects they had managed to save from the encroaching flames.*

After returning to his family from the rescue mission at the church, Grandfather Alexander organized the older boys into a "spark-watch". Armed with wet blankets, they scrambled around on the roof of the family home and prowled the yard extinguishing the many red hot embers that constantly landed on their property. My father told me that if they had to flee their home, the last thing to be done was to free the chickens from their pen. Every chicken for itself!

Next, Alexander joined a group of other neighbourhood men to help Mr.

Sketches found among George Sangster's papers when he died in 1997 at the age of 103. George made the sketches years after the fire, drawing from his memory of the streams of people coming up the hill, fleeing the fire.

Burr the jailer (actor Raymond Burr's grandfather) save the Burr house which stood directly in the path of the flames on the upper side of Cunningham Street, two doors from Seventh Street. The men hauled the Burr family mattresses onto the slopes of the mansard roof and piled bedding on the flat part. They formed a bucket-brigade, soaking everything to protect the roof from burning embers. Then they moved their bucket-brigade next door to Saint Paul's Episcopal Church, but their efforts were in vain and that building succumbed to the flames.

The Burr house survived, because just about then the wind shifted from blowing up the hill from the river to blowing downhill, and the fire then began to feed on itself. Fortunately for the Sangster family, the fire halted at Royal Avenue only four doors from their home!

At morning light, the Sangsters surveyed the damage. Their front yard was piled high with bundles and luggage that people had abandoned out of sheer exhaustion. Eerily, many street lights in the burned-out area continued to work, illuminating blocks of abandoned ruins. Many of the homeless citizens were housed and fed in the Armories. Nine thousand meals were served that week by the ladies of the community, which included Elizabeth Sangster. Clothing, blankets, tents and mattresses were donated or provided from the funds that poured in from cities and businesses across Canada.

Tipperary Park became a "tent city". It was a jumbled stockpile of belongings salvaged at the last minute by families fleeing the fire. One man, realizing that his flock of chickens was doomed by the advancing flames, quickly wrung their necks and stuffed them into a barrel which ended up in Tipperary Park. In the chaos of the days that followed, they completely slipped his mind until citizens complained of the terrible stench emanating from somewhere within the park!

The day after the fire, as the smoldering ruins began to cool,

Circa 1896 - The Sangster Family
Back row: Alexander Sangster, Walker, Lewis, Alice
Centre row: Rufus, Baby George, Elizabeth Sangster
Front row: Nellie, Philip

it became apparent that many cats and dogs, perhaps trapped in cellars, had somehow survived the fire but were badly and painfully burned. At least one Good Samaritan took pity on their plight, and spent that Sunday putting the burned animals out of their misery with a revolver. He was aided in this merciful task by a small army of boys who helped comb the burned-out ruins, spotting the injured pets for him.

My father and two of my uncles took part in that adventure, and often recounted the tale. I asked Dad about the dangers they faced while climbing through the smoldering ruins which could have collapsed, or the possibility of encountering an animal turned vicious by pain and fear. He said they weren't concerned about those things. He admitted that the real danger was if their mother found out. She would have been furious with them had she known they had been that close to a loaded gun!

CR

The Rat Lottery

Everyone had a woodshed or small barn in their backyard where they stored firewood, tools and chicken feed, for nearly every family raised a few chickens. As you can imagine rats were a common nuisance in those days. In Dad's family, they trapped the rats in a cage-like trap, rather than poison them or kill them in ordinary rat traps. When they had accumulated at least 10 rats, they would put the cage on a wagon and pull it to the intersection of Sixth Street where it leveled off at Queens Avenue.

By this time, a crowd began to gather because the boys had put out the word on the children's grapevine that, "The Sangster boys and their dog are going to let some rats go!"

The family dog was named "Jip", and Jip was a Rat Terrier. He lived up to his breed, for he hated rats with a passion and could grab a rat by the scruff of its neck and with a snap of his head, Jip would break the rat's neck. It was done in a blur so fast the eye couldn't follow.

The Sangster boys would wait until the crowd was sizeable. Of course all their friends were there for the sport, but the majority of the crowd was grown men – betting men. The bet was, "How many rats can Jip kill before they get away into the ditches that line both sides of the dirt road?" There was always someone there willing to hold the money and record the bets.

Dad said that the greatest unknown factor was how quickly each rat realized the cage was open and an escape route was suddenly available. The boys would tie a long string on the cage door so they weren't in Jip's way when the first rat skittered out. He said Jip would be poised like a pointer, quivering in anticipation, waiting for the cage to open.

Imagine the speed and coordination of the little terrier when ten rats ran, at top speed, in ten different directions at once! Dad said the spunky little Rat Terrier sometimes got them all! Was that a note of pride I heard in his voice?

∝

Little Devils In The Graveyard

Recently, I dug out my copy of Hellen Pullem's book, *The Not So Gentle Art of Burying The Dead*, a history of New Westminster's cemeteries. She writes that the cemetery once on the high school site was abandoned by white settlers in favour of Fraser Cemetery in 1889, and, "From that time on, few if any white people were buried at the Douglas Road Cemetery and it came to be used by the Chinese until 1914". My father told me he remembered it being used solely by the Chinese community. In his day, it was referred to as "the Chinese cemetery".

At the turn of the last century kids in those days made their own fun, and many parents were blissfully unaware of what their children were up to. When word went out on the kids' grapevine that a Chinese funeral was imminent, young boys from all over town headed to Chinatown at the foot of Royal Avenue to enjoy the spectacle and follow the funeral procession.

Chinese musicians, with flutes and gongs and other exotic instruments, led the way up the hill amid exploding strings of firecrackers intended to frighten away evil spirits. Hundreds of strips of white paper were strewn behind the procession. Each paper strip was punctured by a series of holes, the belief being that an evil spirit would have to weave its way through each and every hole before it could reach the deceased. By then, the deceased would be safely interred and beyond the demon's reach. The boys who followed the funeral procession gathered up these paper strips and later used them as "tickets" when they played circus.

Once the burial ceremony was over, the mounded grave was heaped with cherished possessions of the deceased, and a "feast" to appease the spirits – bowls of rice and vegetables, and sometimes even a small roast pig!

Dad and his chums hid out a safe distance away until all the mourners had departed. Then, when the coast was clear, they gathered at the graveside to enjoy the feast. They weren't spirits, but they WERE "little devils." I'm sure my Grandfather, a deacon at the Baptist Church, would have taken a dim view of such disrespect for the dead, and marched the boys to the woodshed - if he had known*.

I used to tell this story to my students when I taught at New Westminster Secondary School. Some would look at me in horror and say, "You mean there are bodies buried under our school?" I would reassure them that the Chinese of those early days pre-arranged and paid in advance for an agent from the Chinese community to disinter their remains after a number of years, and ship the packaged bones back to their native villages in China.

When excavation began for the Vincent Massey Junior High School in 1949, the engineers and workmen were made aware of the history of the site, and were on the lookout for human bones. I'm not sure any were found, but according to Dad who was Mayor at the time, their instructions were to treat the remains with respect and inter them at Fraser Cemetery.

Little boys of those bygone years didn't follow only Chinese funerals. Sometimes they trooped after a Christian funeral procession if the Firemen's Band had been hired for the occasion. The musicians, leading the procession and followed by a black and glass hearse pulled by black horses, played something somber, like *The Death March*. But Dad told me that as the Firemen marched back to the fire hall they played something much more lively, like, *"The Girl I Left Behind Me!"*

* *Even today most parents are blissfully unaware of some of the mischief their children get into. Some of you will say, "NOT MINE!" Don't kid yourself, my own children are in their fifties and bit by bit I am only now learning about some of their escapades when they were kids.*

"Tin Can Band" taken at Queens Avenue and 7th Street Boy's Central School grounds 1898.
Back row: Rufus Sangster, Willie Thompson, Walker Sangster. Clare Young, Lewis Sangster, Philip Sangster
Front: George Sangster, Howard Schaakie - Photographer unknown

CR

Indoor Plumbing

The very first toilet my dad ever saw was installed on the back porch of the Smith's house in the late 1890s. People didn't trust the idea of a toilet *inside* a house so it was quite common to find them enclosed on a back porch, at first.

Clive and Ken Smith were twins. Clive became my Grade 8 Social Studies teacher in 1948. The Smith twins were chums of the younger Sangster boys, Lewis, Philip and George. On the day the plumber came, all their little chums came to play in the Smith twins' yard, hoping to get a look at this fancy new facility.

Suddenly, young Clive came running down the back steps yelling, "Kenneth! Kenneth! Come and see the water-whirl!" meaning the whirlpool made when the chain on the overhead tank was pulled.

Before the day was over, each and every kid in the neighbourhood got to pull the chain at least once.

When my mother's family, the Appletons, moved into 319 Sixth Avenue in 1905, the facilities were outside, attached to a small barn. Most city outhouses had metal containers that were picked up by the "City Scavenger" weekly. With his horse and wagon, he traveled the city's back lanes in the middle of the night, loading, by lantern light, full cans of effluent onto his wagon and leaving rinsed, empty cans behind in each privy. The contents of the soiled cans were eventually dumped into the river!

The Appletons weren't on the Scavenger's route because they had no back lane. So once a week or so, my maternal grandfather Moffat Appleton, dug a hole and emptied the contents of the privy-can and then immediately filled the hole in. One day, he got called away before back-filling the hole. Later, in the dark, my grandmother Bessie stumbled into it!

My mother, Naomi, a young lady of fourteen, went looking for her mother after visitors had arrived. When she couldn't find her mother in the house, she went outside to look for her. Bessie was certainly grateful when her daughter found her. Young Naomi helped pull her mother out of the hole and then was sent to get soap, towels and a bucket of hot water, while Bessie stripped down in the barn. Naomi was instructed to tell her younger sister Ruth to entertain the guests but NOT TO TELL RUTH OF HER PREDICAMENT! All her life, my Aunt Ruth was a chatterbox and a confirmed mischief-maker. Ruth would have blurted it out, for sure.

Naomi toted the buckets of water out to her mother, then took shoes, stockings, underwear, a dress and some cologne out to the barn to make Bessie presentable for company.

I'm sure my Grampa Appleton got a good tongue-lashing for his neglect. And you can be sure that as soon as a city sewer line was put down Sixth Avenue, the Appletons installed indoor plumbing. Although at first, it too was installed on the back porch. Later, Moffat and his youngest brother, my great-uncle Jack, added a two-room lean-to addition onto the back of the kitchen. The new addition provided a full bathroom with toilet, tub, sink and waterheater, and a large walk-in pantry. The pantry cool-air vents are still visible on the northeast outside wall of the house now owned by our son, Jay.

Until 1942, when a complete upstairs bathroom was added to the house, a commode or chamber pot was available upstairs in case of an emergency during the night. Some people called them "thunder-mugs".

CR

The Great Pie Robbery

At the turn of the last century, the Sangster family lived in a large house kitty-corner to the Armories, and directly across Sixth Street from the old original Queens Avenue United Church. Each summer, the ladies of the church held an evening "pie social" to raise money for the Sunday School. All day long, the devoted ladies baked fruit pies in the church kitchen and set them to cool on the window sills. The mouth watering smell of home baking filled the air.

On one such day, Dad and a pal spotted some neighbourhood "toughs" stealing pies. They decided to become "vigilantes", and waited with their trusty slingshots to teach the pie thieves a lesson.

I should mention that my dad was a dead shot with a slingshot. Many a pigeon pie stretched the Sangster food budget - every bird shot in the head. Imagine how many pigeons it took to feed their family of nine!

Anyway, the two boys waited behind some bushes for the thieves to show themselves. When one fellow slowly raised his head beneath the church windowsill, Dad took careful aim and let him have it in the back of the neck. His target let out a holler, turned and spotted the marksmen and started to chase them!

It wasn't a pie thief at all! It was the huge and fearsome Chief Constable Bradshaw, who had been summoned by the ladies of the church to catch the pie thieves!

Angry because he had been "shot", and mistaking my father and the other boy for the pie-thieves, Bradshaw began to chase them. The two shooters went over fences, through backyards and down alleys for several blocks, until Bradshaw finally cornered them in a barn. The boys hid themselves in a large empty wooden barrel and held onto the lid as tightly as they could.

The Chief Constable began a methodical search of the barn, but the combined weight of the boys and their tight grip on the lid fooled him into thinking it was a full barrel with a nailed-down lid. Dad swore he was sure Bradshaw could hear their pounding hearts!

The policeman was positive he recognized a couple of Sangster boys, so my grandmother Elizabeth was puzzled when Bradshaw pounded on her door and demanded to see Dad's twin, Philip and another brother, Rufus. When the two Sangster boys appeared – clean, cool, and not a hair out of place – the detective realized he'd made a mistake, and lumbered away, muttering to himself.

A quarter of a century later, when CHIEF OF POLICE Bradshaw was addressing a New Westminster civic dinner, he told the story of the unsolved mystery of the pie robbery. He then turned to Lewie Sangster, the youngest Alderman at the head table, and said, "Why do I have the feeling that the sharpshooter of that day long ago, who raised a lump on the back of my neck the size of a bantam's egg, is seated not too far away from me at this very moment?"

When Alderman Sangster's face turned as red as the berries in a pie, Chief Bradshaw knew he had finally solved "The Case of the Great Pie Robbery".

႟

Backrow: G. Bradshaw, E. Pentland, W. Milne, E. Anderson, L. Nixon, R. McDonald, E. Johnston, S. Bass, C. Pittendrigh, P. Bruce
Front row: J. Reid, T. Annandale, F. Hume, Matron B. White
Circa 1923 - New Westminster Archives

Christmas 1902

My dad's youngest brother, George, was also a fountain of information about our city's earlier days. He was an amazing man, with a sharp mind and keen eyesight right up to his death in 1997 at the age of 103. I once asked Uncle George about Christmas in New Westminster when he was a boy, and he told me a little story I'd like to share.

He sat me down and started. "I was about eight years old and our family didn't have much money to spend on Christmas. I wanted Santa Claus to bring me a box of building blocks. Instead, I got something that probably did me more good in the long run - a drawing slate. Maybe that's why I became an art teacher rather than an architect.

"Howard Schaake was my best friend. His family was better off than ours because his father owned Schaake Machine Works on Front Street. So Howard had asked Santa Clause for a pony and cart. He was confident his wish would be granted. On Christmas morning his parents told him his gift was out in the barn. He raced out to the barn and there, in the middle of the barn on the floor was a toy horse and cart, about a foot long. He cried all day. No one could stop him crying, not even me. I always thought it was a cruel joke.

"Our family went to Olivet Baptist Church three times on Christmas Day. We always had a turkey or a goose. There was more grease with a goose. Mother saved the goose grease, then mixed it with strong dry mustard, painted it on a large piece of brown paper to plaster on our chests whenever we had a cold.

"Mother gave me fifty cents to spend on Christmas presents. I bought something for the other eight people in our family and my

Elizabeth and Alexander Sangster's Christmas tree circa 1912 with grandchildren Millicent, Dwight and Kathleen Purdy (Kathleen taught Art in local schools c,1930 – 1950s) - Sangster Collection

two best chums Howard Schaake and Toby Jackson*. I gave all of them a two-for-a-penny pencil from the stationery store. I got Dad a mustache cup for fifteen cents.

"But I bought my mother the most expensive gift of all. I'd heard Mother say she'd like a new set of dishes. I told Mr. Moy the storekeeper this, and he showed me a beautiful set of miniature dishes. You know – dolly dishes. But I was a serious little boy and I thought they were perfect. I'm sure Mr. Moy gave me a bargain, for I only had thirty cents left to spend.

"I can see Mother yet – sitting in her rocker by the window that Christmas morning in 1902 with my gift on her lap, rocking back and forth. First she laughed and then she cried. Then she laughed and then she cried.

"Many years later, after she died and we were looking through her keepsakes, she still had that set of little dishes, carefully wrapped and protected in the very bottom of her cedar hope chest. When I saw them, it brought back a flood of memories. I sat down and held them on my lap, and I laughed and laughed. And then I cried".

*became Mayor of New Westminster 1951

CR

Bath Night

More than a century ago, baths at my dad's house were once a week on Saturday night. This was normal practice of the times. The old galvanized tin tub with the high back was brought in from the woodshed and placed in the middle of the kitchen. On the roaring hot wood stove were several large copper containers heating water. The youngest children were bathed first in a small amount of water, then dried, put in their nightshirts and hustled up to bed. Then the girls. All the males in the family were required to stay upstairs, or outside in good weather, until their female siblings were modestly clothed in their nightwear and off to bed.

Next the boys. As each member of the family took a turn in the tub, more hot water was ladled into the cooling bath water. The girls' mother manned the ladle up to this time, then the father took over the ladle for the young men. When they were all done, he himself added more hot water and climbed in for his weekly bath. His wife would return to the kitchen and they would have a quiet time to discuss family affairs while she ladled in more hot water or scrubbed his back. Then the mother, with the kitchen all to herself, would **finally** get her turn.

Imagine! Eight bodies had already used the same water! No wonder doctors in that era cautioned pregnant women not to bathe in a tub, but only have sponge baths! Good advice, indeed.

After her bath, the beleaguered mother was left with the chore of ladling the water out of the tub into a bucket and emptying bucket after bucket into the sink. After she had cleaned the tub and dried it well and hung up all the soggy towels. She would save the last bucket of bath water to wet a mop and clean up the kitchen floor. THEN the poor woman could climb the stairs and fall wearily into bed.

About 1900, Dad had his first bath in a real bathtub with hot and cold running water. It came at the invitation of his oldest sister Alice, who had recently married Russell Purdy. The newlyweds were living in a house with a bath room – a room that contained only a bathtub. Dad said the experience was one he would never forget. For the first time, HE could control the temperature of the water, and he could fill it up to the brim. And he had complete privacy, including a lock on the door! Heaven!

☙

Tomboy Dynasty

My mother and her sister Ruth were tree-climbing tomboys. They spent many adventurous hours in the big cherry tree in the front yard on Sixth Avenue. Their mother, Bessie, had been something of a tomboy herself. She boasted to me that she could bat a ball farther than most boys at her school in the 1870s in Nova Scotia. Bessie understood her daughters' natural tendencies to be physically active, and encouraged their outdoor activities. She did have one rule, though. Because there were no street lights to indicate the coming of darkness, and because no one in those days had wrist watches, Bessie would say to them, "When Mr. Trapp's Chinaman drives his cows back down Fourth Street for milking, then it's time to come home."

Mr. Trapp's herd of cows was driven daily from Agnes Street to Trapp's Field, a large open grazing meadow bordered by Eighth Avenue, Second Street, Ninth Avenue and Fourth Street. Much of Trapp's Field still remained in the early 1940s and was a great place to fly kites without fear of tangling with electric wires.

On the other hand, my grandfather Moffat Appleton was a stern Anglican with rigid Victorian principles about how "young ladies" should behave, and that did NOT include physical activities. Because of his attitude, my grandmother secretly built each of the girls a pair of walking-stilts. Moffat never did find out about the stilts because Mother and Aunt Ruth hid them inside a big hollow stump across the street on a vacant lot now occupied by the house at 316 Sixth Avenue.

Thankfully, because of her upbringing, my mother didn't discourage my tomboy ways. I too climbed the same old cherry tree, unencumbered by skirts and petticoats,

Lewie Sangster on stilts - Sangster Collection

because my mother bought me blue jeans and high-top runners in the 1940s when such items could only be purchased in the Boys' Department (there were no such things as girl's blue jeans back then).

And when I made the grade seven girls' basketball team, my father took one look at my flimsy white tennis shoes and drove me immediately to Rumble's Sporting Goods on 12th Street and bought me a pair of boys' high-top runners. I was the first girl in town who had ankle-support runners! All the other girls were envious. By the end of the basketball season, several girls on our team wore them too.

Unfortunately, mother drew the line at buying me high-laced leather hiking boots. Every Christmas and birthday I would cut the picture of those beautiful boots out of the Eatons' Catalogue Boy Scout Equipment page, but Mother never gave in to my pleas. However, thirty-five years later when my husband Don and I and the kids began selectively logging our Keats Island property in the 1980s I finally got my boots. I bought them myself – and they even have steel toes!

During the bitterly cold winter of 1949-1950, when for several weeks the thermometer hovered at zero degrees Fahrenheit and none of the school district's furnaces could cope with the unprecedented cold, my mother backed me up when I defied the high school Principal's rule that girls had to wear skirts or dresses to school, and would not be allowed to wear jeans or slacks regardless of the sub-zero temperatures. We could wear slacks TO school, but not IN school. No one took into consideration that boys not only wore nice warm trousers in school, but most wore comfy long johns as well!

Thinking back, when we won that battle, it was a small step forward for women's rights in our town.

I always encouraged my two daughters, Kim and Janet in their tomboy ways. They too climbed the same old cherry tree. It ran in the family. And I always felt that if a girl could hold her own and punch a boy in the nose when she was seven – she could do the same if it was really needed – at seventeen!

CR

Pride Goeth Before A Fall

The beauty of a fresh snowfall soon turns into a minefield of hazards for pedestrians, and slippery sidewalks combined with New Westminster's steep hills create a double hazard.

I remember coming out of the old Eagles' Hall on Blackie Street after a wedding reception many years ago, to find we'd had a surprise snowfall. The men formed a human chain down the steep sidewalk to Columbia Street where most of us had parked our cars. The ladies, in their high heels, steadied themselves by holding onto the chain of men as they inched their way to the bottom of the hill.

Uncle George recalled one incident that took place around 1910 on the steep stretch of road at the foot of Sixth Street below Columbia. By the standards of that era, it was like a comedy skit right out of Keystone Cops. Uncle George told me:

"It was one of those 'silver thaws'", he said. "A dandy. Everything was coated in ice. The woman in question attended our Baptist Church, so I knew her well. She was a big, pompous woman – always looked straight ahead with her nose in the air. You know the type – holier than thou.

"Anyway, she was walking on her way to shop at the Farmers' Market on Front Street. The hill was a sheet of ice. The barber halfway down the hill hollered to her not to come that way, but to go through the Dominion Bank Building, down the stairs and out the Front Street door.

'Well,' she thought, 'A barber telling ME what to do! The very idea!' So she started down the hill, and BINGO – down she went on her backside, sliding down Sixth Street and trying awkwardly and unsuccessfully to get back onto her feet.

"Several people were watching, but nobody dared venture forward onto the ice. Then along came Alex Lamb, a short, portly gentleman. Gallantly, Alex attempted to get her up very gingerly.

"Then BINGO! Down HE went. SHE went down again too, but they were holding onto each others' hands, so they went down the hill together, going round, and round, and round, like they were waltzing, sitting down!

"Well, by the time they got to the bottom where it levels onto Front Street, there were dozens of spectators, all roaring with laughter and holding their sides at the spectacle!

"Boy, was her face red! And his too. It was all very undignified. Especially for a Baptist!" Uncle George recalled with a chuckle.

CR

Sidewalk being ploughed by horse-power on First Street and Third Avenue
Photo - Sangster Collection.

Limburger At The Opera

My Uncles Will and Walter Appleton were practical jokers, and according to family lore, my Grandma Bessie was often the target of their pranks. I never heard of them targeting their father, who was an austere, humourless Victorian. But their prank with the Limburger cheese unintentionally targeted BOTH their parents.

In the latter part of the nineteenth century, even small towns had an Opera House. The local Opera House was home to not only opera, but also vaudeville, dramatic plays, lectures, concerts and any form of entertainment that required the purchase of a ticket. People in those days thought of paid entertainment as a special occasion, and dressed up in their very best.

I don't know what was on the playbill the night of the prank, but I do know Bessie was dressed in her finest. Her evening outfit included a smart little *reticule* - a drawstring bag containing a hanky, a perfume, maybe a small fan and sometimes a small vial of smelling salts. These little evening bags were usually ornate with embroidery, bugle beads, pearls and such. They were individual works of art, lovingly handmade by the owner and proudly displayed on high social occasions such as a night at the Opera House.

Unbeknownst to their mother, the two teenage boys had secreted a rather large chunk of Limburger cheese into her *reticule* just before she left for the Opera House. They pulled the drawstring particularly tight so as to seal in the gaseous fumes of this potent well-aged cheese.

It wasn't until near the end of Act I that Bessie, in reaction to the sad plight of the heroine, felt the need for her handkerchief. She loosened the strings on her beautiful little evening bag and pulled out her handkerchief, at the same time releasing all the pent up gases that had accumulated since they left home.

Immediately, gentlemen began to fan their hands in front of their faces and ladies quickly clamped their lace trimmed hankies to their noses. Folks began to turn their heads and glare with eyebrows raised at anyone sitting in their vicinity with the unspoken question in their eyes, "Was that YOU? I know it wasn't ME!"

Now, for those of you who have never had the unfortunate experience of getting a whiff of Limburger, let me explain: I once was in charge of stocking the cheese display at Woodwards' Food Floor, and I took the opportunity to open a package of Limburger cheese to have a sniff. I had always been curious ever since my mother told me about Bessie's night at the opera. I swear to you that Limburger cheese smells like the foulest burst of flatulence that you have ever had the misfortune to smell! I kid you not!

Now, back to Bessie at the Opera House. Almost immediately, she grasped what had happened and instinctively KNEW who the culprits were. By now, through the process of elimination, all eyes were on her. At least she felt they were. She didn't know whether to sit very still and hope she would disappear from sight or leap to her feet and flee the theatre.

Instead, she touched her husband's hand and whispered, "I'm feeling faint. I need some fresh air." Moffat, who was unaware of the Limburger trick, but quite aware of the stifling odor in the theatre, without a word, escorted his wife up the aisle.

I'm sure my grandmother thought she would never live it down, but I'd be willing to bet no one thought anymore about it and soon settled down to enjoy the rest of the play.

As for the boys, and what happened to them, I'm afraid I don't know. Mother wasn't even born when it happened and I don't think Bessie ever told her. For that very reason, I have no doubt the punishment was severe.

CR

Sleigh Riding

Whenever January slips by without a heavy snowfall, there are bound to be disappointed kids who got shiny new sleds for Christmas. When it does snow, kids head for the sleigh run in Queens Park. But sleigh riding there is tame compared to the old days.

Early in the last century, before motor vehicles, kids tobogganed down the long sloping mile of Twelfth Street from Sixth Avenue to Columbia Street. It was a long half mile back up hill, but Dad told me that kids could get two or even three good "runs" in during a winter evening.

Later, when motor vehicles took over the streets, our city fathers barricaded choice hills for the exclusive use of tobogganers. Tenth Street hill and Sixth Avenue from First to McBride were two. My favourite was Second Street from Tenth Avenue to Eighth. It gave us a steep, breathtaking ride for several blocks, then the gradual upgrade at Sandringham slowed us to a safe stop before Eighth Avenue. Sapperton kids used Sherbrooke Street.

But what about Sixth Street hill? Russell Purdy and George Sangster, two of my uncles, were adults old enough to know better on that New Year's Day in 1919 when they foolishly tried out the steep Sixth Street hill. This is probably the longest hill in our town.

There had been a deep snowfall overnight, and the two men were out for a stroll when they happened to meet Art Lord, the Assistant Postmaster and two of his friends at the corner of Sixth Street and Third Avenue. They were pulling a large toboggan, complete with sleigh bells. They proposed to my uncles that they all take a sleigh ride, "for old times sake". The plan was to ride down the sidewalk as far as Queens Avenue—just one short block.

Uncle George recalled: "Well, by the time we got to Queens we were really travelling and missed the turnoff . Before we knew it, we'd passed Royal, too! Below Carnarvon, Art managed to steer us off the sidewalk onto the road.

"We were hanging on for dear life when we shot across Columbia Street like a bullet, and were airborne halfway to Front Street! When we landed, Art yelled, 'FEET DOWN!' Miraculously, we slid to a stop before we reached the river's edge.

"Suddenly, the police came running and sliding down the hill after us! Russell and I high-tailed it to the right. The others, dragging the sleigh, ran left with the police in hot pursuit.

"When the police found they'd captured the Assistant Postmaster, they let the pair go with just a warning for 'speeding'. Today, they'd call it 'reckless endangerment'".

It's traditional for us West Coasters to brag to prairie folks whenever we have a mild winter, but the child within me can't help but be a little disappointed when it doesn't snow, at least once, during the winter season.

CR

Jumbo To The Rescue

Every fall, when the circus came to town, Dad and his brothers gathered "windfall" apples from their own and many of their neighbours' trees and traded the apples for tickets to the circus. Sometimes they earned tickets by putting up posters around town advertising that the circus was coming. Sometimes they helped "muck out" the horses' stables, and sometimes, they actually got to feed the elephant!

Uncle George told me that he and Toby Jackson once got fired from that job by choosing apples that were the EXACT diameter as the elephant's trunk. They would give the apple a bit of a shove so that it got stuck firmly in the animal's trunk.

The frustrated elephant would do what any human would do if something got stuck up her nose – blow it! The stuck apple became a projectile, and shot like a bullet across the circus grounds, which were the armory's parade grounds and today's City Hall parking lot. Eventually, the apple-projectiles would hit someone and all hell would break loose. At that point, George and Toby hightailed it out of there! If the boys didn't get paid their free tickets, it didn't matter because most little boys of that era were quite adept at slipping under a canvas flap into the big top.

One year when the circus was in town, a city works crew had been working to improve Sixth Street below Queens Avenue. Somehow, the steamroller got away from the driver and ended up on its side in the ditch.

Try as they might, they couldn't get it up-right, and therefore the machine's powerful steam engine was useless. Somewhat like a helpless turtle on its back.

Eventually, someone from the circus happened by and offered to go get the elephant. With proper harness and a couple of experienced "roustabouts" guiding the big pachyderm through the process, the steamroller was uprighted and pulled out of the ditch onto the road. It was all in a day's work for a circus elephant.

I wonder if the City of New Westminster ever got a bill for services rendered?

CR

Grandma Bessie Had A Bird

Around the turn of the last century, before the advent of the "Funeral Chapel", large funeral services were held in churches, while smaller, more intimate services were held in private homes. So my grandmother Bessie was asked to host a private funeral for a distant cousin because the Appletons had a roomier parlor than the family of the deceased. She agreed. My two uncles helped her to rearrange the furniture for the occasion.

My Uncle Walter Appleton, who had done a stint in the Merchant Navy, had recently returned from the South Seas and brought his mother a big white male cockatoo with a handsome yellow crest. The bird usually perched on an ornate metal stand, uncaged, in the parlor, but on the day of the funeral he was banished to the back bedroom. The door was firmly shut.

On the day of the service, the deceased was laid out in the parlor surrounded by candles, flowers and potted palms. A lady organist from the church brought a portable pump organ and was playing suitable background music as the mourners began to arrive. It soon became apparent that there was a shortage of chairs, so my grandmother sent one of my uncles to the back bedroom to get two more.

While the bedroom door was ajar, the cockatoo spotted the organist's very fashionable hat. Her charming chapeau was topped off with a stuffed white dove, perched seductively on a bed of pink tulle with its wings and tail spread invitingly. Instantly in love, the cockatoo let out a lusty squawk and soared into the parlor, landing amorously on the organist's hat!

Pandemonium broke loose! The lady organist screamed, fleeing the house in terror, never to return. Other ladies screamed, and several fainted as that was quite common in that era. Gallant young men dashed this way and that, trying to capture the bewildered cockatoo. It was finally caught and returned to the back bedroom. The funeral service eventually continued, but without the benefit of organ music.

Eventually, the story about the cockatoo was added to our list of amusing family anecdotes. But in those prim Victorian times, and given the somber occasion, the incident was considered "shocking" and was talked about for years. Grandma Bessie soon got rid of the cockatoo, but never really did live down its indiscretion.

The only one amused at the time was Uncle Walter who had brought the bird back from the South Seas. He was heard to remark that he hadn't had so much fun since Bora Bora.

CR

Hangings

In the Old West, hangings were often carried out using the nearest sturdy tree. In New Westminster, hangings took place in the fenced in yard of the provincial jail which in my dad's day stood directly behind the John Robson School site on Eighth Street. Back when the school was T. J. Trapp Technical High School, the remaining jail buildings were adapted for the shop classes, and the basement still contained barred cells.

In the old days, as the date for a scheduled hanging approached, rumours circulated around town about the identity of the hooded hangman. When convicted murderer Charlie Slumac dropped through the trap door into eternity over a century ago, taking the secret of his alleged "lost gold mine" with him, it was rumored that his hangman was the same hangman who had hanged Louis Riel five years earlier.

Eye witnesses at a hanging never knew how they would handle the moment of truth – that moment when they realized this man would die at the hands of another man. A veteran policeman might begin to sob helplessly, a boisterous bully might faint, and on at least one occasion, a new prison doctor couldn't examine the body after his first execution because the pounding of his own heart filled the stethoscope!

By the 1920s the chestnut trees had grown tall along the fence line of the jail and young boys could climb the trees to get a birds-eye view of the hangings. Judge Tommy Fisher's mother told me that young girls were too modest to climb the trees and expose their undergarments, but weren't above jockeying for a position at a knothole in the fence. The Sheriff would patrol the fence and chase them away but they would soon return.

Dad said the jailers even blocked the inside of the knotholes but the kids learned to jiggled out a new knot and then slip it back into place it until it was time for the actual hanging.

Don't forget this was an era of no movies, no illustrated comic books, no television, no ice rinks, no swimming pools and no playgrounds. Kids found their own entertainment and thrills wherever they could. Dad said he spent many an hour watching the chain gang from the Penitentiary lay brick roadbeds. The convicts actually wore a ball and chain! Lower Fourth Street hill is the only remaining example of the work of the chain gangs of long ago.

CR

Skating On The River

My father claimed that the only time he ever played hookey was one winter day when the Fraser River was frozen solid. He was a teenager at the time, so it had to be before 1910. He borrowed a pair of skates, the kind that clamped with straps and buckles onto ordinary boots.

He started down the North Arm of the Fraser River and headed towards Steveston. He fell down often at first, but finally got the hang of it, for he was a strong athlete. Soon he was gliding in long strides and the miles sped by.

By the time he got to Marpole, he realized he'd better turn back if he were going to make it home before dark. Easier said than done.

The tide had turned and was rising fast. The Fraser is a tidal river all the way from Mission to the ocean, and as it rose, great cracks appeared in the ice. At first, he easily jumped over the cracks, but eventually, he had to follow a crack until he found the narrowest spot. Then it began to get dark and much more dangerous.

By the time he reached New Westminster he was exhausted and soaked from nervous perspiration and many falls. He was very late for supper, and everyone was worried sick. He had no choice but to confess to skipping school. His parents were so relieved he was home safe and sound, that he **wasn't** sent to the woodshed.

Dad also realized what a close call it had been. That's why his first time playing hookey – was his last. At least that's what he claimed.

Skating on the frozen Fraser River - New Westminster Archives.

CR

Shoot The Referee!

In the heyday of field lacrosse in New Westminster, they played home games on Saturday afternoons at the oval in Queens Park. Vancouver and Victoria rounded out a very competitive league. The fans gave opposing teams derogatory nicknames - "Boo, Clamdiggers", "Boo, Crabeaters" and "Boo Salmonbellies" were shouted to demoralize the opponents. But New Westminster turned the tables and adopted SALMONBELLIES as the team name and made it a thing of pride. Why Salmonbellies? According to my father, who played for the Salmonbellies when they won two national championships in 1913 and 1914, the riverfront at New Westminster was lined with fish canneries. Salmon was so plentiful in the river that they only canned the upper fillet part of the fish and discarded the underbellies. A frugal homemaker could send a child with an empty bucket to a local cannery and for 25 cents the family had enough salmon bellies for several meals!

Lacrosse competition was fierce. Local store owners hung signs stating "GONE TO THE GAME", and closed their businesses on Saturday afternoons. The BC Electric Tram Company put extra cars on the trams headed from Vancouver to Queens Park via a spur line that ran down Sixth Street, and along Fourth Avenue to the park. Crowds sometimes reached ten thousand. This was a remarkable statistic when you realize that was nearly half the population of the city at that time.

One fateful day, the game ended with a loss for the visiting team. A disgruntled fan drew a pistol and shot at the referee! His friends wrestled the fan down, then hustled him out of the park in the confusion that followed. Luckily, he had missed his target.

Later that evening, Mr. Thomas Furness, who had been a spectator at the game and who was foreman of the City's sidewalk construction gang, emptied his trouser pockets as he prepared for bed. There, on the dresser, resting amidst the assortment of nails he always carried, lay the lead slug from the afternoon shooting at the park! Mr. Furness checked his trousers and, sure enough, there was a bullet hole in the wool fabric!

The story flashed around town. People shook their heads in amazement that, luckily for Mr. Furness, the bullet must have been nearly "spent" when it struck his pocket. The handful of nails did the rest.

○○

New Westminster's sidewalk construction gang. The best dressed worker in the photo is probably the foreman, Mr Thomas Furness - Sangster Collection.

Catching The Greased Pig

In his day, Dad was the fastest runner on the Salmonbellies field lacrosse team and probably the whole Inter-city League. Opposing teams knew that if Lewie Sangster got a breakaway, no one could catch him. In one crucial league game against Vancouver, Dad got his breakaway in the closing seconds of a tie game that would decide the championship.

Vancouver's fastest runner lit out after Dad, and when he realized he couldn't stop Lewie, he reached out with his very long-handled field lacrosse stick and clobbered him on the top of his head just as Dad took his shot on goal. He scored! The blow to the head had knocked him unconscious but he kept right on going, taking out the goalie while scoring the goal!

The referees allowed the goal, the Salmonbellies won, and the attacking player got a game suspension. Dad got several stitches, and for the rest of his life, that scar would bleed if the teeth of his comb scraped the scar tissue, and Dad would mutter a curse on that Vancouver player of long ago.

Lewie Sangster, "Rover" for the Salmonbellies
Photo - Sangster Collection.

Until recent times, there were very strict rules in Canadian sport as to what was "amateur" and what was "professional." The simple answer was that "professional" athletes were paid. "Amateurs" were not.

One 24th of May, Queen Victoria's Birthday holiday about 1913, after a lacrosse game at Queen's Park oval, Dad and his teammates went down to Columbia Street to watch the traditional horse races, Indian canoe races, and other fun that was going on. One of the competitions was "Catch the Greased Pig." Because of his speed, his pals encouraged him to enter, and held his coat and lacrosse equipment while he signed up.

Again, Dad's unparalleled speed paid off and Dad caught the pig!

The prize was to keep the pig, which was squealing and fighting to get free.

When a man offered to buy the pig for five dollars, Dad gladly handed the porker over and then treated his friends to food and cold drinks.

The Vancouver lacrosse team launched a protest with the Lacrosse Commission, claiming that by accepting money for an athletic performance, Lewie Sangster was no longer an amateur and he should be banned from playing amateur sports of any kind, especially lacrosse!

Of course the protest was denied, and Dad continued to play lacrosse for the Salmonbellies, receiving two 14 carat gold watch fobs for the 1912 and 1913 Minto Cup Championships before he went overseas in WWI. I'm sure those beautiful gold mementos were worth a lot more than a $5 pig!

CR

This panoramic photo illustrates the large crowds that attended lacrosse games in Queen's Park oval in the hey day of field lacrosse before World War 1 - New Westminster Archives.

Mmmmmmmm Pigeon Pie

Slingshots were a big part of a boy's life in the years before and immediately after 1900. My dad took much care and pride in the making of a new slingshot. He told me,

"You didn't just pick any old "Y" from a tree. It had to be a hardwood tree – oak, pear, cherry. My favourite was dogwood. After selecting the perfect "Y" I would peel it and carve it so that it had two knobs at the top to keep the rubber from slipping off, and a heftier knob at the bottom of the stem where your hand gripped. Then I would tie a cord joining the two prongs and tighten it until the "Y" started to look like a "U". Very gradually, I'd tighten the cord until the two arms of the slingshot stood perfectly parallel. Then I would place the new slingshot in the warming oven above the big kitchen stove and let it dry out for several days. All that was left to do was add the sling and then practice with it to break it in."

Dad was a marksman. The many pigeons he brought home for pigeon pie were nearly always shot in the head. Dad could talk "pigeon talk". He could "coo" exactly like a real pigeon and a curious bird would invariably stick a head out to have a look. "Thunk". One more bird for the pie.

On one hunting expedition, Dad and a chum decided to climb into the bell tower of the Baptist church where pigeons abounded. While chasing one bird across the rafters of the sanctuary, the other boy slipped. His foot broke through the ceiling above where some church elders were holding a meeting! There was hell to pay for that stunt.

Dad heard a rumour that pigeons could be made drunk and were easier to kill. Because his household was Temperance, there was no source of liquor at home. So he enlisted one of his chums whose father was known to like "strong drink". The boy tapped his father's private stock of an ounce or two of whiskey. They dipped chunks of dry bread in the alcohol and began feeding the pigeons. The birds flocked to the free lunch. Pretty soon the birds were staggering and falling down and completely unable to fly. Quickly, the boys wrung the drunk birds' necks. Both families had large pigeon pie for supper that night.

He never told his parents about the whiskey. I wonder if that particular pie had a better flavour?

CR

Hold Your Horses!

Early in the last century, owning a "horseless carriage" was as rare as owning a helicopter is today. The first car ever to appear on New Westminster streets was put together by my uncle, Clarence McLean, who operated *MacLean's Auto Garage* on Royal Avenue near Sixth Street for more than fifty years. There were two gas-pumps in front of the business, one *regular* and one *premium*. A large hand crank on the side of each pump was turned by the attendant for each transaction, pumping the fuel up into the glass container which sat on top of the pump, ready for the next customer to drive up. Increments in gallons were marked on the glass for the customer to see. If the customer asked for, say, 10 gallons, the attendant placed a nozzle in the customer's gas tank, and down poured the gasoline by gravity feed until the glass tank showed a decrease of 10 gallons. As a child, I loved to watch this very visible process. I particularly liked to watch premium gas because it was a beautiful pink and looked just like Cream Soda pop.

Uncle Clarence was born in the mining town of Leadville, Colorado, and was struck by gold fever at the age of sixteen. He took a steamship to Skagway, Alaska, and then traveled 500 miles by dogsled to Dawson City, Yukon. After a raft of adventures, and never striking gold, he made his way to Vancouver and was attracted to New Westminster in 1904. Sixty years later he told me this story about our city's first automobile:

Unknown Gas Jockey at MacLeans Autoworks.
Photo - Sangster Collection.

"Joe Reichenbach and I decided to build a car, just for amusement. It took us a whole year of grinding, boring and general hard work to get her ready for the road. Every day the fellows would wander into our shop and josh us about our 'infernal machine'.

"When we finally finished, I decided to take her out real early in the morning, just in case the first run might be a flop. Off I drove at four a.m. as far as the foot of Braid Street. Everything went fine until I got back onto Columbia Street, and she **stalled**. It turned out the dry battery connections had been jarred loose by the rough road.

"By this time in the morning, everyone was walking to work. Over they came to watch me peer at the engine. When I got her fixed, I cranked her up. Well! You never saw so many people go in so many directions so fast as when the gas in the muffler exploded in an awful BANG! One poor fellow ran smack into a telephone pole!

"One of the biggest drawbacks to driving an auto back then was the strict rule that horses had the right-of-way over cars. It once took me nearly an hour to get up Eighth Street to Royal Avenue (three blocks) because every time a horse came along I had to pull over to the side of the road.

"That very first car was painted a shiny red, and as I traveled along Columbia Street, owners, clerks and bystanders ran to hold horses at the first sounds of popping and banging in the distance. I guess I'll always remember that little red buggy!"

And now you know how we got the expression, "Hold your horses!"

CR

The Great Escape

On August 9, 1907, two convicts who were working in the B.C. Penitentiary brickyard, slipped under a fence when guard Alex McNeil ducked inside the tower hut to light a furtive cigarette. Then they scaled a wall using a handy ladder and disappeared into a nearby ravine known as "The Glen".

Glen Creek once supplied water to the original settlement of Royal Engineers and later to the Penitentiary. In those days, a planked bridge, known as the Glen Bridge, spanned the ravine as a continuation of Sixth Avenue. In the late 1930s the bridge was replaced by an earthen causeway known as the Glen Viaduct. Today, what remains of the creek that once ran through the present Royal Square site, past the Justice Institute, the Canada Games Pool and under Sixth Avenue runs down what is left of the ravine to the Fraser River. Today it is mostly in an under ground culvert and much of the ravine has been filled in. Up until the early 1940s, the section of the ravine north of Sixth Avenue was the city dump, but was filled in for sanitary reasons. We're told that what's left of the Ravine now is home to coyotes even though the lower part is a beautifully landscaped park.

In the early days the local boys had dammed the creek and formed their own "ol' swimmin' hole". My father learned to swim in Glen Creek, as did most boys of their era. It seems fitting that today, most of the children of New Westminster learn to swim at the Canada Games Pool, only a stone's throw from that pond of bygone years. On that August day over a century ago, Billy Miner the notorious train robber (sometimes known as the *Grey Fox of movie fame*) and a convict named Albert McCluskey, made their way down the steep side of the ravine and came upon five local boys who were skinny-dipping in a pond.

On that day in 1907, three of those naked boys were Sangsters – twins Lewis and Philip, and youngest brother George who told me his version of that day:

"We called it the Penitentiary Dam, and we were forbidden to go there. With me were Jimmy Ellie, Howard Schaake, and two of my brothers. We were playing 'Robinson Crusoe' when we saw two inmates coming down the side of the ravine. They didn't seem to be in a great hurry. Anyway, they hunkered down and talked to us for a minute. We recognized Billy Miner. Us kids had followed the crowd that thronged the train depot the day he was brought to town in handcuffs. We had talked to him many times through the fence. To us he was a kind of hero, I guess. You could tell he liked kids.

"When the convicts stood up to leave, Miner turned to us and, looking each of us in the eye said, 'Now boys, you didn't see us today…… DID YOU?' We all mumbled 'No, sir.' And then the two escapees walked towards the Sixth Avenue bridge.

"It was a little while before the Penitentiary bell began tolling. Up until then I guess we just thought they had been sent into the ravine on some sort of errand, as 'Trusties'. But when we heard the bell we said, 'Gosh, they've escaped!' So we climbed into our clothes as quick as we could and got out of there. We knew there'd soon be someone down there asking questions. And we didn't want to get into trouble.

"We were practically grown up before we ever told our parents about what happened that day at the Penitentiary dam."

The Sangster boys' reluctance to tell their parents was because they weren't supposed to be in the Glen in the first place. That reminded me of the fact that my girl friends and I, whenever the thermometer hovered below freezing for more than a week, would sneak through the bushes on the Penitentiary property and ice-skate on that very same little pond in the Glen. We didn't tell our folks either, because we had been trespassing on Federal land, and we knew it. We could read the No Trespassing signs.

But oh, what a thrill to skate on our very own private skating rink, pretending we were the Olympic figure skater, Sonja Henie!

WANTED!
Billy Miner
Train Robber

ᗉᖇ

How The Trapp Boys Learned To Swim

According to my father, every boy in the prominent Trapp family, when he reached the summer of his 10th birthday, was taken down to the docks and thrown into the Fraser River. Word would get out that "MR. TRAPP IS GOING TO DROWN ONE OF HIS BOYS! AGAIN!"

Every kid in town, it seemed, rushed to the waterfront to enjoy the fun. I'm sure it wasn't much fun for his boys. Mr. Trapp would tie a rope around the kid's waist. The kid would be shivering in his drawers from fright, not the cold. His old man would pick him up and drop him into the water. Then he would stand at the edge of the dock and yell, "SWIM! Dammit, SWIM!" The kid would flounder and sputter and flail until he eventually got the hang of it. I guess the boy knew deep-down that his father wouldn't let him drown. Eventually the kid would be hauled up and everybody cheered!

Dad said he was sure glad his father only **forbade** him to go swimming – anywhere. Of course Dad, like most kids in those days, eventually taught himself to swim, either in the Brunette River or their secret Penitentiary dam, in spite of their parents' rules.

CR

Girls, Girls, And More Girls

Someone calculated that if the dial telephone hadn't been invented, and then the cellular phone, and operators had to handle all the calls placed today using the old cord plug-in switchboards, it would require every female in the country over the age of 16 to be working as telephone operators to keep up!

Since the first phone in New Westminster was connected from Captain William Irving's house on Royal Avenue to his shipping office on the docks, working for the Telephone Company became a first job for hundreds of local girls. It was practically a "rite of passage" after leaving high school.

Of course the first telephone operators were young men, but they soon proved unreliable. They were cheeky, they whittled on the wooden switch boards, and the lads on the evening shift would sometimes connect with the boys at the Vancouver exchange and amuse themselves singing barber shop harmony! Girls were much more reliable.

I'll bet some of you can still remember a steady stream of boyfriends, husbands, and "wolves" in cars picking up or dropping off operators changing shifts at the B.C. Tel Exchange on Clarkson Street.

When I helped my husband Don with the research for his first book, *WIRE SONG, A History of the Early Years of the Telephone in B.C.* I came across a lot of operators' stories. One New Westminster story concerned a young operator who was followed

Working the switchboard. Painting by Kim Benson

home on several occasions by a "creep" (today we would call him a stalker). She managed to give him the slip until one evening she decided to end his obsession once and for all.

She walked up Sixth Street hill to a house just below Royal, walked boldly in and left the front door ajar. Her stalker eagerly followed her in and right down the hall to the kitchen where the girl's neighbour, the Chief of Police, was having his dinner!

For nearly seventy years, the Provincial Mental Hospital, later known as Woodlands School, and now the upscale subdivision "Victoria Hill", was known locally as "Number Nine", although few people knew that NINE was their original telephone number.

For a number of years in the 1940s the switchboard operator there was my girlfriend's eldest sister, Myrtle Hagen.

During the '40s, the radio program *Fibber Magee & Molly* was very popular. On every program, Fibber would make a phone call and when the local operator asked him "Number, please," Fibber would hesitate a moment, then say, "Oohh, is that you, Myrt? How's every little thing, Myrt?" So as kids, we'd phone "9" and when Doris' sister answered, we'd say, "Oohh, is that you, Myrt? How's every little thing, Myrt?", then quickly hang up.

☞

Bigotry Was A Way Of Life

Curious about the local telephone company's discriminatory policy towards the Chinese, I sifted back through B.C. Tel's archives, and eventually tracked its possible origin to an incident on New Westminster's Columbia Street in 1886 involving the local telephone manager, George Pittendrigh.

According to the archives, Chinese workers used to be employed to do all the outside heavy construction. Pittendrigh put an end to that policy when, one day he decided to lend a hand to some Chinese who were setting up a telephone pole. They were just about ready to drop the butt into the hole when the 12 o'clock whistle blew for lunch. So the workmen immediately dropped the pole to the ground. The unexpected fall of the pole caught Pittendrigh by surprise and brought him to his knees. He suffered a severely wrenched back. He swore that Chinese workmen would never again be employed for telephone work.

Here is how telephone poles were raised before mechanization. Painting by Kim Benson

Later that year the local telephone charter was amended to provide against the employment of any Chinese by the company. An act passed by the provincial legislature prohibited the company or any contractor from employing Chinese. Penalties ranged from a $10 fine to imprisonment for 30 days!

This ban remained in the New Westminster & Burrard Inlet Telephone Company charter until 1891. However, the newly created British Columbia Telephone Company made sure their charter made no mention of the subject.

Naturally, this rampant bigotry sifted down to the children of the community. My father recounted an incident in his youth when a bunch of teenage hooligans chased a Chinese man who wore the traditional long single braid down his back and dressed in the traditional pajama. When they finally caught him, they held him down and cut off his long braided pigtail. Dad knew this particular Chinese man, and later, when he inquired around the Chinese community as to why he hadn't been seen around, Dad was told that the man in question had taken to his bed after the assault, and had died of humiliation.

ભ

"You're Next, Mr. Wong"

I once had the privilege of interviewing New Westminster pioneer, Hilda Tait shortly before her 100th birthday.

Hilda had joined B.C. Tel as an operator in 1906 when the local exchange was situated in the Burr Block at Columbia and Fourth Streets. In 1908, when the exchange was moved to Clarkson Street, she became chief operator. A gracious lady, she was very candid about the old days: "Eventually we could call Seattle, and we had two operators for Long Distance. Vancouver was long distance, too. There were only two lines to Vancouver – one each way. So businessmen would call 'Central' (the common term of those days meaning the operator) to have their names put on a waiting list, and we would call them when their turn came to use the Vancouver line. This was about 1910.

"The Chinese would also do business with each other between here and Vancouver. They would call Central, quite irate, saying, 'What for I not get my call, missy? I wait two hours!' And they had, too. Sometimes even longer. That's because the policy in those days was to shift the Chinese business requests to the bottom of the pile. Oh the terrible things we did to them! So we'd say, 'Oh yes, Mr. Wong, you're next!' .

Racial discrimination led to the invention of the dial telephone. Therefore it is not surprising that dial service, which conveniently bypassed the operator, was invented by a German undertaker who was convinced that operators in his small U.S. town were prejudicially steering funeral customers to his non-German competitor.

CR

A Proper Courtship

One day in 1910, my dad, as circulation manager for *The Daily Province*, was walking along Sixth Avenue on his way to investigate a customer's complaint. As he passed 319, a young girl came running around the corner of the house, waving her apron and shouting as she chased a wayward chicken. My dad paused, and leaning on the fence to watch, he loudly cleared his throat to catch the attention of the pretty girl. She stopped in her tracks and looked at him. She blushed to the roots of her hair, spun around and raced out of sight. That blush did it. Lewie Sangster was "thunder-bolted!"

Conveniently, one of dad's schoolmates, Ben Gunn, lived at 315, the house next door. He called on Ben and asked him about the girl at 319. Ben told him there were two girls next door. The Appleton sisters. The older one was Naomi and the younger one was Ruth. Realizing that Dad probably meant Naomi, he asked, "Would you like to meet her?" Dad replied, "You bet!" So Ben invited him to a house party he was having the next Saturday evening and assured Lewie that the Appleton girls would be there.

And thus began the courtship of my mother and father.

In that era, young people were rarely allowed to be alone together. There were the occasional house parties where, in a group, they played "Post Office" (a kissing game), when the chaperones weren't in the room. And of course, they danced. But mostly, the courting was done when the young man "came calling".

Dad would arrive at Mother's house early in the evening carrying a small paper bag. In the bag was a mixture of sugar, cocoa and salt and sometimes a few nuts. Mother would supply butter, milk and a pot and the couple would make fudge over the big wood-burning range. You can be assured that there was a lot of bumping into each other and hand touching as they stirred the fudge and tested its "done-ness" by dropping a sample of the mixture into a glass of cold water to see if it was firm enough to pour into a buttered pan. When ready, the pan of fudge was set out on the back porch to cool while the young couple tidied up the kitchen.

My Aunt Ruth was only two years younger than my mother. She was precocious and pushy and I bet my grandmother had her hands full keeping Ruth out of the kitchen so the young couple had some time to themselves.

When the fudge was cool, they would cut it into squares and share it with Naomi's parents and sister. By that time, there was no excuse for Dad to be there, so he would say his polite good-byes and Naomi would see him to the door where I'm sure a quick kiss soon became the norm.

In 1913, the Appletons paid an extended visit to Sacramento, California. Before they left, Lewis and Naomi had an "understanding". In today's language, they were "engaged to be engaged". Thus began a romance by correspondence.

Dad confessed to me that after some time had passed, he began to have second thoughts. Being the gentleman that he was, he could not bring himself to send Naomi a "Dear Jane" letter, so he took time off from work and booked boat passage to San Francisco, then traveled by train to Sacramento. He hired a hansom cab to take him to the Appleton house on G Street. Naomi was waiting on the porch. "I took one look at her and I KNEW, then and there, that I would spend the rest of my life with her. On my return trip by train to New Westminster, we passengers had an hour to kill in Bellingham, Washington, so I went in search of a jeweler and bought a diamond solitaire ring, insured it, and mailed it to your mother." Mother used to laughingly say, "We were engaged by correspondence!"

Lewis and his blushing bride were married in Sacramento April 6, 1915, Dad's twin, Philip Sangster, was Best Man and Ruth Appleton was her sister's Maid of Honour. They honeymooned

The Appleton sisters, Ruth (14) and Naomi (16) on the porch of 319 Sixth Avenue - The Sangster Collection.

in San Francisco to attend the 1915 World's Fair before returning to New Westminster to begin their married life together. The photos Dad took of the Fair are remarkable. Mother left me a cherished keep-sake from the Japanese Pavilion at the Fair. It is a beautiful fringed pure silk shawl delicately embroidered with Japanese chrysanthemums.

Lewis and Naomi Sangster celebrated their Fiftieth Wedding Anniversary in 1965. Three years later Dad passed away.

CR

Five Brothers – No Substitutes

On the western edge of our City Hall property stands a granite monument to Timothy Mahoney, known as "Tim" to all the boys he coached in the game of basketball at the YMCA. Five of those boys were Sangsters – Walker, Rufus, the twins Lewis and Philip, and George, the youngest. Under Tim's expert coaching the five Sangster brothers (no substitutes) began to beat all comers in the game of basketball.

Talk of war with the Kaiser was in the air. All five boys were in the Reserves, so they, along with their coach moved their practices to the Armories and became the Westminster Regiment official basketball team. They were hot. Their father, Alex, became their manager and the Sangster boys won the Inter-City League. The Provincial Tournament was on the horizon and the Westminster Regiment team was the touted favourite when suddenly war broke out, and Walker, who was Quartermaster for the Regiment, was soon on his way to France.

Backrow: Cunningham, Alex Sangster, Tim Mahoney
Frontrow: Rufus, Walker, Philip, Lewis and
Reclining: George Sangster - photographer unknown.

In the early weeks of World War I, Captain Walker Sangster, centre on the Sangster brother's basketball team, was killed "going over the top" by a German sniper as he led his troops out of the trenches. Combatant officers in WW I, by order, wore all their identifying insignia on their tunics and they carried only a pistol! They were easy targets for snipers and the officers on the front lines often didn't last long. My Uncle Walker's body was never found. And that was the end of the basketball team.

The four other brothers tried to enlist immediately. They rejected George - too young. Rufus was talked out of it as he had a wife and child. Philip was signed up immediately, but Lewis was rejected because of ingrown toe nails. Dad was devastated. He went directly to his family doctor and had painful surgery on his feet. As soon as he healed, he too signed up.

The twins, Lewis and Philip, made a pact. They would never accept a promotion and would remain "Buck Privates" and they would join different Regiments so the likelihood of them fighting in the same battle would be a remote possibility. They made these decisions in the hope of sparing their mother another tragic telegram.

During the fighting in France, the twins tried to keep track of each other's Regiments. During a lull in the fighting, Dad heard that Philip's group was just down the road. Carefully slipping away, he located one of Philip's Sergeants and inquired of his whereabouts. The Sergeant stepped to the entryway of a nearby bunker and yelled, "PRIVATE SANGSTER …..REPORT!" No answer. So Dad stuck his head into the bunker and yelled, "ILIP-PHAY"! Immediately he heard a voice reply, "EWIS-LAY!" Their childhood use of Pig-Latin brought the brothers together in a bear hug. It was October 30, 1916—their 25th birthday!

Later in the war, Dad got word that Philip had been wounded on a nearby battle field. Dad was a Battalion Scout, so running through hostile territory was nothing new to him. He searched for hours on the battlefield with no luck until he met a soldier who said that Philip had been captured. It was true. It was later confirmed that Philip had been wounded, taken captive, operated on without anesthetic and eventually "exchanged" along with other Canadian prisoners for German prisoners. Uncle Phil was left with a permanent limp.

Dad's talent as an athlete and outstanding sprinter was the reason he was recruited as a Battalion Scout. There were no walkie-talkies in that war, and messages were sent and replies received by runner. This was a dangerous job, and enemy snipers were on the alert for lone soldiers traveling with speed. Sensitive messages were memorized in case of capture. Dad was young and confident and often took shortcuts through enemy territory if his message was urgent.

To boost morale among the Canadian troops in France, it was decided to hold a track meet called the Canadian Corps Sports and all battalions sent their best athletes back from the Front to a training centre. The 47th Battalion included my father in their roster. Dad told me, "We athletes ate the best of food, slept in real beds, and were kept warm and dry. We got hot baths and professional rub-downs whenever we needed them. After a couple of weeks we competed in the Games. I was in all the sprints and actually came second to Tom Longboat, the Canadian Indian who eventually went to the Olympics! It was great to be treated like a valuable race-horse, but the minute the Games were over they shipped us back to the trenches – to the mud, and the rats, and the lice and the damp beds. We were never dry. It wasn't long before I succumbed to double pneumonia and was invalided out and sent back to England."

Dad was not expected to live. In those pre-antibiotic times, pneumonia was considered a death sentence, especially if it was in both lungs. Recently, our daughter Kim got interested in websites about WW I and actually found Dad's medical report from France. The Transfer was written and signed by Captain John McCrae, the Canadian Medical Doctor who wrote *In Flanders Fields*. Ironically, Capt. McCrae himself caught pneumonia and died two months later.

Back in England at the rehabilitation hospital in Folkstone, Kent, Dad slowly gained his health back. Eventually, he got word that Philip had been part of a prisoner exchange and was on his way back to England.

One morning at Parade, they announced that any soldier able to travel could get the day off if he signed up to go to an RAF air show at a nearby airfield. Although most of the soldiers were still recuperating, they figured a day off was a day off, so most of them went to the air show to watch the fly-boys do their stuff. Actually, the air show was really a recruitment show, and tables were lined up prepared to sign up any soldier willing to transfer to the air corps. According to Dad, the demonstration was really great, except for the fact that three planes crashed and all three pilots were killed! Guess how many soldiers signed up to transfer to the Air Corps.

Major McEwen MD and Pte. Lewis Sangster
on leave together in London
- Sangster Collection.

Dad kept in touch with many home town boys who were overseas. His diaries were full of the names of his school chums. One of his close school pals was Bruce McEwan. Bruce already had his MD when he signed up so was automatically commissioned as a Major in the Medical Corps. After meeting up with Bruce in London, they spent a great day together seeing the sights. The next morning, Dad was summoned to Report. He was reprimanded for fraternizing with someone above his rank and given extra KP. Someone had seen him and Bruce together and turned him in. No one turned in Bruce. These were the kind of rules Canadian boys did not understand. They came from Canada, a "classless society" where officers were just ordinary guys like them who had got promoted, whereas the British Forces officers were from the "upper class" and NEVER fraternized with the men. ໑

Tales From The Trenches

I often wondered why my father's War stories were always upbeat and interesting while many or most returning soldiers refused to talk about their war experience. It wasn't until I saw the surprisingly authentic movie, "Passchendaele" that it came to me. I knew Dad had been at Passchendaele and as I watched that movie which was based on a true story, I suddenly realized why Dad wasn't more traumatized by his war experience. As a battalion scout, HE NEVER HAD TO KILL! In fact, Dad didn't carry a weapon if he could help it. The weight slowed him down. Speed was of the essence!

Let me share some of his experiences. Sometimes the scouts were told to forage for themselves. Always in twos, they would pester local farm wives for food. But more importantly, for a warm, dry place to sleep and the use of the farm wife's flat-iron (or was it glad-iron?). The irons came in two parts – a handle with a clamp, and the heavy iron smoothing part. Often there were two or more of these heavy parts kept hot on the top of the wood stove. When the iron being used cooled off, it was ejected from the clamp to the stove top and the handle was clamped onto a fresh hot iron.

Now, these Canadian soldiers weren't trying to have neatly pressed uniforms amid the mud and squalor of the Front. They were only trying to rid themselves of as many lice and their nits (eggs) as possible. Dad said that as the hot iron was pressed down a seam in a shirt or trousers, you could hear the "psssst, pop, psssst, pop" of the nits and "cooties" as they fried. He said he hated lice worse than the rats that sometimes slept on his chest in the bunkers or pill-boxes. A rat could be chased away, but not a louse.

The best night's sleep he ever had overseas was when he and his buddy were allowed to sleep in a barn. The grain harvest had just finished and a whole bin in the barn was full of bran. The two young soldiers snuggled down into the bran, pulling it over them like a blanket. The bran seemed to contain its own warmth, and the dryness of the bran sucked every bit of dampness out of their clothing.

Being continually wet was one of the worst tortures in trench warfare. Their socks rotted on their feet. They were constantly berated to keep their feet dry but it was an impossibility. On one of the first days Lewie Sangster bedded down inside a pillbox, soaking wet to his skin, a British sergeant entered with the daily "tot of rum" – the traditional right of all British servicemen, not just sailors. He filled each man's tin mug and when he came to Lewie, my father said, "No thank you, Sergeant, I promised my mother I would never touch alcohol and I signed a pledge." (Dad was a good Baptist boy).

The old Sergeant bellowed, "HOLD OUT YOUR MUG! NOW DRINK IT DOWN! THAT'S AN ORDER!" Dad choked down the unfamiliar burning liquid blinking tears between coughs. "Now listen to me, sonny. While you're in this God-forsaken war you will down your tot of the King's rum, and then you'll wrap yourself in TWO blankets and fall into your bunk. It's the one sure thing that might extend your life in this hellhole!" Dad said it was the best piece of advice he ever got in the army. The rum made you perspire heavily, and when you awoke you were dry and the outer blanket was soaked in your sweat.

He told me that they became toughened to the sight of dead bodies. Sometimes bodies were stacked high awaiting a burial detail, and it was not an uncommon sight during the lulls in fighting to see a soldier propping a mirror on a stack of corpses as he shaved, using a mug of hot tea which was the only hot liquid they ever got. Being clean-shaven was compulsory, even in the trenches!   By the way, in WWI, soldiers were encouraged to NOT shave their upper lip as the belief of the times was that shaving your upper lip weakened your eyesight! Go Figure!

Dad described a weird happening: He witnessed three officers in a tent with the canvas sides rolled up. They stood around a table covered with ordinance maps. Suddenly out of nowhere, a stray shell made a direct hit on the tent. One officer escaped unscathed. One officer was severely wounded. Not a trace of the third officer was found!

At one of the farmhouses that he and his buddy went to, the farmwife sat them down at the kitchen table and gave them soup and bread. Heaven! All the while she kept up a conversation with two other women who were visiting her kitchen. On the stove were several large copper pots of hot water. She reached up and took a large washtub off the wall where it hung on a nail and began to fill the tub with hot water. Then she laid out towels and soap. Just then her husband walked in. He was very grimy like maybe he'd been down a mine. To the shock of the two Canadian lads, the man began to undress until he stood buck naked and stepped into the tub. His wife brought him a well prepared pipe and a flaming twig from the fire. He took several long drags and then contentedly puffed away, still standing in the tub, while his wife washed him from head to foot with a soapy rag, all the while keeping up a running conversation with her two lady friends. I'm sure neither of those boys could ever imagine their own Canadian fathers putting on such an immodest spectacle!

I think we often forget that many of these young WW1 soldiers were green as grass and very unworldly. On Dad's first leave to a French city, he spent the day like a tourist. When Nature called, he entered a public toilet which was basically a long outhouse with about ten holes in a row. He sat down and no sooner got settled when a big, stout French woman walked in and sat down on the hole right next to him, opened her bag and took out her knitting! Dad froze. He looked neither right nor left. He barely breathed. After what seemed like an eternity, the woman put away her knitting, attended to business, straightened her clothing and left. Dad got out of there as quickly as he could because that was just about all the embarrassment a Baptist boy could endure.

Irving Berlin wrote, "How you gonna keep 'em down on the farm, after they've seen Paree?" Today we'd call it culture shock.

After Dad was sent back to England to recuperate, he received word that Philip had been part of a "prisoner exchange" and he, too, was back in England. The twins made arrangements to meet in London.

"Philip was quite the cut-up," Dad said. "At Madam Toussaud's Waxworks, we were looking at a display entitled, *Soldiers of the Empire*. Each wax figure wore the uniform from one of the Commonwealth countries. Each figure had a cardboard tag attached to it describing the rank and country of origin. With a twinkle in his eye, Philip stepped into the display and struck a pose as if he were a wax figure too. Just then, two English women rounded the corner and began to study the display. Philip didn't move a muscle as the two women began to search his tunic for his cardboard tag. Just then, Philip loudly cleared his throat and stepped forward and gave them a snappy salute! The two women screamed, and Philip and I beat a hasty retreat! Philip was a born actor. He should have gone into show business."

ᘉ

Hello Central

As my father's troop train wound its way through the Fraser Valley, he realized his bride and the folks at home had no idea when his train would be arriving. He had wired from Montreal that their troop ship had docked and that they would be boarding a CPR train shortly. They couldn't predict when they would reach Vancouver because troop trains had no schedule and were often relegated to a siding while scheduled trains commanded the right-of-way.

But now the end was in sight, and barring unforeseen circumstances, an arrival time could be determined, so Dad quizzed the Conductor, who consulted his railroad timepiece and gave him an arrival time. There wasn't time to have a telegram delivered, so a phone call was in order. The Conductor informed Dad that shortly they would be stopping at Whonnock in the Fraser Valley to take on water. That would take about ten or fifteen minutes.

As the train slowed to a stop, Dad leaped off the train and commandeered the station phone. When the operator asked, "Number, please," He gave her the Appleton's phone number in New Westminster where his wife, Naomi had been living with her parents for the last three years while he was overseas. It rang, and rang, and rang. No Answer!

He begged the operator to try again, in case it was a wrong connection.

Still no luck.

In desperation, my father contacted the operator once more.

"Operator, I'm a returning soldier and I haven't seen my wife for over three years. There's no answer at her house, and I want to let her know what time to meet my train." The operator was wonderful. She took down all the pertinent information, and as Dad's train made its way to the coast, she kept on trying the phone number until finally someone answered.

When Dad debarked at the Vancouver CPR Depot, there was his bride. Both her parents, her sister Ruth, both of Dad's parents, and his sister Nellie had accompanied her. But Dad only had eyes for Naomi. He had married her in April and joined the 131st Battalion in October. So theoretically, she was still a bride, having only enjoyed married bliss less than a year. Exactly 9 months later, my brother Ross was born!

Oh yes, there was also the driver of the car that had made the trip from New Westminster, It was a great big touring car, but I can't, for the life of me, remember who that Good Samaritan was.

That operator who helped Dad out was typical of the days before dial phones. There was no 911. But there was always a friendly voice on the line whenever you picked up the receiver. She could summon the fire department, the police, a doctor or an ambulance. In small towns, if the doctor wasn't home, she'd track him down too!

Newly-weds Naomi and Lewis Sangster, 1915 - photographer unknown.

The operators were "no nonsense" girls. It isn't any wonder, for their supervising operator was literally breathing down their necks. In the larger phone exchanges, some chief operators actually wore roller skates so they could roll the length of the long switchboards and check up on any girl who might be slacking off!

When my sister-in-law Bonnie Benson Peterson was an operator in the mid fifties, we had a code. If she took a call that I placed, after I gave her the number, she would reply, "Thank you, madam." And I knew it was her.

My grandma Bessie liked to tell of the time she waited, and waited for Central to come on the line and ask, "Number, please". Getting impatient, my grandmother muttered, "Hmph. She must have gone to take a pee," and an indignant voice retorted, "I did not! You nasty thing!"

CR

Divine Retribution

As a young man, and then as a newly-wed, my father worked in the City Treasurer's Office. In those days before World War I, everyone in town came into the City Hall, in person, to pay his or her electric light bill. There were so many Chinese in those days, for New Westminster still had a large Chinatown at the foot of Royal Avenue, that Dad learned to count in Chinese so he could ask for the correct payment from a Chinese customer to pay the electric bill, and then count out the change in Chinese, if required. To this day, I can count to 100 in Chinese the way he taught me!

When Lewie left City Hall to go overseas with the Westminster Regiment boys in 1915, everyone wished him God speed, and his Supervisor assured him his job would be waiting for him when he returned from "Killing the Hun". While overseas, he received a package containing letters from all his co-workers at City Hall (see list following), including Mayor Wells Gray, who later became premier of British Columbia Here is a quote from Mayor Wells Gray's letter to Dad:

City Treasurer's office, clerks Santo Brown and Lewie Sangster
- Sangster Collection.

March 30, 1917

Dear Lewie:

I am writing you a few lines for the purpose of letting you know that we are all pulling for you, when the news arrived here that you were very ill.

I can assure you we all felt greatly concerned but hopeful that your good clean life* would mean everything in the strain upon your system...

Your position with the City will be all O.K. also, but I suppose when you return you will be after MY position.** Well I will try and hold it for you...

Good luck, As always,

Your friend, Wells

When Dad finally returned home from overseas, nearly three years later, he reported to City Hall to resume his duties in the City Treasurer's Office. "Sorry," he was told, "but you were gone so long we had to replace you. We gave your job to young Al So-'n-so". Dad was furious. He felt betrayed and indignant that they would break their word to a war veteran. I'm sure many other vets got the same treatment.

So Dad, who always had the "gift of the gab", took training with the Mutual Life of Canada and became a Chartered Life Underwriter, an insurance agent, successfully selling life insurance up until his death in 1968.

Over a decade later, in the 1930's at the height of the Great Depression, the city was stunned to learn that more than $30,000 had been embezzled from the City coffers! A huge sum in those lean years—close to half a million today.

The thief was caught, tried, and sent to the B.C. Penitentiary to serve his time. His name? You guessed it! It was the very same guy who was hired to replace Lewie Sangster while he was overseas.

"Humph!" My father would say whenever he told the story of the City embezzlement. "Served them right! That'll teach them not to go back on their word to a veteran! I call it Divine Retribution!"

---

* Pte. Sangster was sent from the trenches back to England with double-pneumonia and was expected to die. Mayor Gray's prediction that Lewie's "clean life" would help him survive, referred to the fact that Dad was an outstanding athlete who neither drank alcohol nor smoked.

** Wells Gray's prediction came true! J. Lewis "Lewie" Sangster DID aspire to the Mayor's chair, and in November 1948, he was elected Mayor of the City of New Westminster.

Pte. J. L. Sangster received a package while overseas that contained letters from every person who worked in the New Westminster City Hall with him before he joined up and went Overseas with the Westminster Regiment. The letters were dated March 30, 1917.

Someday these letters will be bequeathed to the City Archives.

LETTERS FROM CITY HALL

Mayor Wells Gray
City Jailer C. E. Pittendrigh
City Clerk W.A. Duncan
Assessment Commissioner F. Broad
Superintendent Board of Works L. J (illegible)
City Treasurer Stan (illegible)
Assistant Treasurer George N(illegible)
License Inspector (illegible)
Building Inspector Y.Y. (illegible)
City Engineer H. Stewardson
Assistant City Clerk T. J. Thomas
Caretaker P. Tuney
Health Inspector H. Pearce
Engineering Clerk G.R.W(illegible)
Plumbing Inspector J. C. Neig
Meter Man Dick (illegible)
Policeman E. Johnston
Electric Light Clerk Ronald (illegible)
Police Sergeant Ed Pentland
Water Roll Clerk J.C.Robson
Detective W. Burrows
Meter Man Deight (illegible)
Roll Clerk Santo Brown
City Electrician James C. Digby
Ambulance Driver Wm. Sharp

CR

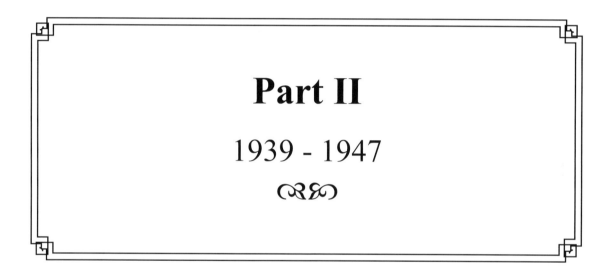

Part II

1939 - 1947

ॐ

Their Majesties King George VI And Queen Elizabeth

In the spring of 1939, there was great excitement and anticipation at our house as my father and mother made preparations to be presented to King George and Queen Elizabeth. I still have the cutaway coat, pinstriped pants and silk top hat my father wore that day. Mother practiced the required curtsy over and over as I, aged five, stood on a chair and pretended to be the Queen. At first, Mom wobbled. Once, she actually took a tumble, but eventually, her curtsy was perfect.

On the big day, I was sick in bed. But my Grandma Bessie, who was looking after me, bundled me up and stood me on a kitchen stool at the foot of our driveway so I could wave my miniature Union Jack as they drove past our house on Sixth Avenue. Dad had bought a full sized British flag plus red white and blue bunting for the front of our house. My sister Norma was with her school at Queen's Park and my brother Ross managed to

Their Majesties at Queen's Park Oval - Ross Sangster

snap a great photo of the king and queen as they circled the Oval.

The royal couple were met at the old station near the front of the Penitentiary by Mayor and city aldermen accompanied by their wives. A three-foot-wide red carpet was rolled out the length of the splintery old station platform for Their Majesties to walk on as they emerged from their open touring car to board the Royal Hudson train. The royal entourage stood on the red carpet long enough for each civic dignitary and wife to be officially presented. The gentlemen bowed, the ladies curtsied and everyone wore gloves as they shook the Royal Hands. Mother always treasured her gloves. "These gloves shook the hands of the King and Queen of England!" she would say proudly. I often wonder what became of those gloves.

The red carpet was later cut into four foot sections and each civic official was given a length of carpet as a souvenir. Our piece of royal red carpet was a welcome-mat inside our front door for more than two decades until it wore so thin it had to be discarded - with regret.

Alderman Sangster and wife, Naomi, all dressed up to meet the king and queen - Sangster Collection.

Mother loved to tell how, as Queen Elizabeth stood on the red carpet awaiting the presentations, the Queen glanced down at one of those little step-stools used by passengers to step down from the train. It was too close to her feet, so she reached out a "royal" foot and casually flicked it out of her way. She stole my mother's heart with that simple gesture – so regal, yet so down-to-earth. Elizabeth Bowes Lyon never did lose the human touch. A great and endearing lady, fondly remembered by all.

ℭℛ

The Big Band Sound

Mart Kenny and his Western Gentlemen were Canada's answer to Glenn Miller. In 1938, the "Big Band Sound" was what young people wanted to dance to, and my brother Ross audaciously wrote to Mart Kenny to hire him for a Duke of Connaught High School dance. Kenny accepted! So the boys' fraternity, *Rho Delta Rho*, rented the Arenex and invited the public to a fundraiser dance for their club.

When the bus-load of musicians arrived in town too early to get into the Arenex, Ross invited them over to our home. The neighbours were all eyes as the big bus eased into our driveway with a long banner on its side proclaiming, *MART KENNY AND HIS WESTERN GENTLEMEN.*

Typically, my mother took it all in stride and set about making something for her guests to eat. Meanwhile, the orchestra members took her at her word and made themselves at home, using the upstairs bedrooms to change into their tuxedoes. As I recall, several overloaded fuses were blown by their new-fangled electric shavers.

As an impressionable four-year-old, another of my vivid memories of that first visit is following singer, Norma Lock (later Mrs. Kenny) around the house, totally awestruck by her shimmering evening gown and her captivating voice as she walked about vocalizing.

Before leaving to play for the dance at Queen's Park Arenex, the band members had a quick sandwich and a slice of my mother's special angel food cake, which was made with 13 egg whites, as there were no "mixes" in those days. When Mart Kenny tasted the cake, he got a faraway look in his eyes – like he'd rediscovered a long-lost love.

That night was the first of many engagements by the Western Gentlemen in our city over the years to follow. The next time, a telegram was delivered to our house addressed to my mother informing her, *Will arrive such & such a date and time. Please bake an angel cake. –Mart Kenny*

I still remember that day in my childhood whenever I hear Mart Kenny's theme song, *"The West, a Nest, and You."*

ᘯ

Civic Picnic 1939

Before the world became so complicated, the City of New Westminster held an annual picnic for its employees and their families.

In the summer of 1939, the City hired a steamship for a cruise to Sechelt Park on the Sunshine Coast just north of Vancouver.

The ship docked at the New Westminster pier and happy families strolled aboard carrying picnic baskets, swimming gear, balls and bats and blankets. Everyone was in a happy mood. The sun was shining and everything was right with the world.

The war drums were sounding in Europe. But in New Westminster on that bright summer day, we were looking forward to a scenic boat cruise and then games, races and a picnic lunch at Sechelt. People lined the rails to wave goodbye to landlubbers, and as we cruised down the south arm of the Fraser River there was a holiday feeling aboard as couples and family groups strolled the decks or joined a group for a sing-song or commandeered a table for a game of bridge or rummy or cribbage.

But that all changed when we reached the mouth of the river. A stiff headwind was blowing on the Gulf of Georgia and huge waves and rollers began to cause our ship to roll and pitch. Before long, passengers began heading to the nearest washroom, but when they all began to fill up, people with greenish faces headed for the railings. Soon every inch of railing space was taken up and people began searching for receptacles - buckets, waste-baskets or anything in their picnic hampers or beach equipment like a paper bag or even a bathing cap!

Eventually, people just threw up on the floor where they sat. The poor crew soon lost the cleanup battle. Children were crying. Adults were moaning. Even those who considered themselves "good sailors" succumbed to *mal du mer* simply because of the stench and their close proximity to people retching and gagging.

My mother later told me that she had laid beach towels on the floor for our family to use, and between waves of nausea and vomiting, I said, "Mommy, tell the captain to stop at the **first island** he comes to!"

Eventually we reached Sechelt and soon everyone got rid of their sea legs, cleaned themselves up and I'm pleased to say that everyone had a great day. The crew of the ship pulled out the hoses, and when we returned to the ship for the trip home, the ship was sparkling clean. Word had it that one city employee had lost his false teeth overboard, and that only two persons on board had not been sick – the Captain and a stalwart St. John Ambulance nurse!

I don't recall any other Civic Picnic cruises. This wasn't because of the terrible seasick experience, but rather World War II had broken out, and fuel was soon rationed, so non-essential trips using any form of transportation were considered unpatriotic.

Years later, at a family gathering of my new husband Don's relatives, I met that stalwart St. John Ambulance nurse who didn't get seasick all those years before. Her name was Nellie Featherstonehaugh and she was my new Grandmother-in-law, who we called "Grandma Nel". She remained stalwart, and every year she passed her St. John Ambulance test to keep her certification current. The last test was administered when she was 100 years of age. She passed with flying colours, and lived to be 103!

It must have been her hardy Viking heritage.

CR

My Own Liberace

His name was Frankie. I never knew his last name. He was our piano-tuner and every year or so he came to tune the baby grand piano that took up one whole corner of our living room.

Even as a preschooler, I sensed Frankie was different. He had shoulder-length hair and always wore gloves even in warm weather. And whenever Mother and Dad discussed Frankie, I sensed they were using a kind of code-language that I was not privy to.

Frankie was a concert pianist who played in a symphony orchestra and tuned pianos to augment his meager musician's income. When he arrived at our house, mother would greet him and lead him to the piano. He would remove his gloves and outer garments. Then, from a small leather case he would produce a shiny tuning-fork which rang a beautiful, perfect "C". That was all he needed. From that point on, he tuned each black or white key using only his well attuned ears and a tiny ratchet. Mother said Frankie had "perfect pitch".

Today's piano tuners use an electronic tuner. There was one in the Band Room at New Westminster Secondary School (NWSS) where I often was the substitute band teacher. The tuner was plugged into an electrical source, and any band instrument could be tuned to it, even the kettle drums. It had a circular face which had a design of concentric circles on it. By playing a specified note into its mike, the circle would spin either clockwise or counter-clockwise. A clockwise spin denoted that the note played was sharp and a counter-clockwise spin meant the note played was flat. Today, using this type of device, piano-tuners tighten or loosen each piano wire until the gadget spins neither right nor left.

Frankie used his tiny ratchets on our piano strings too, relying on his own ear until the satisfactory sound was produced by each key.

All during this long, technical procedure, I sat quietly under the baby grand, clutching my favorite doll, and waiting for the moment when Frankie was satisfied with his handiwork. Then, after stretching all his fingers to warm them up, he would begin to play.

And how he could play! He introduced me to Beethoven, Tchaikovsky and Brahms. His pianissimos gave me goose bumps. His crescendos made my heart thump. Sometimes he would stop in the middle of a sonata or concerto and make a tiny adjustment to one of the piano strings. And then he would continue with my private and privileged concert.

I was always sad for me when it was over. Frankie would don his clothes, including his gloves, and Mother would give him a cheque and escort him to the door.

Years later, I understood the caustic jeer yelled at boys who were overdue for a trip to the barber…"GET A VIOLIN!!!" for in those bygone days, only male musicians could legitimately wear long hair.

When the hippy era dawned, boys brave enough to grow their hair long were often the object of jeers. One handsome young lad on the Richmond Junior lacrosse team was the first of their league to have hair that hung below his helmet. Whenever he found himself tussling in a corner for a loose ball, someone in the crowd would holler, "Hit him with your purse! Hit him with your purse, Shirley!"

Don and I were young parents when the Beatles came on the scene. We loved their music. In fact, Don attended the Beatles Concert at Empire Stadium in Vancouver as chaperone to several neighbourhood teeny-boppers. We eventually allowed our boys to grow their hair into Beatle haircuts. Only recently, our youngest son, now in his fifties, confessed that while he was a student at Spencer School, one of his close chums was not allowed to bring our son to his house to play after school because of his Beatles "mop top". The boy's parents believed our son was obviously a bad influence on their son. The boy's parents probably figured the Benson parents were far too liberal - might even (God forbid!) be hippies!

CR

Christmas 1940

One of my early Christmas memories is from 1940 when at age six, I asked my mother how Santa got into our house. Because we didn't have a fireplace with a chimney, my sister and I always hung our stockings on the foot of our beds. Mother gave me one of her wise-mother looks and said, "Come with me". She took me down the basement and showed me, high up in a corner, the old coal shute that hadn't been used in decades. It seemed logical to me that Santa could easily get into our house that way so I didn't question it.

On Christmas morning in my Christmas stocking, along with many little toys, was a Japanese orange, a couple of marzipan fruit, and (the tip-off) a large, pink-paper-wrapped Rogers' reknowned "Victoria Cream" chocolate from Victoria, B.C.

When I again expressed my skepticism about the existence of Santa Claus, my mother scowled and took me into the kitchen. First she looked under the kitchen counter into the little wooden box which we had bought from the grocer only two days before. The box had been pried open and a couple of Japanese oranges were missing. Next she looked in the cupboard on her personal shelf where she kept her "goodies". A box of marzipan was open and so was the beautiful burgundy chocolate box from *Rogers'*. It too, was missing a couple of "Victoria Creams". "The old rascal!" said Mother. "I'll bet Santa's having trouble finding candy, just like everyone else. With all the wartime shortages, I'm sure he knew I'd understand his problem."

I continued to be a believer for a couple more years because, after all, Mother knows best.

Christmas 1946, Evelyn with nephew Craig Walton. - Norma Walton

Our City's Very Own Lake

In very cold winters, the city fire trucks would flood the upper Moody Park playing fields near Eighth Avenue and Tenth Street. Those upper fields didn't have any drainage and huge swamps of water formed in that area from fall until late spring. It was the closest New Westminster ever came to having its very own lake, and it was the perfect place for an outdoor skating rink.

If there was a snowfall, somehow the ice got cleared. Someone shoveled it. Probably Tenth Street neighbourhood kids brought their shovels across the street. They were the ones who got the most use out of the rink.

I particularly remember being taken to Moody Park by my older sister Norma and her friends. Mother had made nice warm ski-pants for me out of a torn pair of my brother's heavy wool army pants which I think were called "battle dress". It wasn't too long before I began to whine to my sister that I wanted to go home. I was cold, and my knees hurt. My sister and her friends were having a great time. There were lots of boys there.

Finally, I began to howl and my sister relented and took me home. I think she was embarrassed by my antics. I remember she was really mad at me. When we got home, Mother undressed me and she gasped when she saw my legs. The heavy rough wool army pants material had worn the skin raw on the inner sides of my knees. My tender seven-year-old skin wasn't as tough as a soldier's. From then on, when I put those ski pants on, I wore my nice soft flannelette pajama pants underneath.

When New Westminster was granted the Canada Summer Games in 1973, all sporting venue improvements were paid for by a three-way split between the Federal, Provincial and Civic governments. So New Westminster dug up the Moody Park upper fields and lay drainage pipes so the fields could be used all year round for soccer and softball, and paid only 33 cents on the dollar! It was a bargain. But we lost the only "lake" we ever had.

My sister Norma and me
- Sangster Collection

CR

"Pay-toll-o" Bridge

In the 1930s, in the depths of the Great Depression, my father was an Alderman. He was the youngest on council and like many young men, progressive in his thinking. When it became known that the Provincial Government was planning a new bridge over the Fraser River, the city council began discussing the city's participation in the planning of the new span.

When Dad learned that the proposed new bridge would have only two lanes of traffic, just like the present bridge (two lanes for vehicles had been built above the old train bridge) he was aghast. He proposed that the new bridge be SIX lanes, to prepare for the future when all families would have an automobile.

He was practically laughed out of the council chamber. "Don't be ridiculous," he was told. "Only the well-off will have cars. We're in a Depression, son!" Anyone who knew Lewie Sangster, knew he could be very stubborn. Especially if he believed he was right. So Lewie stuck to his guns, and finally convinced other council members to back his plan for six lanes.

The government compromised by making the bridge FOUR lanes, and named the bridge for "Duff" Patullo, B.C. Premier at the time. It was a toll bridge for more than twenty years, and people began calling it the "Pay-toll-o" Bridge.

The toll was 25 cents, the equivalent of about $3 today. Frequent crossers bought books of tickets at a reduced cost. My job, as a little girl, was to hand the ticket to the toll-booth operator on the Surrey side of the bridge. It made me feel very important until one day, as I handed over the ticket, our fingers touched, and "Zap", a jolt of static electricity shot up my arm and scared me. From then on, I refused to hand over the ticket.

Another of Dad's Depression Era ideas was also rejected. Because the Municipality of Burnaby was bankrupt and went into receivership, Dad proposed that New Westminster BUY, (at 25 cents on the dollar), all adjoining Burnaby land, as far as Royal Oak! This would have given our city two lakes, and more available industrial, residential and park lands. Until the day he died, he bemoaned the short-sightedness of that Depression-era city council.

Hindsight is 20/20. Too bad Lewie Sangster's progressive ideas were rejected. A lot of bridge accidents and fatalities could have been prevented.

Before the the Patullo bridge was built, the road to Surrey crossed the top of the railway bridge - Sangster Collection.

℞

The Battle of the Snowballs

During the years of World War II, 1939 to 1945, our town had two army camps. One was set up on empty property where the New Westminster Secondary School complex sits today. It used to be bush, bounded by Sixth Street, Tenth Avenue, Eighth Street and Eighth Avenue. Soldiers awaiting transport overseas to the Pacific Theatre were camped there. The sight of soldiers marching down our neighbourhood streets was a common one.

The other army camp was the wooded area of Queen's Park from the back of the Arena parking lot to Sixth Avenue. Barbed wire and all! To school children who went to Spencer School it was quite common to see a tank or other military vehicles rumble down Sixth Avenue and turn into the park!

As the men marched smartly past our school when we were outside for recess or lunch we would flock to the sidewalk's edge to cheer and wave. The guys would wave back and I'm sure we caused many a lump in the throat for these men who had left sons and daughters, brothers and sisters, at home in faraway parts of Canada.

Many wives and children from all over Canada followed their men to the Lower Mainland. Rental accommodations were scarce. Many of these wives trudged from door to door to ask if any spare room was available. I remember helping Mom spring clean the front bedroom as the door bell rang. A woman clutching the hand of a small boy, asked, "I saw you removing curtains, is that a room you could rent me?"

Many big old mansions were divided up into small rental units. My best friend's family rented out their living room/dining room to a soldier's wife and child. She had a hot plate and a toaster only. She got water from the main kitchen and shared the only bathroom with the host family of six.

During the winter of 1942, when I was in Miss Hilda Smith's grade two class, a platoon of soldiers marched by during lunch hour. There had been a beautiful snowfall the night before, and the snow was fresh and fluffy. As we stood at the sidewalk's edge, cheering, one of the soldiers bent down, scooped up a handful of snow and let fly a well-placed snowball.

The fight was on! The soldiers broke formation and attacked. Our Grade Six boys counterattacked. Everyone got into the fun. Boys and girls from Grade One to Grade Six joined in the melee until the school bell summoned us to class and a red-faced sergeant brought his men back into line. But that wasn't the end of it.

After we took our seats back in the class room, sitting smartly "at attention"—backs straight, feet flat on the floor, hands clasped and resting on the desk, Miss Smith stood at the front of the class and slowly looked each of us in the eye one by one, and scowled. Finally, she spoke. "I am SO ashamed of you!"

What followed was a ten minute lecture on our gallant soldiers, patriotism, the War Effort, Spencer School pride, etc., etc., etc. We began to squirm. Some of the girls began to cry. She made us feel so ashamed and unpatriotic for throwing snowballs at "our heroic fighting men".

We were all sentenced to thirty minutes detention after school. It felt like a thirty year sentence as we sat at our desks, backs straight, feet flat on the floor, hands clasped and resting on our desks – and heads bowed, trying to make our seven-year-old brains comprehend just what we'd done wrong.

೧೩

I Remember Eddie

When World War II started in 1939, the conflict was in Europe, half a world away from New Westminster. But when the Japanese navy attacked Pearl Harbour, Hawaii on December 7, 1941, the war was suddenly on our horizon. When a lighthouse off Vancouver Island's west coast was shelled by a Japanese submarine shortly after, war was suddenly in our own front yard.

Fear of invasion coupled with decades of racial discrimination triggered a roundup of citizens of Japanese descent and seizure of their property. Soon more than 20,000 citizens were stripped of their rights and forcibly uprooted from their homes. Many had been born in Canada, yet they were evacuated from "the coastal defense zone" and transported to isolated internment camps in British Columbia's interior.

One of the darkest chapters in Canadian history had begun. And sadly, the shadows would even reach into the classroom of Miss Hilda Smith's grade two class at Herbert Spencer School.

I remember Eddie Ando. His mother had a hairdressing salon near the corner of Sixth and Sixth and his father was a millworker. Eddie's best friend was Herbie Lee whose Chinese parents ran a fruit and vegetable store a few doors away. Each morning, Eddie and Herbie would call on me so we could walk to school together. I know Eddie was still around on Valentine's Day, 1942. He knocked on our front door after dark to bring me a valentine. I remember seeing his father standing discretely in the shadows waiting for him.

Then suddenly one day, Eddie was gone from our lives. We never walked to school together again, and Herbie had lost his best friend. When we asked where Eddie had gone, Miss Smith told us only that Eddie's family had moved away.

A decade later, when I was a student-teacher at Herbert Spencer, long-time teacher Honey McAskill told me this story:

"I had stayed late at school to do some marking. It got dark early in the winter, so I hurried to get home. Air raid drills could come without warning, and street lights were out during the "blackouts" and I didn't want to be on the street when that happened!

I overtook two little boys who were hurrying along ahead of me. I recognized Eddie and Herbie. I could hear them talking, and I heard Eddie, the little Japanese boy say to his Chinese friend, 'Come on, Herbie, we gotta hurry. Those damn Japs might come over and bomb us tonight!'"

Eddie and Evelyn 50 years later. Photo by Don Benson.

I remembered Eddie, and for fifty years I wondered whatever became of him. And then Eddie came back into my life when the phone rang one day and a voice said, "Evelyn? This is Eddie!"

It seems a reporter from the Japanese-Canadian publication, *The Bulletin,* had run a story based on an article I had written for a local paper about losing my friend Eddie. Eddie had read her story in *The Bulletin* and recognized himself as the lost friend.

It really is a small world. Eddie now lived in Coquitlam and commuted to New Westminster to an impressive office at the Quay overlooking the Fraser River. Don and I met with him after his phone call and he recounted to us what had happened to him and his family all those years ago:

"I remembered you, Evelyn, and sometimes wondered about you and our friend Herbie. I remembered Spencer School and some big tough kids from the Loyal Protestant Orphanage. I always walked softly around them and they left me alone.

"I wasn't told any more than you were about why my family had to leave, only that we had to pack up what we each could carry in a suitcase. We were taken to the PNE grounds, and then by train from Vancouver to Taylor Lake near 93 Mile House where our group built a new village on an old ranch.

"My father and the other men all worked for the *Sword Pulp Company*, cutting pulp-wood for shipment to Port Mellon. The kids in all grades attended a two-room school. I will always remember that Nellie Squires, who had been our Grade One teacher at Spencer, somehow tracked me down and sent me a picture book version of *Bambi* as a gift!

"After the war was over, in 1947 we moved to Ashcroft so I could attend high school. After graduation I joined the RCAF and was sent for training to London, Ontario. I became a Flying Officer and Navigator, but my eyesight eventually fell below air-crew standards, so I left the RCAF and came back to the Lower Mainland and attended UBC to get my commerce degree and I became a chartered accountant.

"In a way, I've come full-circle back to our community. My daughter teaches dancing and my son plays lacrosse. If you look out the window, there, you can see the Timberland Lumber Company where my dad used to work before we were taken away. And now Timberland is one of my clients."

That dark chapter in Canadian history is over and Eddie and his family are living proof of what a miscarriage of justice it was. Isn't it ironic that the same government that uprooted Eddie and tens of thousands like him because "they weren't to be trusted," would, ten years later make him an officer in the Royal Canadian Air Force, so he could "defend his country"?"

Note: Eddie Kimiaki Ando B.Comm. C.A. died June 11, 2005 of leukemia

CR

World War II On The Home Front

War was declared in September of 1939.

During the war years, rationing became a way of life. To save gasoline, Dad turned off the engine, put the car in neutral and coasted downhill, while we all prayed the brakes would hold. To stretch meat coupons, Mother observed "Meatless Tuesdays". A new product came on the market to help housewives cope with meatless meals. It was called *Kraft Dinner*, and we loved it. I still do!

To conserve butter coupons she made us try an odd-tasting new product called "oleomargarine" which looked like lard until we added do-it-yourself colouring at home. The result didn't fool anyone because no matter how long you mixed it, there would always be a few tell-tale streaks of orange colouring still showing. The Canadian Milk Producers' lobby feared people would stop using butter if margarine was put on the shelves coloured yellow like butter!

People did a lot of trading of ration stamps. Teetotalers traded their liquor stamps for tea and coffee stamps. People on special diets traded sugar stamps for my dad's honey. A boy we knew fell into the river and nearly drowned and all he could think of, as he struggled under water, was that he had the family ration books in his pocket and his mother would kill him!

We saved tin foil, and tin cans full of bacon grease which were sent to the munitions factories. We knitted. We donated used clothing. We invited servicemen to our homes for Sunday dinner while they waited in B.C. for transport to the Pacific war zone.

Adults bought War Savings Bonds at Columbia Street "bond rallies" promoted, in person, by stars like Jack Benny and Joe E. Brown. Children brought their quarters to school every Friday to buy War Saving Stamps. In art class we drew and coloured posters that said, "Make Hitler Yell Uncle! – Buy War Savings Stamps", and other such patriotic slogans.

We sang, "We Heil, phhhhhht! Heil, phhhhhht! right in der Fuhrer's Face!" and "Rosie, rat-a-tat-tat, the Riveter" (we kids loved songs with sound-effects).

Thinking back, I'm embarrassed to remember one little boy in our neighbourhood who was taunted and harassed constantly throughout the war years simply because his name was Adolph as in Adolf Hitler.

Adults went to the movies mainly to see the newsreels. These censored film clips rarely showed any defeats or setbacks. The audience would cheer every time they showed an enemy plane shot down and boo loudly whenever they showed *Der Fuehrer*.

If single young women couldn't make wing tips for Mosquito Bombers at the Pacific Veneer Plant, or join the CWAC, WRENS, or WAFS, they volunteered at Westminster House, (today known as the Galbraith House), our canteen on Eighth Street at Queens, to serve donuts and coffee to the servicemen. There were games rooms, reading rooms and a generous supply of stationery for the boys to write home to their moms and sweethearts.

Local girls also flocked to the popular afternoon "Tea Dances" featuring the big-band sound on records. The theory was that during the afternoon, no one could get caught in a blackout drill. But in truth, I think mothers thought up the idea to keep their daughters from going out with servicemen after dark.

Speaking of blackouts, we built plywood covers or sewed blackout curtains for our windows. We placed buckets of sand in strategic places throughout the house in case of incendiary bombs. We stocked a First Aid kit. In 2004 I came across our kit in the corner of a shelf in the basement. Some of the medicines and supplies were still in their original wrappers so I donated that WW II First Aid kit to the New Westminster Museum. My sister Norma's husband George Walton was the air raid warden for our block. With flashlight, hard hat and A.R.P. armband, he patrolled the neighbourhood during blackouts until the siren blared an "all-clear". If a window showed even a pin-point of light the air-raid warden would yell, "Douse that light!".

With sugar rationed, and the stores bereft of candy and gum, we kids had to find ways to satisfy our sweettooth cravings. My chums and I would squirrel away sugar, a teaspoonful at a time, without our mothers knowing. When we had accumulated a combined total of two cups of sugar, we'd get together at a house where the mother was out. We'd make fudge, then clean up the mess as quickly as possible. Sometimes we were so nervous of being caught that we didn't cook it long enough. When that happened, we ate the runny, gooey, sugary mess with a spoon! To us it tasted just as good.

My brother, Ross, whenever he was on leave, would bring home chocolate bars from the PX at the army base. What a treat! And one day after a swim at Hume Park, Doris Hagen and I spotted a line-up at a Sapperton corner store. Someone yelled, "Chocolate bars!" We got in line and spent our busfare on *CrispyCrunch* bars, (one per customer) and walked that long walk home – happily munching that heavenly treat.

No one got a new bicycle during the war years. Second-hand bikes were the norm. Bicycle tires were patched and re-patched. My first bike was a second-hand maroon CCM that I bought from Jack Calbeck's sister. New cars were also a thing of the past.

Nylon first made its appearance during the war years. It was invented and used primarily for parachutes. A few lucky brides were wed in gowns of parachute material, no doubt swiped from an airbase by a brother or sweetheart. Nylon stockings were a rarity. Many girls painted their legs, complete with a stylish seam up the back drawn with an eyebrow pencil. When a shipment of nylons arrived at Collisters Dry Goods on Columbia Street, the line-ups began before dawn and stretched for blocks. One pair per customer, so ten-year-old me was dragged into the line-up by my sixteen year old sister to claim an extra pair for her. These sheer stockings were so precious to the women during the war that they put on gloves before they handled them and drew them up their legs for fear that a hang-nail or a ring might snag them! A new profession was invented – mending runs in a stockings. I recall seeing a woman seated behind a counter in Collisters, a nylon stocking stretched across the mouth of a drinking glass using a magnifying glass as she plunged a teeny-tiny crochet hook up and down with lightning speed, mending a "run" in the stocking.

Everyone tried to do SOMETHING for the War Effort. We children attended Saturday Matinees at the Edison Theatre and patriotically paid ten steel coat-hangers for admission. I even remember paying for my ticket with a soup can full of bacon grease for the munitions factories.

Even the "movie serials" of the day often had a patriotic theme as the hero chased a Nazi spy, or narrowly prevented a "saboteur" from blowing up the Empire State Building or a munitions ship in New York harbour.

I even ate my vegetables for the War Effort. "Think of all those poor starving children in Europe," my mother would say.

CR

Doing Our Bit For The Boys Overseas

Mother and a group of her friends met once a week, in the war years 1939 – 1945, to sew for the War Effort. She called it her "Red Cross Club". They made and rolled bandages from old bed sheets, knitted socks, toques and mittens and made "Ditty Bags".

A Ditty Bag was a draw-string pouch into which went one pair of socks and jockey shorts, a razor and blades, toothbrush and toothpaste, a comb, washcloth and soap, etc. But these fillers cost money, so the ladies of the Red Cross Club had to raise cash to buy their supplies.

To meet this need, the ladies made quilts and raffled them off at twenty-five cents a ticket. The quilting bees were held at our house for two reasons: first – Mother owned a large quilting frame*, and second – we had a very large living room to set it up in and it could stay there, leaning against a wall until the next quilting session.

When the frame was put together and the quilt securely pinned in place, the four corners were supported on chair-backs and the ladies sat around it and hand-sewed, or "quilted" the padded comforter.

Every quilt was unique. Each one a work of art. The one I remember most was made entirely of men's silk ties – very elegant and shiny and colourful.

On quilting nights, my job was to sit on the floor under the quilting frame and wait patiently for a needle and thread to suddenly fall down, dangling like a small puppet. I would rescue the needle by pushing it back up close to the spot it popped through. The owner of the needle would grab it and I pull it up and continue her quilting.

These dropping needles did not happen too often, and after a while, the ladies forgot I was there. From my vantage point under the quilt, I got an early education in childbirth, infidelity, death, illness and other serious happenings in the lives of the ladies of the Red

Cross Club. Before I was even nine years old!

* *Two 1 x 2 boards 8 ft. long and two 1 x 2 boards 10 ft. long with heavy double-fold canvas tacked along one edge of each board to which the quilt was pinned. The corners were held together by "C"clamps.*

ᐃᕈ

Women In Wartime

My mother was a nineteen-year-old bride when my father went overseas in 1915 during the First World War. She moved back to her parents' home and then shocked her Victorian father by taking a job. She clerked in the Post Office, "to free a man for active service." During WW I, women were conductors on trolly buses, helped bring in the crops and worked in the many factories involved in the war effort and even volunteered to go overseas as nurses and ambulance drivers.

My neighbour and friend, Iona Pearce, was also 19 when she left her small Vancouver Island community and signed up with the newly-formed Canadian Women's Army Corps (CWACs) at army headquarters in the old Vancouver Hotel in 1941 during the Second World War. After a brief indoctrination period at Vancouver's St. Mary's Priory, Iona was shipped to Alberta for basic training. Iona told me:

"After we were issued uniforms at the priory, we learned basic marching on the streets of Vancouver. At first, people stared. Some laughed, and others made rude remarks, like saying we'd been recruited to be mattresses for officers! They could be very hurtful.

"But later, during the height of the war, we were in great demand to parade at War Bond Rallies to attract the crowds. People were proud of us by then. They cheered!

"Most of the girls, me included, had never been away from home before. Many were literally right off the farm. There was a lot of homesickness. But the lack of privacy was worse! Dozens of women living in close quarters – eating, sleeping, undressing, bathing. It was really hard to get used to. Especially for the very shy ones.

"We were proud of the uniforms, but everyone hated the army-issue underwear - serviceable cotton KHAKI bras and panties! Most of us kept a hidden supply of civilian undies which we wore whenever we thought we'd get away with it. If you got caught, you got punishment – KP (kitchen) or latrine duty.

"I was trained in stenography. While I was stationed at the old Vancouver Hotel as an Ordinance Clerk, I was there the day the munitions ship *Green Hill Park* blew up in the harbour. Windows broke and stuff flew around. We went on full alert – tin hats and all – because everyone thought the Japanese were bombing the harbour!   It wasn't until weeks later that we heard that the longshoremen had tapped into some whiskey barrels being shipped to the boys in the Pacific, and the fumes built up in the hold. Then some poor sucker lit a cigarette and BOOM!

"I stayed in the CWACs after the war to help process the boys returning from the Pacific Theatre. In Victoria, I processed the ones who had been in Japanese prison camps since the fall of Hong Kong at the very beginning of the war. I'll never forget it. It was heartbreaking. They were walking skeletons. But boy, were they glad to be back!

"I try to attend Remembrance Day at the Cenotaph. I always shed a tear or two because if you were in the service in wartime, you never forget it."

I'm proud to report that my mother's sister, Ruth Stewart, who was in her late forties during WW II, was a welder in a wartime factory in California – all five foot nothing of her! She told me that dwarfs and midgets were highly prized employees and were paid accordingly because they could get into tiny places to weld or rivet.

Although my Auntie Ruth liked the pay, I know she felt she was doing her bit for her three sons – two in the navy and one in the marines.

❦

Funny Papers

I'm not sure if I've outgrown reading the comic strips in the weekend newspapers, or if they're just not as entertaining as they once were. I think it's the latter. In our day we called them the "funny papers".

I miss *Prince Valiant* and its beautiful art work. I miss *Li'l Abner* and the hillbilly humour in the community of Dogpatch in Kentucky. That comic strip, and later comic books came out in the 1930s about the same time as Erskine Caldwell's *Tobacco Road* opened on Broadway. Later, *Li'l Abner* was made into a Broadway musical.

The big, handsome country-boy hero, Abner Yokum, his Mammy and Pappy Yokum and their pet pig Salome were a likeable family, ever-ready to aid anyone in peril. Other characters included, Hairless Joe, Marryin' Sam, Lonesome Polecat who kept the community supplied with Kickapoo Joy Juice the local moonshine, and my favourite, Joe Bf*&^%$#nik, a sad little fellow who carried his bad luck around in a dark cloud that was always raining on him. The heroine (usually the damsel in distress) was the voluptuous Daisy Mae who tried vainly every Sadie Hawkins Day (April 1) to capture Li'l Abner in the Annual Bachelors race which would result in an immediate wedding. Of course the female anti-heroine, Wolf Gal had the same goal in mind. For years, magazines contained mini comic strips advertising *Five Minute Cream O' Wheat* where

Mammy cooked up a bowlful for Li'l Abner so he would have the strength to save Daisy Mae from some villainous situation.

The Teeny Weenies wasn't a comic strip but a beautifully drawn panel that fascinated children and stirred their imaginations. The Teeny Weeny characters were little people about two inches tall who appeared to live in somebody's untidy back yard. They all looked alike but you could tell the difference by their costumes – Dunce, Old Soldier, Cowboy, Lady of Fashion, Indian, etc. While the Teeny Weenies were tiny, everything in their world was normal size. This meant they could ride on the back of a mouse, swim in a bowl of water, use a nasturtium leaf for an umbrella or feast on a single gumdrop. Many are the hours I spent as a child building "Teeny Weeny Towns" in my mother's garden. A generation later, my daughters did the same with their tiny plastic "Troll Dolls".

As far as comic BOOKS went, my outright favourite was written by a psychologist and first appeared during the Second World War – *Wonder Woman*. My girlfriends and I said, "It's about time!" Here was a gal from the lost world of Paradise Island ruled by a wise and courageous Queen, who sent Wonder Woman to the world of men to help us win the war.

Not surprisingly, Wonder Woman became a powerful role model for some young readers who eventually became feminists. That's because before her, comic strip heroines like *Tillie the Toiler* and *Brenda Starr, Girl Reporter* were adventurous, independent and even rebellious, but Wonder Woman had a golden lasso and bracelets that deflected bullets!

I don't think my girlfriends and I were the only ones who speculated that Wonder Woman could have flattened Batman and Robin together in a fair fight!

Another regular feature on the weekend "Funnies" page was *Ripley's Believe It Or Not* which kept right on going long after Robert Ripley died in 1949. During W.W. II there was quite a stir around town when New Westminster was mentioned in *Believe It Or Not*, when two Royal City soldiers won the prestigious Victoria Cross, the highest award for bravery in the British Empire.

The unbelievable part wasn't that Private Ernest "Smokey" Smith and Major Jack Mahoney – against incredible odds – both came from the same town in Canada, but that they both lived on the very same street—Fifth Street. And perhaps even more unbelievable than that, the lady who lived between them on the very same street was named VICTORIA CROSS! I remember Miss Cross—a tall, thin, severe-looking local spinster who wore rather drab, out-dated clothes. An intimidating figure to small children.

CR

Central Heating

My sister Norma and I shared a bedroom when we were children. We thought it was normal for water to freeze in the drinking glass on the bedside table on frosty nights.

In those days, our house had only one heat vent, a big fancy grill in the floor between the living room and dining room. It's still there but only for show. I remember standing on the grill on winter mornings, my flannel nightgown billowing around me as I wriggled into my school clothes.

We were fortunate to have an oil furnace. It was considered "advanced" over wood and coal or even sawdust furnaces, but I envied my chum, Denise Ivens, her sawdust pile. Whenever a fresh load of sawdust was delivered to her driveway, we spent the first day "skiing" down the pile before her brothers shoveled it through a window into the basement bin. It was great fun but tended to make our underclothes slivery.

At our house, the oil truck deliveryman filled the two 50 gallon drums in our garage. Then, with a hand-pump like the kind that you used to see on a well, dad filled gallon jugs, carried them down the basement stairs and poured the stove-oil manually into the furnace reservoir. This was "advanced"?

Having only one heat vent, and that one was on the main floor, didn't do much to heat the bedrooms. So we compensated by wearing flannel gowns or pajamas and cozy, warm, knitted "bedsocks". And when the temperature took a nosedive, we would also wear our cozy kimonos, and pre-heat the bed with a hot water bottle. No wonder most of us slept with our heads under the covers back then! Bald men wore nightcaps.

We had a little electric heater which we placed in the bathroom if it was someone's bath night. And in the kitchen every fall, Dad would install a tin, wood-burning space-heater and would poke the tin stove-pipe into the chimney hole still there from the old, old days when there was a wood and coal range in the kitchen.

In those days, most children were responsible, in some way, for keeping the house warm. Some cut kindling and split firewood to keep the woodbox full. Others carried large buckets of sawdust and dumped them into the "hopper" on the side of their woodstove or furnace, or carried buckets of coal called "skuttles" to sit by the fireplace. Piles of cordwood dumped in the driveway or back lane had to be split and stacked in a woodshed or under a porch. To kids, the tasks seemed endless and we longed for warmer weather.

But distant pastures always seem greener. Because my family had no wood-burning stoves or fireplaces in our house, I often volunteered to cut kindling at the Hagen's house while my friend Doris was finishing her dinner. Their wood was nice, clean "planer-ends" from a lumber mill, and easy for a young girl to cut. To Doris and Johnny Hagen, it was just plain work. I suppose they envied me my hand-pumped furnace oil.

Keeping warm was something you worked at in the old days. How spoiled we have become. Although it's fun to recall those times long ago, whenever it turns cold I wouldn't trade my thermostat for all the nostalgia in the world. ❧

W. S. Collister Drygoods

I can't remember when I last had a store clerk's personal attention. In fact, today's shoppers can't even FIND a store clerk, let alone get any personal help. This sure wasn't the way when my mother shopped.

When we went to *W. S. Collister Drygoods* on Columbia Street to shop, the clerks were eager and plentiful. At the glove counter, there were nice little stools to sit on and a tiny little pillow to rest an elbow on while the clerk patiently fitted a glove on "Madam's" hand. Most gloves were made of kid-skin and took great patience to get them on. It was fascinating to me, as a child, to watch the clerk work the soft leather onto each of my mother's fingers and then scrutinize the result to make sure she had chosen the correct size for "Madam". If a purchase was made, the customer received her new pair of gloves in its very own glove-box embossed with the name, W. S. Collister.

Mother invariably said, "Put it on my bill," which was a big disappointment to me because all the clerk had to do was write it up in her sales book and give Mother a copy. I always hoped for the day that she would pay in cash. THEN I could watch the fun as the clerk put the sales slip and the cash in a little tin box with a lid and, reaching up, would attach it to an overhead cable, give it a tug, (or was it done with a lever?) and "Swooooosh" the little tin trolly-car would zip up the cable to the mezzanine office where a cashier would check the sales slip, put the correct change into the little tin cable-car and, "Swooooosh" it would return to the original clerk who would count out the change to her customer. I was quite happy to stand and watch these little cable-car-cash-boxes zoom back and forth, like a miniature train-set in the air. Mother could take all the time she needed, for I was thoroughly entertained by the overhead spectacle.

At the stocking counter, the clerk wore gloves. Each pair of stockings came in a squarish, flat box about a half inch deep, just big enough to hold one or two pairs of neatly folded silk (later nylon) stockings. The little boxes of stockings were stacked behind the counter by shades – dark, medium, light, black, white and each box also gave the size. She would lay one box at a time on the counter, open the lid and carefully fold back the smooth, white tissue paper that surrounded each pair of stockings. She would then gently shake open the top of one stocking and insert her gloved hand. Then, holding up the stocking to the light she could demonstrate the colour and sheerness. All stockings had seams up the back. Sometimes the seam was a feature of the stocking, worked in a darker thread with maybe "clockwork embroidery" at the heel.

To my little-girl eyes, one of the special things at Collisters was the display dolls behind the corset counter. These were perfect miniature womanly-shaped mannequins about 24 inches tall clad in the latest undergarments crafted in a miniature size. I often wonder if these miniature mannequins were the forerunner of the Barbie Doll. I know I would have given my ten-year-old teeth to have such a glamourous doll. Dolls in my day were strictly "baby" dolls, or maybe "little girl" dolls like my Shirley Temple doll.

Mother didn't buy her "corselettes" at Collisters, but rather at the Corset Shoppe that featured personal fitting. It was a tiny shop right next to the Columbia Theatre. The shop had a glass display window with all the latest undergarments for women, and evening line-ups for the late show at the Columbia Theatre slowly filed past this window. It was embarrassing for some men who averted their eyes, and a source of ogling and salacious comments from many of the younger men. In gold lettering on the door it said, Madam So-and-so, Corsetier.

Back at Collisters, I always liked it when Mother took me upstairs to the milliner's department. A whole wall was covered in wooden pegs displaying the latest hats for the current season. It seemed like hundreds of hats to me. After Mother had explained to the clerk what she was looking for – mentioning a special coat or dress with which it would be worn, the clerk would bring several for Mother to try on. If a particular choice was up high on a peg, the clerk would use a long pole she kept handy to gently lift down the hat. Mother would be seated at a small table with a triple mirror, and would try on each hat that was offered. If none of them were to her liking she would get up and stroll the length of the hat wall and perhaps point out other selections.

In the meantime, I would be trying on the same hats she had just rejected, admiring myself in the 3-way mirror and pretending to be quite grown up.

Dad bought his hats at *M. J. Phillips Store For Men*, also on Columbia Street, and he often let me tag along. Dad never took as long selecting his hats as mother did. But I liked to go with him for a very special reason. You see, all men wore hats in those days, and when they went to an indoor function, they removed their hats and left them at the door on a hat rack or a table that had been provided. But most men's hats looked alike except that they were blue, or brown, or gray, or black. So how did the men know which hat was theirs? Easy. Once a new hat was selected, the clerk took it into the back room and using a punch-machine, punched the customer's initials in the leather hatband. In Dad's case, "JLS".

So a quick glance into the inside hat band he knew the hat he'd chosen was his. But even before that, he could spot his hat amongst others by the *feather in the band*. And THAT's where I came in. Because after the initials had been punched into the INSIDE hatband, I got to choose the exact feather for the OUTSIDE hatband. The clerk would show me a box filled with little clusters of feathers. They were beautiful little works of art. Someone with an artistic eye had bound together tiny bouquets of feathers in wonderful combinations of colours. Some feathers were even speckled and I tended to choose one of them. The choice was mine, and mine alone. Dad waited patiently and didn't interfere. Once I'd picked out my favourite, he'd let me tuck it into the hat band then he'd place the new hat on his head, give it a tilt and say, "How do I look?"

He'd wear his new hat out of the store, and I'd carry his old one, feeling proud that I had been a part of a special father/daughter ritual.

CR

Going To The Beach

In my dad's youth, he and his chums WALKED the many miles to Crescent Beach along the train tracks. It was called Blackie's Spit in those days, and the boys carried everything…heavy canvas tents, food, water, utensils, clothing, lacrosse sticks, -everything.

As an adult, my father's first car, a Model T Ford coupe, was used to take his family to the beach. It took some maneuvering. Dad sat behind the wheel. Mother squeezed up close to him. Grandma sat close enough to Mother so that there was about six inches of seat for my grandpa who perched sideways on the seat with his feet planted firmly on the running-board while clutching my brother Ross, aged about 5, on his lap. The door was tied

Young Lewie Sangster (left) and two chums tenting at Blackie's Spit circa 1905 - Sangster Collection

open so it couldn't swing closed and bang my grandfather's knees! So with four adults and one child aboard, they drove merrily to the beach, and if they passed a policeman on the way, the cop would smile and tip his hat!

In the 1930s and 1940s, most families didn't have a car, so going to Crescent Beach or White Rock by train, or to Stanley Park or Kitsilano Beach by B.C. Electric tram required a lot of planning and a very early start. But it sure beat walking.

Some families looked forward to only one trip to the beach during the summer, and that was to the Annual Sunday School Picnic. These events were highly organized outings, with foot races, softball games, swimming, sing-songs and plenty of prizes. Each family packed a lunch and the Sunday School provided a special "treat" – vanilla ice-cream Dixie Cups with

Our model T Ford and Ross Sangster (5) and a young cousin 1924 - Sangster Collection.

little wooden spoons – delivered to the picnic park packed in canvas duffle bags filled with dry ice.

During the war years, when cars weren't being manufactured, our family was lucky to have a 1939 Pontiac sedan. But with my parents and my grandmother in the front seat, and my sister and her friends in the back seat, there wasn't room for me and my girl friend. So we got to ride in the trunk! Yep, in the trunk - with the lid up, of course.

Dad would put a bent nail through the metal arm that held up the trunk lid so that it couldn't fall down. We'd sit with our feet on the rear bumper. A box containing a big pot of hot, home-made baked beans was wedged between us, all swathed in blankets to keep it hot until lunch time. Packed all around us were the rest of the picnic goodies and the usual assortment of beach towels and beach toys. My friend and I would sing songs and wave to the people in the car behind us, and to other trunk-riders in cars going in the opposite direction.

Sometimes our destination would be Alderside, out along the old IOCO road, where we'd spend the day with the Sibleys, the Hamms, the Clarence McLeans, the Ken MacKenzies and the Slim Sindons. Alderside was given its name by my Dad's sister, Nellie McLean.

I did my first swimming there, if you could call it swimming. I'd hang onto the shoulder-straps of my father's wool bathingsuit and he'd swim waaaay out to the diving raft. He'd carry me up the ladder and we'd sit on the raft for awhile and I'd wave to Mother on the beach which seemed miles away. Mother didn't approve of me piggybacking so far out in deep water. She didn't swim, and had a real fear of water. Of course, I couldn't swim either, but I had unwavering trust in the powerful breaststrokes my father used to carry me from and to the beach.

When twilight came, families gathered around a bonfire and sang camp songs and nostalgic songs from World War I like, "There's A Long, Long Trail A-winding", "Keep The Home Fires Burning", "Pack Up Your Troubles In Your Old Kit Bag", "It's A Long Way To Tipperary" and many more, led by one of the most enthusiastic sing-song leaders who ever lived – my father, Lewie Sangster.

It was dark when we headed home from our day at the beach. The beans had all been eaten, so the blankets were wrapped around us trunk-riders to keep out the evening chill.

Lewie, Norma (6), and Ross (15) at Alderside - Sangster Collection

Those were simpler times. We didn't travel at breakneck speeds on freeways, but took our time and enjoyed the ride. And we didn't have laws that forbade us the fun of riding in the trunk of a car. That was just an unforgettable part of a family trip to the beach in bygone days.

CR

The Beekeeper

Lewie Sangster was our town's unofficial Bee-chaser. He kept several hives of bees in the backyard of our home on Sixth Avenue where he showed four decades of visiting elementary school students how to locate the queen bee in a hive. A born showman, he always worked on the bees without a veil or gloves for protection, and to the delight of the school children, he would allow handfuls of bees to crawl over his face. Before a class left, each child was treated to a piece of comb honey fresh from the hive. He always instructed the children: "Bees are really peace-loving and friendly. If you don't harm them, they won't harm you."

Each spring, Lewie was swamped by phone calls from frantic citizens who were intimidated by honeybee "swarms" as big as footballs, hanging from their lilac bush or front porch. Bees swarm in the spring if their hive is too small, or if a new queen has hatched and the old queen was exiled with her own retinue. On one occasion, he got a call from the Warden at the B. C. Penitentiary. A swarm of bees had settled on a bush in the exercise yard and the prisoners were refusing to go outdoors! In those days, the Pen taught just about every trade in the book – except beekeeping. So Lewie rushed there, put on his usual show and soon had the queen and her bees captive in a nice wooden hive which he took home in the trunk of his car. A box of bees (including a queen) cost $30 by mail order in those days.

A clever reporter put the story on the wire service under the headline, "ALDERMAN RESCUES QUEEN FROM PENITENTIARY". It caught the imagination of newspaper editors everywhere, and the story flashed around the world. Apparently some of the penitentiary inmates weren't impressed. Dad heard one of them quip, nodding towards the mental institution next door, "They should lock this guy up over there!"

Our basement always smelled sweetly of honey. The boxes of honeycomb that Lewie brought in from his many hives around the Lower Mainland were processed there. Lewie lovingly filled jars with the golden liquid to give to his friends.

The nectar from different blossoms made different colours and flavours of honey. Dad always said clover honey was the best, so in 1950, when they were building the new high school and playing fields, Dad sent me and my new boyfriend, Donny Benson, up to the empty fields where Mercer Stadium is today with sacks of clover seed which we scattered to the wind. That summer, Dad had his own bumper crop of clover nectar for his beloved bees.

Overnight guests at our house were always treated to toast and comb honey for breakfast and often went home with a golden jar for their families. Every November 11th he took a gallon to the armories for the hot-buttered-rums served after the Armistice parade.

Lewie died in 1968. When the family went down to the funeral parlour to view his body, laid out in his best suit, Mother leaned over him and plucked a bee stinger from the lapel of his suit. "That man!" she exclaimed, "He was out tending his bees in his very best suit!" Next day, at the graveside, which was covered in nearly a hundred floral tributes, a lone honeybee buzzed from flower to flower. Mother turned to me and whispered, "Your father would have been so pleased."

After the funeral, we contacted the B.C. 4H Club and a group of young people from Vancouver Island came and gratefully accepted all his bee-keeping equipment. We hope it gave them as much pleasure as it did Lewie Sangster.

Lewie Sangster tending his beloved bees, circa 1960. Sangster Collection.

Our basement always smelled deliciously of honey. Even years after Dad passed away and all his equipment had gone to the 4F club, I often got a whiff of honey as I descended the basement stairs.

Talk about a sweet memory!

CR

Honey In The Basement

Why did my father "keep bees"? For the honey, of course! Bees don't give you honey in nice, neat jars or tins. Bees keep their honey in the hive in beautiful geometric six-sided cells neatly built onto wooden frames which the beekeeper hangs in their hives. The bees intended this honey for their winter food.

So after the honey seasons were over, and before winter set in, the beekeeper harvested his honey. He would take the lid off a hive, carefully lift off the top box of hanging frames of honey, set it on the ground and then replace the box with another in which the hanging frames were empty of honey. He then put the lid back on the hive. Over the winter months he placed an upside-down gallon jar of sugar-syrup to sustain them until spring. By the mid 1940s he began adding the new "wonder drug" sulphathiazide to ward of any bee disease.

I often watched while, ever so gently, Dad would lift each frame of comb honey from the box he had removed from the hive and shake it in front of the hive to dislodge the bees that were still on it. When all ten frames had been cleared of bees, he would pick up the box (called a *super*) and place it in the trunk of his car and bring it home to our house and store it in the basement.

Our basement was where he "extracted" the honey. Extracting was a long, careful process requiring patience and devotion. Each six-sided honey cell on each frame of honey had been "capped over", or sealed with a lid of wax. My father would carefully remove the "capping" with an electrically heated copper knife which looked somewhat like the short sword a Roman soldier might carry. All the capping was removed from both sides of each frame of comb honey and then, two at a time, the uncapped frames were placed in the "extractor".

The extractor was a large steel drum about the size of an oil drum. It had a bottom but no top. The extractor held two frames of "uncapped" honey at a time in two vertical rectangular metal baskets. A crank handle on the side of the drum was then turned and all the honey on one side of each frame was flung out into the drum by centrifugal force. After a few minutes the frames were reversed and the crank turned and the honey on the other side of the frame was flung into the drum.

When all the frames had been "extracted", we filled jars with beautiful golden honey from a spigot near the bottom of the extractor. Dad gave most of his honey to friends as gifts, but during the WW II years he traded his honey for SUGAR ration coupons so he had enough sugar to make syrup to feed the bees during the winter months. If someone insisted on paying for the honey he charged 25 cents a quart.

Turning the crank on the extractor was often my job. I have a 1939 colour 16 mm movie film of Dad working on his bees and about ten seconds of the film is me, aged 5, wearing a red sun suit and turning the crank on the extractor.

CR

May Day And The Queen Of The Bees

On the second Friday of May, hundreds of New Westminster school children would lie in bed straining to hear the loud report from a special cannon roll across the city at eight a.m. to announce that May Day was on.

On a clear, sunny May morning, the decision to fire the gun was easy to make. If the sky was leaden, and it was pouring rain, the gun wasn't fired and it became just another school day until the next Friday.

But a problem arose on those days when **it might** rain – and then again **it might not**. Then the decision could be a tough one. There was no weatherman listed in the phonebook. There was no Internet and no TV Weatherman to consult.

Should the official May Day Committee risk having our May Queen and her suite soaked? To answer that question, J. J. Johnston or another committee member would phone the "bee man", Lewie Sangster, and ask him to go out to his back yard and consult with another queen and her retinue as to whether the weather would clear up. Within minutes, he would have the answer from the Queen of the Honeybees.

Honeybees fly about two miles from their hive and cannot risk being caught in the rain and forced down because of wet wings. That would mean certain death. So bees have to be infallible in predicting rain.

Dad would study the bees' activities in the several beehives we always had in our back yard. If the bees were flying in and out of the hive with no hesitation, it meant there was no chance of rain. If they stayed inside the hive, it meant that rain was imminent. But if they milled about on the doorstep of the hive, and brave "bee scouts" took short test flights, he'd watch to see how the other bees responded to the reports that were brought back. Then he'd return to the phone and tell the May Day Committee his decision.

Dad loved New Westminster, and May Day had a special place in his heart. Until arthritis slowed him down, he'd put on his tuxedo and escort one of the May Day girls into the oval and enthusiastically dance the "Lancers" with her at the May Day Ball that night.

I often accompanied Dad to the Lancer rehearsals at Queen's Park Arena and sometimes filled in if one of the girls, or even a man, was absent. If the organist, Fred Nelson, couldn't make it, Dad would hand me the microphone and I would "Diddle, diddle, dee," the four different tunes needed to practice the four "sets".

Many girls from past May Queen Suites that I have interviewed over the years remember fondly the prominent "gentleman" who escorted them that day and led them through the complicated steps of the traditional, elegant "Lancers".

What are "Lancers"? you might ask. Lancers are circle dances thought

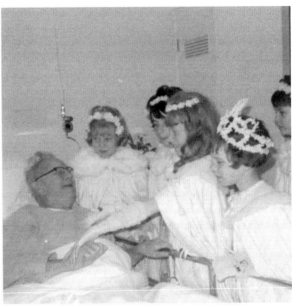

May Queen Lori Clarkson and her entourage visit ex-mayor Lewie Sangster in Royal Columbian Hospital May 12, 1968. Photo Evelyn Benson

to be the origin of North American square dances. Each circle has four couples. There is no "caller" for the intricate moves. The dances are carefully taught by an instructor. Lancers come to us from Victorian times in Great Britain when all well-bred young people took dance instruction. They became very popular at Military Balls where Royal Lancers (cavalry) were proficient at this popular dance form and taught the local ladies wherever they were stationed throughout the British Empire. It is believed that the Royal Engineers under Colonel Moody brought the "Lancers" to the pioneers of New Westminster. They are still danced each year at the May Day banquet, nearly a hundred and fifty years later!

Between 1895 and 1968, Dad missed taking part in only four May Days – three when he was overseas during World War I, and his last May Day in 1968 while he was in the Columbian Hospital. The May Queen and her attendants visited him at his bedside. He passed away that very night.

Dad claimed the bees were never wrong about the weather over the years, and he took pride in having the final say about May Day. And I felt privileged, when the weather was in question, to be the **very first kid in town** to know whether it was May Day or not.

CR

A May Day Remembered

Before our celebrated week-long Hyack Festival was born, May Day festivities were packed into a single dynamite day and evening, usually the third Friday in May. Every kid in town from Grades two through nine was involved in rehearsals for the big day: folk dances, gymnastic drills, bicycle drills, square-dancing and maypole dancing were part of every May Day, and took weeks of rehearsals to perfect.

We learned to dance around an invisible Maypole in the school gym. The school Music Teacher would play the music on the piano. Sometimes she would be busy or absent and so we learned to sing the words to the Maypole dance to accompany ourselves:

"Come lasses and lads, get leave of your dads, and away to the Maypole high;
For every fair has a partner there, and a fiddler standing by;
And Jimmy will dance with Jane; And Johnny has got his Joan;
And it's trip it, trip it, tri-i-ip it, trip it, tri-ip it up and down;
And it's trip it, trip it, tr-i-ip it, trip it all around."

Maypole dancers - City Archives.

In May, 1941, Jaquie Overand was crowned May Queen from Spencer School, and a few lucky Grade Ones were chosen to be the Flower Girls that lead her into the stadium. Usually it was little girls only who were chosen for this privilege, but that year, Nellie Squires our Grade One teacher, went against custom and chose girls AND BOYS to lead the Royal Party in! The girls wore the usual little pastel silk dresses, and the boys wore royal blue velvet short pants and vests over white ruffled shirts. Regular Little Lord Fauntleroy's! Because I was the shortest girl I was paired with the shortest boy, Eddie MacKenzie who, by the way, eventually grew to over six feet. We led the procession, and the couples that followed us were progressively taller and Ann Cassidy and Paul Harding, who were both a head taller than Eddie and me, brought up the rear.

The May Day Ball, held the evening of May Day at Queens Park Arena, was THE social event of the year for kids. Dressed in our very best, we joined in the Grand March, two-by-two behind the May Queen suite and their adult escorts. Down the centre of the Arena floor we'd march. Then the Queen and her escort, usually J.J. Johnston, peeled left and the next couple peeled right and marched down the sides of the Arena floor until

Left to right: Ronnie Giles, Denise Ivens, Rodney Hostman, Maryanne Hockey, Ken Ingalls, Doris Hagen, Ron ?, Wilma Gilley

TWO couples met and four-a-breast marched down the centre of the floor. Then FOUR peeled off to the left and four to the right meeting at the far end to form eight-a-breast. EIGHT-a-breast was all that could be accommodated and the lines disintegrated. Then we danced the first waltz with our partner.

Later, we all cheered as the Queen and her entourage formed three BIG circles and performed the intricate maneuvers of the traditional Royal Lancers. An evening of dancing and socializing followed, during which new sweethearts were discovered and some young hearts were broken.

I was escorted to the May Day Ball of 1941 by little Eddie McKenzie accompanied by his mother. He presented me with my very first corsage. Pink carnations as I recall. I never received another corsage until our High School Christmas Formal in 1950. It was a gardenia and it was presented to me by a really cute guy named Donny Benson.

CR

Left to right: Paul Harding, Ann Cassidy, Luella Wadey, Ed Harrington, Donna Nevard, John Richards, Eddie McKenzie, Evelyn Sangster, and Miss Nellie Squires.

Shirley Temple Days

As May Day approached, new clothes and new shoes were the order of the day, and in my case, a new hair-do was a **must**. My hair was naturally straight, so early in May I was dropped off for a dreaded "permanent wave" to affect a stylish "Shirley Temple hair-do" of bouncy ringlets.

Isobel Sell's beauty salon was set up in two rooms of her home at 514 Sixth Avenue. The house is still there with two shops tacked onto the front. Mr. Sell, a chiropractor, ran his practice out of the same house, which meant that an interesting assortment of townsfolk rang their front doorbell on any given day.

At nine o'clock on the morning of the first Saturday in May, my mother left me at Mrs. Sell's with a sandwich for my lunch as I would be there until mid-afternoon. In those days, a "permanent wave"

Author in ringlets. Sangster Collection

took several hours. The "instant" home-permanent had yet to hit the market. The quick and easy new "cold wave" which didn't require electrical heat, was disdained by Mrs. Sell who called it, "new-fangled".

After shampooing, Mrs. Sell sat me on a board laid across the arms of a barber chair, then began winding strands of my hair onto two-inch long metal curlers. She then daubed on an evil-smelling solution that hinted of ammonia and skunk-cabbage. Next, she wheeled over a tall electrical machine that looked like a prop from a Frankenstein movie. She positioned this contraption over my head. The many dangling wires with metal clamps on the ends were then attached to each of the metal curlers on my head. When all the wires were attached she threw the switch, and I swear the house lights dimmed!

Each of those dangling wires with the metal clamps was suspended by an individual pulley. And as time passed, the weight of all that metal caused me to slide further and further down, until Mrs. Sell would rescue me by giving each wire a sharp tug and UP IT WOULD GO, like a window blind, hauling my poor little scalp with it. The pain in my neck would be temporarily relieved until, once again, the weight would slide me down.

But the intense heat and the neck-ache from the weight of the clamps and even the occasional scalp-burn were all worth it when Mrs. Sell unplugged me and began brushing out my hair, forming individual fat Shirley Temple ringlets around her finger. I can still remember the feel of those ringlets bouncing like a head full of coiled springs as I skipped home along Sixth Avenue humming "On The Good Ship Lollipop". NOW I was ready for May Day. ଔ

Encroaching Urbanization

Our urban bushlands and forested areas have mostly disappeared and many wild animals have evolved into city dwellers. The last time we drove away at 4:30 a.m. to catch an early flight, we watched a pair of coyotes trot down the center line on Sixth Avenue.

Unfortunately, some of nature's creatures have fled or died out because of encroaching concrete and asphalt. How long has it been since we've seen a pheasant? Or a toad? Or a garter snake? These harmless snakes were so plentiful in the 1940s that Buddy Greenall from Fifth Street collected a whole bagful of the slithery creatures and let them loose in the hallway at Spencer School one warm spring day. You never heard such screaming!

Buster Gunn, Ross Sangster, and Forbes Gunn showing no fear of the beehives in our backyard circa 1929
- Sangster Collection

Needless to say, Buddy got THE STRAP.

During that era, Dad kept several hives of bees in our backyard, and garter snakes often lived under the hives. Each day, when the "housekeeper bees" nudged any accumulated dead bees out the hive entrance, a snake would make a meal of as many as were discarded. One particular garter snake that was around for a while, used to sun itself on the wooden stringer of the back fence behind the row of bee hives. It appeared to be watching Dad perform his beekeeping duties. Perhaps it was looking for a handout.

As late as the mid-sixties, my own sons collected snakes. I made them keep them in a large open box in the back yard. I'll never forget the day our three-year-old Janet walked into my kitchen clutching two snakes in each tiny hand! "See Mommy! Pretty snake!" As I assured her of their beauty, I gently eased her out the door, praying all the while that she wouldn't drop them in the house. A snake down a heat vent was an odorous nightmare mothers today don't have to worry about.

Now that the B. C. Penitentiary farm lands are gone, we don't see pheasants around town anymore. We used to see them strutting among the rows of vegetables in the Pen grounds, or swooping across Sixth Avenue. Sometimes they found their way into nearby yards.

One morning in the early 1940s, my mother looked out our kitchen window to see a big beautiful cock pheasant in our garden. She phoned Dad at his office downtown, and he said, "Don't disturb it. I'll be right there!" He rushed home, grabbed his shotgun, stepped out the back door and, "BANG" - roast pheasant for dinner.

It goes to show how things have changed. If someone discharged a gun in their yard today, we'd hear sirens coming from all directions. But in those days, a man could climb onto a bus carrying his shotgun after a day of hunting along the Brunette River or on the Queensborough wetlands of Lulu Island. The only thing the driver would say to him was, "Get anything?"

CR

Grocery Shopping

I try to avoid the mega-stores. I find myself wandering among what seems to me like acres of groceries. The brand selections are overwhelming – aisle after aisle, choice after choice. It is mind-boggling.

My mother didn't have that problem. Grocery shopping wasn't a chore - it was a social occasion. The other shoppers had familiar faces and most were known by name. Babies were compared, snapshots were admired and the latest "news" was exchanged.

My mother shopped at the B&K at Sixth and Sixth where the Westminster Savings Building stands today. In later years the B&K moved to the opposite corner. Roy Bussey, the manager, knew all his customers by name. Most customers had an account, so children could be sent shopping with a note but no cash. The purchases were "put on the bill" which was paid at the end of each month.

As she entered the B & K, Mother would go directly to the counter at the rear of the store and Roy would get out his little invoice pad.

"Now let me see,…..I need a box of Corn Flakes, a pound of butter, two tins of peas. Not the big ones, the little tiny sweet ones." You notice Brand names weren't mentioned as Roy carried only one brand of any commodity. As each item was listed, Roy would send a clerk to fetch it off the shelf. If it was temporarily out of stock, Roy would make other suggestions and Mother and he would discuss the relative merits of each.

Coffee was freshly ground by the clerk, not the customer, in a big, shiny red grinder. Cheddar cheese was on a big flat wheel in the center of the store with a cutting knife hinged in the center like a big paper-cutter. The customer would indicate the **exact** size of the wedge she wanted cut.

Bulk-buying was the norm. Bins and barrels of dried items like rice, lentils and macaroni were measured into paper bags and weighed on an overhead scale to the customer's exact specifications… "That's too much!" or, "Well, maybe just a smitch more."

The purchases were placed in a cardboard box. When all the selections were made, the "box boy" carried it to your car, if you had one. Otherwise, it was delivered to your house later in the day by bicycle. Being a box boy for a grocery store was often a boy's first salaried job. He would need a bicycle, of course, and a special carrier on his handle-bars that would hold a large cardboard box.

During the war years when many food items were scarce, we would sometimes find added "treats" in our box of groceries when it was unpacked at home – bananas from South America, a jar of maraschino cherries, hot chocolate powder or even chocolate bars! Of course they had been added to the bill, but none of Roy's "best customers" ever complained about these added surprise wartime luxuries.

Nostalgia is fun, but we must remember that the "good old days" weren't all good. The lack of choice in those days made for monotonous meals. Winter meals were particularly boring as the choice of fresh produce was very limited. Remember, no one had a freezer. Potatoes, turnips, carrots and cabbage supplemented by canned peas, corn and string beans were served meal after meal after meal. Fresh off-season produce from California or Florida had practically stopped being trucked this far because of gas rationing during WW II.

Today most of us have freezers, and we don't have the time to shop the way our mothers did. So it's back to the mega-store where the choices are wonderful, but shopping is more of a chore than a social outing. What choice do we have?

CR

Dairyland

A Dairyland milk processing plant and horse barn was once located at the north end of the Westminster Mall complex bordering the lane that runs through to Fifth Street. At a long loading-dock facing Sixth Street, trucks delivered large metal cans of raw milk fresh from Fraser Valley dairy farms, to be bottled. Homogenized milk and milk cartons were still in the future, so each glass milk bottle had a five inch layer of pure cream at the top. In theory, you pressed the little cardboard lid tightly to the bottle, up-ended it, and gave it a few shakes to distribute the cream throughout to create "whole milk". I say "in theory" because early-risers sometimes cheated and poured pure cream on their cereal. In winter, when the temperature dropped below freezing, the cream on the top of the bottle would freeze and expand, pushing the little cardboard cap out of the neck of the bottle and rise like a popsicle made of pure cream. Yum!

There were no milk deliveries on Sundays, so that's when us kids climbed over the locked gate and played "stagecoach" in the empty wagons at the Dairyland plant.

There was a loose board on the high wooden fence at the back of the stables, and a favourite "double-dare" of those days was to climb through the fence into the grounds of the Hollywood Sanatorium, known locally as "Hollywood San". We were convinced that the place was full of "crazies" and the occasional scream coming from the barred windows only helped to confirm our fears!

Creamo Dairy (later Dairyland) wagon on Sixth Avenue - Sangster Collection.

Each milkman trained his horse to memorize his delivery route, so he could load his basket with bottles of milk and cream, and make his deliveries to several houses in a row. While he made the deliveries, "Old Dobbin" would pull the wagon three or four doors up the street, or around the corner, and wait patiently for his driver to catch up.

The milkmen were like public watchmen. They kept an eye on the elderly and those who lived alone. If yesterday's milk was still on the porch, but the customer hadn't notified the milkman she'd be away, there could be a problem. He would knock on the door, and if he didn't get an answer, he might confer with a neighbour, or even notify the authorities. If the inside of a window was covered with flies and no one answered the door, that was an ominous sign, and the police were quickly summoned.

After our society lost its daily deliverymen, it wasn't too long before we had to invent organizations like Neighbourhood Watch.

My husband's grandfather, Dick Featherstonehaugh, delivered milk for Dairyland back in the early days. He had many "milkman stories" to tell, but this is my favourite:

"Most customers left their empty milk bottles on the front porch, but one of my customers nailed a wooden apple box just outside a window off the front porch so she could retrieve her milk without stepping outside.

"One morning the box held no empty bottles. There wasn't even a note changing her order – a very unusual occurrence. She was a two-quarts-day customer. I stood there on the porch, undecided whether to leave the two quarts anyway.

"Apparently the lady of the house awakened just then, and realizing she'd forgotten to put out the empties, she leaped out of bed and rushed to the window. When she snapped up the window-blind, it caught the hem of her nightgown and lifted it clear up over her head! I don't know whose face was redder – hers or mine.

"From that day on, there was no more little wooden box under the window and her empties were lined up on the porch just like everybody else's."

CR

Moody Park

Moody Park playground had a wading pool. My friend Denise and I would put on our bathing suits, pack a lunch, grab a towel and head for Moody. If it was a very hot day, we'd run through every lawn sprinkler on the way to the park. In the block of Sixth Avenue between Seventh and Eighth Streets, where Royal City Centre Mall is today, many of the houses had picket fences. Denise and I would walk along the stringers, arms out, balancing like tightrope walkers.

One day, as we walked the fences, we decided to stop for lunch on a beautiful green lawn with lovely shade trees. We thought it was a small park. Suddenly, a woman appeared and demanded to know what we were doing in her yard. It was Mrs. Dashwood-Jones. Her house sat at the back of the lot, nearer Princess Street not like all the other houses in the block that faced Sixth Avenue. We were really embarrassed. She should have been flattered that we thought her beautiful yard was a park. When Woodwards bought out that block in the 1950s, the Dashwood-Jones mansion was saved and moved to the corner of Sixth Street and Tenth Avenue and became a Rest Home.

One summer, Denise's brother Russell Ivens went to work at the *Stubby Pop Factory* in the 600 block Princess Street. On our way to Moody Park, we would tip-toe up to a side window of the factory and peer in. If we spotted Russ, we'd tap on the glass and he'd come to the window and slip us a couple of bottles of pop. Denise preferred "Lime Rickey", but my favourite was "Mandalay Punch" (grape), but whatever the flavour, it tasted especially good because it was FREE.

Once a summer, Moody Park was home for a week to the *Crescent Shows*, a typical carnival of the day. Rides, games of chance and other attractions drew a steady crowd. I can still smell the cotton candy and popcorn. I can still hear the music and noise of the rides. Our favourite was the "Rollo-Plane" because it was the scariest and Denise and I were confirmed daredevils.

One year, the big attraction was a trailer in which, for ten cents, you could see a polio victim in a real Iron Lung. The "carny" shouted over the loud-speaker, "COME and SEE the GIRL in the I-RON LUNG! She TALKS. She BREATHES." The loud-speaker would blare the sound- effects of the mechanical iron lung pumping air in, then the wssshhhh sound of air escaping. Denise and I paid our dimes and filed through the trailer feeling sad for the beautiful young girl who would never walk again, tied forever to this great mechanical thing. Later that day, as we headed home, we spotted the same girl standing behind the trailer, smoking a cigarette!

CR

Deliveries

Mother purchased many of our family's needs conveniently, right at her own back door.

Chinese vendors trudged door to door with poles across their shoulders suspending two baskets loaded with fish fresh from the river that morning, or vegetables fresh from a truck garden down Trapp Road. In later years, "the Chinese vegetable man" toured our streets in a Model T Ford truck – a favourite target for pint-sized fruit-snatchers.

The vendor soon got to know the lady of the house's preferences. Here is a purported conversation that took place between the vegetable man and my Great Aunt Jesse. She was a stout, no-nonsense lady who always had a very florid complexion:

"Wong, do you have any tomatoes?"

"Oh yesee, missee. Plenty nice tomatoes."

"Are you sure they're fresh?"

"Oh yesee, missee. Flesh. Very flesh. All same pick this morning."

"That's good. But are they ripe? I don't want half-ripe tomatoes."

"Oh yesee, missee. They lipe. Velly lipe."

"Nice and red?"

"Oh yesee, missee. They velly led. Nice and led. All same colour your face!"

Needless to say, Great Aunt Jessie found another source for her family's vegetables. Too bad she didn't find a better sense of humour.

Bakeries competed for the door-to-door bread trade. Our 4X Bakery man, carrying a basket loaded with a selection of baked goods, tapped on the back door, then loudly announced his presence, "BAKER!" Mother would make her selection there on the back porch.

Communications with the milkman were carried on by correspondence, using little notes left tucked into the neck of the empty bottles lined up on the porch. She could order milk, cream, butter, buttermilk and cottage cheese. By leaving a note, the customer could sleep while the milkman filled the daily order in the chilly pre-dawn hours.

The week's soiled laundry, tied up in a table cloth and left on the back porch, was replaced with neat, brown-paper packages containing the previous week's laundry. Men's shirts were returned starched to perfection and carefully folded and pinned around a stiff piece of clean, white cardboard which I quickly commandeered for my many childhood art projects. Dad's collars were separate from his shirt. He attached them to his shirts using brass collar buttons. The collars came well-starched in a cardboard ring to keep their shape. Household linens were neatly pressed and folded. Clothing items, on request, could be returned dry, or "damp", wrapped in wax paper and ready to be ironed.

Before the invention of the steam-iron and permanent-press fabrics, housewives would "damp-iron" to get the wrinkles out. If the item to be pressed had somehow dried out, dampness was added from an old glass vinegar bottle with a stopper in it that had holes like a watering can. Professionals, I am told, like tailors and laundry-workers would put water in their mouths and spray it over the garment! Mother never did this.

Housewives ordered cleaning compounds and utensils from the *Fuller Brush Man*, and herbs, spices and medications from the *Watkins Man* or the *Raleigh Man*. Remember *Snap*, a hand-cleaning compound made from fine sand and smelling like sassafras? Or *Carbolic Salve* often used as a poultice?

The children's favourite delivery man, especially during hot weather, was the Iceman. After waiting in ambush for him to park his truck and then wrestle two 25lb. blocks of ice off the tail-gate with gigantic ice-tongs, and carry them into a nearby house, neighbourhood children would dart forward, snatch broken pieces of ice, then flee. A rare and treasured prize was a piece of salted ice, a product used in hand-cranked "freezers" used to make homemade ice-cream.

How many remember garbage service "delivered" right to your back yard? We didn't have to lug garbage bags or cans out to the street. In fact, we could forget that garbage even existed, except when we put it in the galvanized tin receptacle near our back porch. The garbage-man walked into our back yard carrying a large two-handled tin wash tub. He wore a cap, heavy leather gloves and a leather or canvas apron with legs to keep himself clean. In those days, before plastic garbage bags, raw garbage was dumped directly into your garbage cans and raw, slimy, maggoty, stinking garbage was dumped into the garbage man's large wash-tub which he then hoisted onto one shoulder and

4X Bakery wagon (formerly Shelley's Bakery) on Carnarvon Street near the court house. Sangster collection.

carried it out of your yard and dumped it into an open dump truck. It was a smelly job that no one envied. Cans, workers and trucks were always surrounded by clouds of flies. We've come a long way! Things are much cleaner now. Even his title has been cleaned up to "sanitary worker".

The computer may allow us to shop from home, but it doesn't allow us to feel and touch and smell what we are buying, nor bring the products to our doorstep. A computer doesn't have a friendly face, or know the latest gossip. Those privileges belong to the past.

CR

Penny Candy

"See a penny, pick it up and all the day you'll have good luck!" is an old saying from when I was a kid. I still pick them up even though there is nothing that can be bought with a penny any more. Penny matches cost two cents and the day of the penny candy is gone forever. And when was the last time you saw a machine that registered your weight and printed out your fortune - all for a penny?*

Many of us can still recall the joy of clutching a shiny copper penny and heading for the neighbourhood confectionery store. In Sapperton, it may have been *White's*; in Queensborough it was probably *Sprice's*; in the West End kids may have gone to *Mathers'*; down the hill kids would go to *Langley's*. The kids in our neighbourhood went to *Bussey's Courtesy Corner* at Sixth and Sixth right where the plaza entrance to Royal City Centre Mall is today. Mr. Bussey had lost an arm in WWI and I recall with amazement how he deftly popped air into a tiny brown bag, carefully held it with the stump of his left arm and filled my childhood candy choices with his right hand.

From the time I learned to read, until 1951, a huge sign sat atop Bussey's store announcing, *"THE FUTURE SITE OF WOODWARDS DEPARTMENT STORE"* until it faded to unreadability. No one really believed what it said. But in 1946, Mr. Bussey sold his corner lot and three others to Woodwards for a whopping $22,000. The rest of the block soon followed.

Now lets get back to those mouth-watering penny candies.

There were "two-fers", "three-fers" right up to "ten-fers"—meaning two-for-a-penny, three-for-a-penny, and so forth. The clerk would open up a miniature paper bag and wait with infinite patience for your choices. The choices seemed endless: jawbreakers, licorice whips, suckers, candy bananas and strawberries, peppermints, jelly beans, toffees, jujubes, butterscotch drops, horehounds and many more. Remember wax lips? Chicken bones? Humbugs? Redhots? Remember candy buttons that came stuck to a long strip of paper ready to be nibbled off one at a time? Remember all-day-suckers shaped like a horseshoe? My favourite was root beer flavoured.

Most storekeepers had the patience of a saint while waiting for a child to make her choices and then change her mind again and again. Sometimes they'd reach the end of their patience and say, "That's it! No more changes! Take it or leave it!"

It was the same in far away Scotland in the 1850s when my grandmother, Lizzie Christie took her penny to the local "sweet shop" and said, "Gi'e me a penny's worth of leafanders, and lavenders, and roond-balls, and yellow lang things…….make a' the rest broken rock…….and throw in a few a'monds. If ye please!"

Yes, penny candies have gone the way of the dodo bird and the Five & Dime stores. But I'll keep picking up pennies, and who knows? With inflation, perhaps people will start dropping nickels and not bother to pick them up.

Say, would a nickel bring five times the luck of a penny?

* As of 2013 the penny was no longer minted in Canada—soon to disappear forever.

CR

Ninety-Five Cent Day

Woodwards Family Department Store on East Hastings Street in Vancouver held a special sale day on the first Monday of each month called "Ninety-five Cent Day". Later in the 1950's, inflation required that it be called "Dollar Forty-Nine Day".

Until I started school in 1940, I accompanied my mother on the B.C. Electric Tram Central Park Line to the Vancouver tram depot on East Hastings Street only a couple of blocks from Woodwards. My Grandma, Bessie Appleton also went along for the bargains.

Mother always made me walk ahead of her in the crowded store, "So I can keep an eye on you," which didn't make sense to me because every time she stopped to admire another bargain, I kept on walking and would suddenly find myself minus a mother which was very scary for a five-year old! I pleaded that she let me follow behind her, but to no avail. "How can I keep my eye on you?" was always her response.

One of the ninety-five cent bargains both ladies sought were cotton "house-dresses", so-called because they were only worn IN the house while doing housework. Some ladies referred to them as "wash dresses" because they could be thrown in the wash. No housewives wore slacks in those days.

When Grandma had made all her purchases, Mother parked us in the *Ladies Rest Area*, a few rows of chairs just outside the Ladies Restroom, while she finished her bargain-hunting. While we waited, I always made several trips to Woodwards Ladies

BC Electric Tram Depot under construction on Columbia Street at the foot of Eight Street - Sangster Collection.

Restroom because it had several **child-size toilets** – perfect miniatures of a regular-sized toilet. To a child, this was a wonderful convenience. I've never seen them anywhere else. I guess they became extinct, just like Woodwards.

It never seemed to fail that, whenever we were at Ninety-five Cent Day, my mother and grandmother had this conversation:

"Don't look! There she is!"

"Where?"

"Over there! Right by that pillar! Don't let her see us!"

Mother would grab me and the three of us would scurry away to a safe spot.

"I don't see her now. We're safe!"

" I can't **stand** that woman!"

As a child, I could never understand why this woman was so feared that we had to hide from her. It wasn't until I was an adult that I asked my mother about her. It seems she was a relative who had left her husband and run away with another man. She left her child behind. In those days, this was practically unheard of. Because of this, the women of my family would have nothing to do with her. She was definitely a *persona non grata.*

I always looked forward to the tram ride to or from Vancouver. The old trams had wicker seats that creaked as you swayed with the moving tram. And at the end of the line, the conductor would move down the aisle flipping the backs of the wicker seats, "bang, bang, bang," until all the seats were facing the opposite way for the return trip and nobody had to ride backwards.

The conductors wore black suits and vests with a gold chain and pocket watch and a black, peaked-brim pill-box hat. They walked through the cars calling out the stops in advance: "JUBIL-EEE", "FRASER AAAARM", ROYAL OOOOAK! The trip to Vancouver took about the same time as today's state-of-the-art Skytrain!

New Westminster Archives.

❧

Pharmacies

Today we are so spoiled. Our drug stores supply almost all our needs except perishable food and liquor. Today we can buy clothing, furniture, appliances, electronics, basic groceries and, oh yeah, prescriptions and toiletries. The privately-owned drug store was once the norm. There were: Davis the Druggist, Linn's Drugstore, Cunningham Drugs, Ryall Drugs to name but a few in our small town.

In our house we had a very small medicine cabinet. Mostly it held the basics: Lavoris Mouthwash (cinnamon), Wampoles Milk of Magnesia (vanilla), Pinauds Lily of France aftershave, Watkins styptic pencil, Iodine, Band-Aids, Bayer Aspirin, Rose Hair Oil, Pepsodent Tooth Powder and Arid Deodorant. Our cabinet also contained a straight razor. And on the wall, next to the cabinet, hung my father's leather "strop" on which he sharpened his razor. I loved to stand and watch him lather and shave with that lethal razor. And while he shaved – he sang! I always knew when it was Sunday because he only sang hymns, like "Guide Me O Thou Great Jehova" and "All Hail The Power Of Jesus' Name".

Not many people used deodorants in the 30s and 40s. There was only one brand – Arid. It came in a jar about an inch deep and it was pink. You opened the lid, ran three fingers around the firm contents, then raised an arm and spread it on your armpits. Then you switched hands and did the other armpit. It had a faint strawberry smell. Hardly any men used deodorant. It was considered "sissy" by most men. My dad, who was a salesman, thought it was a great invention. Body odor, known in our day as "B-O", was commonplace. I can remember riding on a crowded bus and having to get off and walk home because of the smell of "B-O" that made me gag.

When we took gym classes across the street at the YMCA, the girls' classes of Duke of Connaught High School had to cut through the boys' gym to get to the other gym. We'd gather at the closed door. Someone would ask, "Is everybody ready?" then fling open the door. We'd all take a deep breath, then hold it as we ran through the boys' gym on one breath. (We were too polite to hold our noses.) And that was in the 50s!

To entice men to be more aware of their personal odour, Proctor & Gamble put out a bath soap called Lifeboy that had a rather antiseptic smell. Their catchy, musical radio jingle ended with the line "Lifeboy really stops B-O, 'beeee ohhhh'" (sounding like a fog horn).

Today's drugstore has so many brands of toothpaste I'd hesitate to count them all. In our day it was tooth POWDER and only one or two brands. You didn't sprinkle the powder on your brush, which was quite wasteful. You put a little powder in the palm of your hand and pressed it with your damp toothbrush. My dad preferred a toothpaste that came in a flat metal tin about half an inch high. You wet your toothbrush and rubbed it around the cake of firm pink paste. I thought it tasted awful.

Disposable diapers hadn't been invented yet. When they first came on the market in the late 50s, they were so expensive that most mothers only allowed themselves that luxury when travelling. Another product that was a boon to mothers was Cream Rinse to delangle hair. My two daughters had long, blonde extra fine hair and combing out those long strands were a chore and caused many a tear. I used to lie them on the kitchen counter with their long tresses in the sink as I poured water over and over trying to get the snarles out without the painful use of a comb.

There were only three brands of feminine products, Modess, Kotex and Tampax and one-size-fits-all. Women who clerked in drug stores were required to wear white uniforms and shoes to make them look like nurses without the caps. When business was slow, one of them would go into the back of the store, out of sight, and wrap all the feminine products in **plain brown paper** before they dared put the boxes on the shelves. It always seemed rather silly to me, because the boxes had a very distinctive shape and it didn't fool anybody.

Condoms were kept under the counter and had to be asked for by name brand. It was said that this was particularly painful for young men if the only clerk in the store was female. Today, the only products kept out-of-sight are cigarettes!

CR

Rat Invasion

When rats invaded the Queens Park neighbourhood in the mid 1940s, they chewed the fur off my Christmas Indian Head moccasin slippers and stole my mother's silk stockings. Where did this plague of rats come from?

Well, in those days, the city garbage dump was located in the Glen ravine, right next to today's Canada Games pool in the same area as the Fire Hall and the Recycling Depot. A pall of acrid smoke perpetually hung over the dump and sometimes, as the wind shifted, those in the area of Spencer School would get an unmistakable whiff of decaying garbage. The plastic garbage bag had not yet been invented, and neither had the home-freezer, so open piles of refuse, predominately made up of thousands of tin cans dotted the dump landscape.

Before the dump was moved, my sister's husband George Walton would sometimes take me and my girlfriend Denise with him to the dump at dusk to shoot rats with his .22 rifle. We'd wait quietly, patiently watching a small mountain of tin cans. Then, when we heard something rattle, one of us would point the flashlight—FAST. Two curious, beady eyes would stare back, and BANG! One less vermin-carrier in the old city dump. George would let us girls each take a couple of shots. To a pair of tomboys like Denise and me, this was heaven—shooting a real gun at a real live target you could really hate—rats.

Then the city closed the dump and began shipping New Westminster garbage to the new Terra Nova landfill in Coquitlam. In only a few weeks time the rats ran out of garbage-food and began migrating to nearby neighbourhoods, including the upscale Queens Park area, in search of food. On the way to Spencer School each morning, kids would count how many rats had been run over on the roads during the previous night!

At first, each family kept the invasion to themselves, thinking they were the only ones to have, "Shhhhh, R-A-T-S" on their property. Soon neighbours began comparing notes on the best way to tackle the problem. We all put out rat poison, and rat traps that looked like gigantic mouse traps. I still shudder to think of the day I accidently stepped on a rat trap in our basement and had to hobble all the way upstairs to find an adult strong enough to open the trap and release my bruised little foot.

Dad cornered a grandfather rat the size of a cat in the basement, and dispatched it with a handy golf club. We kept the .22 rifle behind the kitchen door for the determined rats that tried to eat through the bottom of our galvanized tin garbage can. Dad, an Alderman, admitted it was an oversight, by the city, not to have hired exterminators to attack the rat population at the dump site before it was abandoned and the rats ran out of food. Again, hindsight is 20/20.

CR

The Spectre of Infection

Infection. The word no longer strikes terror into a mother's heart. For whether it's in our throat or our finger, a quick prescription from our doctor for an antibiotic, and practically overnight the infection is gone.

Our grandparents would have called that *a miracle,* for before the discovery of penicillin and sulpha, the first of the "wonder drugs" of the 1940s and 1950s, the word "infection" was to be feared – with good reason. A simple wound to hand or foot could require endless hot compresses, yet still lead to amputation! Lung infections like pneumonia meant mustard chest-plasters, steam tents and bedside vigils, back when prayer was often the strongest medicine available.

Simple head colds could develop into ear infections that required repeated syringings with a carbolic solution. If that failed, it was off to the hospital for the dreaded mastoid operation, a procedure now known only in Third World countries. In 1898, my mother, Naomi Appleton, at age two, had this operation done on her family's dining-room table with her father handling the anesthetic and her teenage brothers acting as "go-fers" for the doctor! Her mother was locked out of the room as she was too upset to witness her baby "under the knife".

Only decades ago, the most common operation was a tonsillectomy. Making it through childhood and adolescence without "having your tonsils out" was a rarity, because if a child had more than one bout of infected tonsils, then surgery almost always followed. Some tonsillectomy patients were as young as one or two years of age.

If a person's appendix should rupture before it was safely removed, the patient's chances of surviving the resulting infection – they called it "septic poisoning" – were not promising. The only cure for an infected tooth was extraction. Very few people had a full set of teeth, and nearly every child had a mouthful of cavities in those pre-fluoride days. Simple boils had to be painfully lanced.

A strep-throat simply had to run its course. Then we waited anxiously to see if the infection had selected a secondary target – like the heart. If that happened, the rheumatic fever that resulted often required that a child be kept in bed, at home, for sometimes a year or more to prevent further heart damage. Some kids lost a year of schooling and their mothers were driven to distraction trying to keep them entertained in those days before television and video games.

No wonder doctors made house-calls! In the days before antibiotics, waiting until office hours to see your doctor could actually mean the difference between life and death. The battle against infection was mostly waged at home. Our mothers were the front-line troops, and their dedication knew no bounds.

Mothers' home-spun treatments were primitive by today's standards. As a preventive medicine loaded with vitamin D, cod liver oil served by the tablespoon ranked high on the list. Because of its strong fishy odor, I was never subjected to this horrible stuff because my mother couldn't stand its smell. Today's delicious, fruit-flavoured vitamins have to be hidden away from children. In our day, it was the children who hid! Our parents seemed to believe that if a medicine didn't taste bad, it wouldn't do much good.

Poultices were our mothers' weapon for fighting external infections. Poultices worked on the "osmosis principle" to draw out the poisons, so they had to be thick and gooey. Both white bread and sugar, or white bread and softened soap mixed into a paste worked well to draw out the infection.

For a puncture wound, when a kid stepped on a rusty nail, it was the "hot soak" – and I do mean HOT! My mother would put my foot in a pan of hot water and Epsom salts. Then, when I tried to pull my foot out, yelling, "It's too hot!" she'd hold my foot down and pour in more hot water. Talk about tough love!

Earaches were treated with drops of warm camphorated oil and a hot water bottle. During my mother's childhood, her father blew hot pipe-smoke into her ear to relieve pain. As no one in our family smoked, my mother sometimes blew her hot breath into my ear. On a recent television show, an M.D. recommended using a hot hair blow dryer to relieve earache. See! Mom and Grandma knew what they were doing!

Flannel cloth soaked in camphorated oil was wrapped around our necks to soothe a sore throat. Mustard plaster pasted on the chest and back was the treatment for a stubborn chest cold, but would blister the skin if the mixture was too strong. Mothers covered the mustard with brown paper before wrapping on wide strips of flannel, to keep the generated heat in.

Remember iodine? Remember how it hurt worse than the skinned knee? Today's kids only know Iodine as one of the elements on a Periodic Table in chemistry class.

My grandmother knew a cure even MORE painful than iodine. She would wrap an injured finger in gauze, then stick the finger in the neck of a bottle of turpentine, then up-end the bottle. YEEOW!

Home-remedies often caused life-long dislikes for certain foods. My dad hated mustard. His mother used to make him drink hot water laced with mustard to induce vomiting when he had a stomach ache. And my husband was forced to drink hot onion juice if he had a bad cold. As a result, when we were first married, I had to prepare his stew and salads without onions – a real hassle.

Then one Sunday years ago, we went on Harold Maiden's family fish boat to picnic at Pitt Lake. After lunch, Don had the nerve to rave about Mrs. Maiden's flavourful potato salad compared to mine . I said, "That's because hers has ONIONS, you turkey!" Today, onions are one of his favourite foods.

In 1942 my mother contracted scarlet fever and an ambulance came to take her to the isolation building of Vancouver General Hospital. The New Westminster health inspector nailed a RED sign on the front of our house that said "QUARANTINED". Then he ordered us out of the house while he fumigated each room with something like a smoke-bomb. My grandmother, my sister and I were isolated from all human contact for about two weeks. Mother was in insolation even longer. Dad was allowed to have one business suit fumigated so that he could go to his one-man office. Thankfully, no one else contracted the dreaded scarlet fever which was THE most common cause of childhood deafness.

They say that over-prescribed antibiotics are helping many germs to develop immunities. They are called "super bugs". The day may come when antibiotics are useless and we will have to revert back to some of Mother's home remedies. That's why I am passing Mother's along to future generations before they are lost forever.

A word about modern medicine and surgery: In my day, every school had children with crossed eyes or a cleft pallet. Harelips were common and surgical repair of this facial deformity was visibly obvious and often disfiguring. Cruel taunting by classmates was not uncommon. Before fluoride, every child had cavities, and rotten teeth produced painful gum boils.

Today, we never see club-foot, goiter, chronic leg ulcers, disfiguring facial birthmarks or leg braces due to polio. I vividly recall seeing a young girl my age being wheeled in a large baby carriage. She was hydro-cephalic. I remember asking my mother why the girl's head was three times the normal size.

I wonder what cures the future will bring?

CR

Look Ma, No Hands!

In my day, they were called roller **skates**, not roller **blades**, and you could hear the noise of their metal wheels on the concrete sidewalks or asphalt roadways for half a block. Today, the roller blade generation wears helmets, elbow-pads and knee-pads as standard equipment. In our day, you could always tell a roller-skater by her skinned knees.

Our favourite skating rink was the divided stretch of Fifth Street between Sixth Avenue and Fourth Avenue because there was almost no traffic, and the road surface had smooth, re-tarred stretches, where we could practice our "fancy stuff".

Author on roller skates. Sangster Collection.

A skate-key on a string was worn proudly around the neck of each roller-skater, like a medallion from an exclusive club. The purpose of the key was to tighten and adjust the clamps that secured the skates to the soles of our leather shoes. But first, you had to adjust the length of the skates to match the length of your shoe, and then tighten them with the wing-nut on the bottom of the skate. One size skate fitted all shoe sizes.

Teenagers, and adults too sophisticated to street-skate, could skate in the basement of the Knights of Pythias Block at Agnes and Eighth Street. They rented boot-skates with wooden wheels for 25 cents, and skated on a hardwood surface. The set-up was similar to public ice skating sessions where you skated to recorded music in a counter clockwise flow.

My husband's aunt, Elma Lund McIntyre, told me about roller-skating in the 1940s:
> "We called it The Rollerdrome, and some of us teenagers who were serious about roller skating formed a club called the Royal City Rollers. There was barely enough room to practice our spins because there were two or three wooden posts close together in the middle of the skating rink. We practiced routines, and got so good that some of us traveled to other rinks to put on shows, and were paid either money or a gift for our performance. Mother made me a wine corduroy skating outfit with a blue satin lining. My skating partner was Harold Pound, and I remember going to North Vancouver and Birch Bay to put on demonstrations. One time, we went all the way to Calgary."

Boys played street roller-hockey in some neighbourhoods. Also, boys would attach cast-off roller skates to a plank, then nail a wooden apple box with handles onto the plank and use the device as a scooter. Come to think of it, that contraption was probably the forerunner of the modern skateboard after some kid let go of the handles and yelled, "Look Ma! No hands!"

⳩

Ye Old Swimming Hole

My father learned to swim in the dammed-up creek that runs through Glenbrook Park. In his day, kids referred to it as the Penitentiary dam.

The first public swimming pool in town was a cement rectangle in Queen's Park behind the Arenex. It was eventually filled in because the sunlight never reached it to warm the water, and the large trees that surrounded it dropped needles, cones, leaves and branches into it.

In the Depression years of the 1930s, unemployed men earned their "Relief Money" from the City by labouring to create Hume Park, which included a new swimming pool—this time in the sunshine. My girlfriends and I would ride our bikes out to swim at Hume Park. The pool was a rough concrete rectangle with no showers, no filters, no heat. It had a hand-cranked wringer to lighten the water-load in the heavy cotton or wool bathing suits of the day. But it was the only public outdoor pool in town, and we thought it was great!

If you loved swimming, you knew the schedule by heart: **Mondays:** closed for filling, straight from the water-main, ice cold with a little chlorine added. **Tuesdays:** sparkling clean and clear but so C-O-L-D it took your breath away. If you liked having the pool all to yourself and you mastered the art of jumping in and out REAL FAST, then Tuesdays were for you.

Wednesdays: still heart-stopping cold. **Thursdays:** a few hearty regulars were in the pool and (sun permitting) the water temperature might tempt the hardier kids to try swimming across the pool once before scurrying for a towel and a brisk rub. **Fridays:** tolerable temperature but starting to get a bit murky.

Saturdays: the water temperature was heavenly, but it was wall-to-wall bodies with hardly a spot you could jump into, let alone attempt to dive into.

Sundays: family picnic day and hardly room to turn around in the pool. The water temperature was now approaching that of bath water, but it was so murky, somewhat the colour of tea, that if a swimmer sank to the bottom in distress, the life guard might not see her. And, you guessed it – more chlorine, so that at the end of a swim our eyes were red and swollen.

They closed the pool earlier Sundays so they could drain it and scrub it and start the whole process all over again.

Before Dr. Salk gave us polio vaccine, if there was a polio outbreak in the Lower Mainland, the pool was closed indefinitely and movie theatres were also avoided.

Saturdays and Sundays were the days my friends and I skipped the pool and went wading in Brunette Creek instead. This was strictly forbidden, for our mothers thought the naturally dark brown waters of the creek were far too dirty and unsanitary. So, how come when they closed the pool due to a polio scare, they didn't close access to the creek?

It seemed a miracle when the Kiwanis Club opened the first pool at Moody Park in 1949. Heated filtered water was a real treat. The only thing missing was the old hand-cranked mechanical wringer to wring out our bathing suits.

CR

Me Tarzan. You Jane.

Every Saturday, we went to a matinee. The playbill always included several cartoons, a news reel, a "short-subject", a serial, and two features – one of which was usually a Western.

The *Metro Theatre* on Twelfth Street and the *Sapperton Theatre* drew local kids. My friends and I preferred the *Odeon* on Sixth Street at Fourth Avenue, but depending on who had the best "feature", we often went downtown to the *Edison* or the *Columbia.*

Short Subjects were ten-minute reels of a comic nature. My favourites were *Lew Lehr's Monkeys Are The Craziest People* which featured some very clever chimpanzees dressed like humans, doing human things like grocery shopping or having afternoon tea.

Serials were addictive. Each episode left the hero or heroine facing imminent death – tied to a stake with flames licking about them, dangling from a frayed vine over a thousand foot canyon, tied to the tracks as the train raced towards them or chained to a table as a spinning gang-saw got closer and closer and closer. No way could we NOT return the following Saturday!

Nyoka, The Jungle Girl was my favourite, (being a tom-boy) but we liked *Jungle Jim*, too, and because it was wartime, lots of serials focused on catching spies and saboteurs. When Hitler appeared in the newsreel, the kids booed and threw stuff at the screen.

 We each had our favourite cowboy. And every cowboy sang and had a funny-looking comic sidekick. *Roy Rogers & Smiley Burnett, Gene Autry & Andy Devine* and *Hopalong Cassidy & Gabby Hayes.* "Hoppy" topped my list, with his black outfit trimmed in real Mexican silver to match his silver hair. But it was his laugh, deep and musical, that I remember most. I can close my eyes and still hear "Hoppy" laugh. Every cowboy show had a chase. During the chase, boys in the audience shot off their cap-guns until the smoke from the exploding caps fogged the air in the theatre.

The feature films at a matinee were chosen for children: *Blondie and Dagwood, Charlie Chan, Dick Tracy, Buck Rogers, Tarzan.* I think maybe Tarzan was the best. For weeks after, we'd take turns being, Jane, Boy, Tarzan or the Chimp, as we climbed and swung in the big cherry tree in my front yard. I never could quite master the Tarzan yell, no matter how hard I beat my chest.

CR

Predators

These days parents walk their children to and from school. Some even drive them a few short blocks, causing traffic jams in front of schools. Children are "street-proofed" - told not to talk to strangers and never, never get into a car or even approach a car. They are told that when walking home they should stay near the inside edge of the sidewalk and stay in groups whenever possible.

Today's children are made aware of the kind of harm that could befall them. Child predators seem to be everywhere. Is it because there is an increase in their activity, or are they just more often reported to authorities? I realize the moral standards in our society today seem lower than in the past, and certainly TV and movies have played their part, but child molesters were around in my childhood too.

My mother told me, "NEVER take candy from a stranger!" From the tone of her voice I knew it would be dangerous to do so. But because she didn't clarify WHY, I assumed that the candy would be poisoned, like the apple in Snow White!

On the children's grapevine, we often heard the terrifying news that one of our schoolmates, or someone they knew, had been "chased". It would go something like this:

"Did you hear about Peggy?"

"No. What?"

"She got 'CHASED'!"

"Oh no! Where?"

"Down at White Rock. She was putting pennies on the railroad track when a man came up behind her and tried to grab her. But she pulled away. She ran, and he chased her!"

"Did he catch her?"

"No. Thank goodness! She got away!"

I don't think any of us had a clue as to what would happen if the guy had caught her. I'm sure we would never have heard anything about it at all if he had, because the police kept these crimes out of the papers so as not to embarrass the families or the child. It happened. Probably more than we'll ever know. Children often didn't even tell their parents about "being chased".

I didn't tell my parents about the only encounter I had with a predator.

It was at the Odeon Theatre during a Saturday matinee. Denise and I were sitting together watching the show when her cousin Ann Ivens slid into the seat next to us. She was spooked. She told us that she had changed her seat twice, and both times the same man came and sat behind her and began to stroke her hair!

I told Ann to take a seat a couple of rows in front of us and we'd watch for him. Sure enough, after a minute or two, a man sat down behind her and reached forward. Quick as a flash, I jumped into the aisle and hit the man with my umbrella. "GET OUT OF HERE!" I shouted, as the astounded creep ran up the aisle with me in hot pursuit. I got in a couple more hits as I shouted, "MY FATHER KNOWS MR. YOUNG THE MANAGER!" (You can see I was a bossy child.) "DON'T YOU EVER COME BACK!"

Denise and Ann and I laughed so hard people were "shushing" us.

I never did tell my parents or anyone in authority about the incident. Nor did we ten-year-olds realize that Ann may have had a close call.

I've been told I was a precocious child. I guess it's true.

CR

Ice-Cream Eddie

We called him "Ice Cream Eddie" because he sold ice cream from the trunk of an old Model T Ford coupe he drove up and down city streets. The honk of his hand-squeezed bulb-horn brought children from all directions clutching nickels. On top of his car was a display board he used to express his opinions on any particular matter that was currently on his mind.

Typically, he had three cardboard tubs of ice cream nestled in canvas jackets packed with dry-ice (solid carbon dioxide used for refrigeration). The flavours were usually chocolate, vanilla and strawberry, but once in a while, he had something really exotic, like maple walnut.

In 1942, Eddie Mills ran for city council and, to almost everyone's amazement, he was elected, beating out veteran alderman Harry Sullivan by 200 votes! The popular opinion was that many citizens thought Eddie's running was a big joke, so they gave him a vote for the fun of it. Joke or not, Eddie was officially on council and then the fun started.

At the back of his property on Dublin Street, contrary to city bylaws, Eddie had the last "outhouse" in New Westminster. When the City tried to force him to install an indoor toilet and connect to the sewer system, Eddie refused, and a feud started.

Eddie was eventually brought to court and fined $10. He said he didn't have the money, but offered to work off the fine by sweeping the streets. The Judge agreed to that solution, and even agreed that Eddie could sweep the streets of his beloved West End. But when Eddie reported for duty at the Board of Works, it was raining. When he demanded a full set of equipment—boots, slicker & hatso he would be dressed properly for the job—the request was refused. So Eddie Mills presented himself at the gates of Oakhalla Prison for the purpose of serving his time in lieu of paying a fine. The Warden refused to admit him.

Eventually, the sewer business was settled, and Eddie Mills didn't get re-elected. According to Alderman, Tommy Radbourne, another West Ender of the times, Mills moved somewhere up the Fraser Valley. For years, he wrote to Radbourne, complaining about some issue or other until eventually the letters stopped. And another City character had passed into history.

∞

Sounds Of The City, Echoes From The Past

Don Benson

There are memories of fragrant smells – Christmas trees, baking bread, new-mown grass; memories of the sense of touch – a snowflake on the cheek, kitten ears, a loving hand. And then there are memories of the special sounds of downtown New Westminster in the 1940s.

Where I grew up, two blocks from the Fraser River, the remains of a little creek trickled through a wooded ravine and a wood-planked sidewalk stretched the entire block. Because only a few neighbours owned cars, the roadway was ideal for playing pickup lacrosse and street games like *Kick-the-can* and *Red Rover*.

At the time, I didn't appreciate that our family lived in a unique place "wired" for sound. For, in addition to the wooden sidewalk with its hollow echoing sounds of footsteps, the Trans-Canada telephone wires ran outside our upstairs front windows, and the singing sounds made by the bare copper wires in a high wind later inspired my first book, *Wire Song*. Also, in the two rows of attached houses that made up our tenement complex, eight families shared the same little back yard, creating a symphony of domestic sounds close at hand. The special sounds of the bustling Fraser River waterfront drifted up to us around the clock.

The first nearby morning sounds were the snorting and clip-clops of the milkman's horse, the jingling of glass milk bottles in his wire basket, and the tinkling of coins in the empty bottles as he jogged back to his wagon.

Later, a screen door screeched open to let out the kitchen sounds of kindling crackling in a wood stove and the metallic clatter of stove lids before banging shut. Soon the wooden sidewalk echoed the footsteps of folks hurrying to work. Later, a hand-mower clattered and whirred across a lawn. A clothes line pulley squealed under its burden of wet wash.

Sawmill sounds drifted across the Fraser from the south bank. Gang-saws screamed, conveyor belts clanked and clunked. Each mill whistle had its own personality. Some tooted. Others whooed or shrieked.

Double-ended gill net fishing boats made up most of the river traffic. You could pick out the different boat engines by the sounds they made, from the deep drone of a Chrysler Marine to the distinctive sound of my favourite, the two-cycle Easthope engine. Easthopes had a single cylinder, and sucked in gas before firing each stroke with a "putt" sound. When slowed right down, an Easthope misfired, then backfired – putt…..put-putt…..BANG!

Near the river, steam locomotives shunted box cars. Even standing still they broadcast a chorus of sounds – the hiss of escaping steam from the valves, the whoosh of air and exhaust from the stacks and the steady clang, clang, clang of the bell. When a steam locomotive started to move, the wheels slipped around at first without gripping the rails, making the slick, steel-on-steel sound like sabers rubbing.

Columbia Street, our main street, boasted some of the early electric traffic lights, and each time the light changed, a loud bell clanged to alert drivers and pedestrians.

Cars were noisier then, and the sounds made by the various makes and models were quite distinctive to boys who studied them. Powerful cars like the straight-8 Hudson and V-12 Lincoln squealed around the corner from Columbia to get a running start and roared, then strained up the steep hill, as the driver determined how far his car could climb up the hill in third gear before he had to double clutch, VROOOOM, down into second gear.

Other sounds of the city that have faded away over time include the yelps and howls from free-for-all dog fights, the sound of steel roller skate wheels on concrete sidewalks, the ding-dong of a hand-held school bell calling kids to classes and the rattle of "Ice Cream Eddy Mills" Model-T Ford followed by the HONK, HONK, HONK of its bulb-horn and his familiar shout, "ICE-CREAM!"

Probably the evening sounds of our street were typical of the times. Mothers called the kids playing street-games like Kick-the-Can or Run-Sheep-Run in the lingering twilight. Each kid's name was called loudly and slowly using musical syllables. Kids with names like mine tried to get home before they were called. That's because the guys called me "Don" and the girls called me "Donny", but my mother hollered for "DAWW-NAAALD!"

Later, a father whacked an armload of stove wood on a chopping block. Cedar kindling, as it sprang away from the block made musical sounds, - like a xylophone. An open window let out the sounds of laughter, applause or music from a radio program, perhaps *Amos 'n Andy* or *Inner Sanctum*.

The BOOOOOM! Of the nine o'clock gun at Stanley Park over twelve miles away rolled across the Lower Mainland and was answered by dogs near and far.

While World War II was raging, air raid practice drills were mostly scheduled, but sometimes they were sprung without warning. With the first ominous wail of the siren, folks rushed to close their blackout curtains. If a chink of light showed outside, the Air Raid Warden from your block shouted, "Douse that light!".

The last conscious night sounds for a kid back then might be the clickety-clack of a steam-driven passenger train crossing the Fraser River trestle bridge, then puffing faster and faster, heading east in full cry, and leaving the sound of its haunting whistle-call behind, to echo down the years.

ℭℜ

Indian Baskets

Their names were Lena and Rosie. They were sisters. Each spring for more than twenty-five years in the 20s, 30s, and 40s, they traveled to New Westminster from the Chehalis Indian Reserve near Agassiz to trade their handcrafted baskets for used clothing.

They trudged from door to door, packing huge bundles on their backs. But the bundles were relatively light, as they contained handwoven cedar-bark baskets in all shapes and sizes, beautifully decorated with geometric native patterns worked into the golden reeds in dark cherry bark. All these lovely baskets were tied up in a big, white bedsheet.

Many housewives of New Westminster used the baskets to hold their knitting yarns or mending. Some of the larger baskets had soft buckskin handles and were carried over the arm when doing the marketing. Being cedar, the baskets could be scrubbed in a tub of soapy water during "spring cleaning". My mother's large collection got an annual scrubbing because Mother affectionately called her baskets "dust-catchers".

The weave of these baskets was so tight that, if kept wet, they would swell and become completely watertight. For this reason, a papoose basket would have a hole deliberately woven into the bottom of the cradle to allow any accumulated liquids to drain out!

No cash ever changed hands. Only used clothing or household items were bartered. My mother told me that one day she was bartering for a particularly beautiful basket but nothing she offered in exchange was good enough. Just then, my father walked in from gardening wearing one of his oldest suits. In those days, there was no such thing as leisure wear. People wore their good clothes as work clothes once their "Sunday best" became a little shabby or outdated.

When Rosie saw the suit, her eyes lit up. It turned out that her husband was about the same size as Dad, so a bargain was struck and my father had to go and change his clothes then and there. Apparently, items of clothing still being worn were more highly prized than "cast-offs".

Lena and Rosie were never allowed to leave our home until Mother served them afternoon tea. She always used her best china tea pot and served it in the parlour.

About 1945, the two sisters came to New Westminster for the last time. They told my mother they were getting too old to make the long trek from Harrison each spring. Sadly, there would be no more basket-trading because the younger women on the Reserve didn't want to learn how to weave. They complained that the cedar ruined their hands, and anyways, they could make cash money working at the canneries.

Fortunately for today's collectors, some native bands are encouraging their young people to learn the old crafts. But because hand-weaving is labour-intensive, even the smallest basket will cost a collector hundreds of dollars.

There was no bartering on that last visit. Instead, Lena and Rosie presented Mother with a gift—two perfectly woven cups and saucers with a matching lidded sugar bowl and cream pitcher. Each piece was exquisitely crafted.

Lena & Rosie's gift. Mother's collection eventually totaled more than fifty! Photo by Evelyn Benson.

A while back, I showed one of the woven cups and saucers to a native artisan at a B.C. Native craft fair. Her eyes widened with interest. She offered me a pair of Haida motif earrings crafted out of 14 carat gold in exchange. I appreciated her offer, but somehow couldn't bring myself to even consider the trade.

CR

Spirits

Bessie Lena Bishop Appleton died in the little front bedroom of the family home early one morning in 1943. I awoke as my dad called out to my mother, "Naomi! She's gone!" After they went downstairs to call Dr. Bruce Cannon who lived only two doors away, I slipped into her room, kissed her wrinkled cheek and whispered, "Good bye, Grandma."

I was only nine. For the past three years, after the death of my grandpa, she had lived with us. She taught me to knit and embroider. She was always home when I came home from school, sitting in her rocker by the den window. She loved apples, and when she finished one she would open her hand and show me a stem, several seeds and the hard center membranes of the fruit, and proclaim, "My name is Appleton, and I like apples by the ton!"

She would tell me stories of growing up in Nova Scotia. Like, how the children would drive the pigs out at low tide on the Bay of Fundy to eat seaweed and root out shellfish. The children were always reminded by their parents that, "When the pigs suddenly raise their heads and turn tail and run for shore – RUN!" It meant that Fundy's riptide was on its way! Grandma Bessie said that one day her chum wasn't paying attention, and didn't notice the pigs racing for shore. He drowned.

Several weeks after my Grandmother died, I was given the front bedroom as my very own. I was so pleased to have my own room until a kid at school said, "Aren't you scared, sleeping in the same bed as a DEAD PERSON? Aren't you scared a ghost will get you?" I came home in tears and said I'd never sleep in that room again!

My mother sat me down and said, "Evelyn, did you love your Grandmother? Did she love you?" Of course my answer was yes. She continued, "Do you think your Grandmother would ever harm you? Don't you realize how lucky you are? If your Grandmother's spirit is in this house, then you have a guardian angel looking out for you, making sure you are safe." From that day on I slept well, knowing I was especially protected.

Do I believe in spirits? Let me tell you two odd occurrences: I bought new wallpaper for the den. Before we could hang it, we had to patch a hole in one wall. Don cut away a piece of the old plaster and filled in the hole. When I examined the old piece of plaster I peeled away several layers of ancient wallpaper. The bottom layer, from the time of the

Appleton's occupancy around 1910, was nearly IDENTICAL to what I had purchased! But there's more! Then when we built the addition for Janet and her family, she and I went to choose wallpaper for her new kitchen. She wanted something in keeping with the Victorian charm of the rest of the house. After much deliberation, she and I agreed on a dark blue and brown pattern. Then months later, when Don repaired a section of wall in the original kitchen, guess what? You're right! The original layer of wallpaper in the kitchen was nearly IDENTICAL to what Janet and I had chosen.

Janet made the comment, "You know, Mom, I think Grandma Bessie must be looking over your shoulder every time you choose a new wallpaper for this old house!"

CR

My Friend "Penny Henny"

When I was a child, one of the sure signs of spring at our house was our annual trip to Bolivar's Hatchery in Surrey. Today, the hatchery is gone, and the land is a subdivision called "Bolivar Heights."

I would watch in wonderment as Mr. Bolivar himself opened drawer after drawer in the incubators to show me hundreds of tiny, fluffy, newly hatched yellow chicks. Sometimes I'd actually get to see a tiny beak peck away an egg shell and watch a wet, wobbly newborn chick test its legs.

Then Mr. Bolivar would select twelve "cockerels" (male chicks) and put them into a cardboard box. I held the box on my lap in the car, listening to the "peeping" all the way home. I never figured out how he knew which ones were male, so don't ask.

The author with Penny Henny 1942
- Sangster Collection

Like many New Westminster families in the '40s, we had a chicken pen in the back yard. But the baby chicks were too delicate to be put outdoors in February, so for several weeks the noisy little fluff-balls lived in a large cardboard box in our den. My job was to keep clean newspapers in the box and mix their special mash. Every once in awhile they would escape! What fun we had chasing little yellow chicks all over the house until all twelve were safely back in their box.

Once they graduated to the outdoors, the cockerels grew and fattened and eventually became Sunday Dinner. The sound of crowing roosters in our yard and in most neighbourhoods was common until about 1950.

One spring, Mr. Bolivar made a mistake. Instead of twelve baby roosters, he gave us eleven – and one hen. The cockerels pecked at her, so I rescued the hen and she became my special pet. I named her, "Penny Henny".

She roamed free in daylight, but slept in a box in the basement at night. For several years after we stopped raising chickens for meat, Penny Henny laid a large, brown egg every morning in a nest she had built under our back porch. Each day she strutted and clucked to announce her accomplishment. She followed me to school many times. I felt like Mary and her little lamb. She always came running whenever I called her name, and at sunset, she would tap on the back door to remind us to let her in for the night. We would open the door and she would hop down the basement stairs and into her box of her own accord!

In October 1944, *The Columbian* newspaper described Penny and me at the Royal Columbian Hospital Fall Fair: "One of the highlights of the evening was little Evelyn Sangster who sat astride her bicycle with her pet chicken perched confidently on the handlebars, attracting large crowds to the Kiwanis lottery booth." Penny was a common sight in our neighbourhood as she rode around on the handlebars of my bike. In fact, she often rode dressed up in doll clothes, complete with hat! But that night at the Fall Fair she was a novel spectacle to the crowds. The Kiwanians sold lots of lottery tickets because of my dear chicken.

Eventually, as she matured, Penny began to fly over our fence and uproot our neighbours' vegetable gardens. She just couldn't resist those nice, tender green shoots when they first appeared in the spring. The neighbours were very unhappy. So we sent her to "board" with twenty other Rhode Island Reds in a large chicken pen in Walter Brown's backyard on Fifth Street. Every day I would ride over there for a visit. I would call through the fence, "Here Penny, Penny, Penny!" And out of the crowd of look-alike chickens, she would come running. I'd open the gate and out she'd strut.

One summer afternoon, after a ten-day absence at summer camp, I raced my bike over to Brown's to take Penny for a ride. To my amazement, the chicken pen was EMPTY! I was dumbstruck. While I was away, Mr. Brown had sold all his chickens – and Penny too! I never dared ask their fate. And I never saw Penny again.

She was the only childhood pet I ever had, and she was so very special. I mourned her for a long, long time, and never again spoke to my father's friend, Mr. Brown.

CR

The Blue Laws

The "Blue Laws" dictated what could and could not be done on Sunday. Church attendance was high years ago, and many people believed that Sunday was a day of rest. The laws of the day reflected this.

All drinking establishments were closed. All retail stores were closed, with a few exceptions. New Westminster drugstores worked out a schedule so that ONE pharmacy remained open from two to five on Sundays, and the schedule was posted in all drugstore front windows. Gas stations had the same sort of arrangement, with posted dates of who was open on which Sunday. It sure didn't help to run out of gas Downtown, when the only open gas pump was Uptown. People tended to "gas up" on Saturdays.

No movie theatres were open on Sunday. Eventually, the city fathers allowed the newly-formed New Westminster Symphony Orchestra to perform on Sundays in the Columbia Theatre if there was no charge. A basket for donations was allowed at the door.

Local bootleggers did a booming business on Sundays. Many taxi drivers kept a "supply" in their trunks. Private clubs, like the Westminster Club, allowed members to have a personal liquor locker, but members had to pour their own booze on Sundays and bartenders could only pour mixer and supply ice.

When Dad was a boy around 1900, Sundays were even stricter. His family went to church at least twice on Sundays and sometimes even three times! Preparation for the Sabbath began Saturday night. All playing cards, games, toys, and sporting equipment were put away - sometimes under lock and key.

Even bicycles were locked up. There WERE exceptions. For example, when Dad became a Telegraph Messenger and was scheduled to be on standby on a Sunday, his bike was released. After all, his wages went into the household coffers and a family of nine needed every penny it could get. Don't forget, the Sangsters were from

The Bensons heading out for a Sunday Drive. Backseat: Scott, Janet, Kim and Mark; Frontseat: Evelyn, Jay and Don - Sangster Collection

Scotland!

So until the "Blue Laws" were repealed, and Expo '86 had a lot to do with making our shopping and liquor laws more in line with the U.S. and Europe, we were Sunday captives. Now you know why that quaint custom, "The Sunday Drive" was invented. What else was there to do?

CR

The Sunday Drive

Evelyn Benson (1981)

On Sundays, all seven of us would drive
To a new adventure –
To the park, to feed the squirrels
And watch the swans;
To the mountains, for blueberries and sun
And off-season snow;
To the beach, to run on sand and fly a kite,
Or feed the gulls
Whose swooping, diving, squawking antics
Made us laugh.

As we drove, we counted Volkswagens,
And convertibles and red barns;
We thudded over logging roads
That wrecked our springs,
Yet still we laughed and sang
And stopped to watch a waterfall;
The noise, the confusion, the lack of money
Didn't seem to matter,
For those were the years when our kids were young,
And so were we.

Street Games

Often dusk was approaching when street games found us hunting for or hiding from other kids somewhere in our neighbourhood. Sometimes we made a lot of noise, but it was mostly that delightful, almost musical sound of children having fun, and the neighbours didn't seem to mind.

For most street games, two teams were chosen alternately by two captains after one of them yelled, "Second captain, first pick!" or "First captain second pick!"

In one popular game, *Run, Sheep, Run,* the captain of the team whose turn it was to hide, arranged special code words with her team. For example, "blue" might mean the hunters were getting closer, and "yellow" might mean they were hunting farther away from the secret hiding place. The hiding places were in neighbourhood yards. No one seemed to mind us trespassing. We hid in garages, under porches, behind sheds, under hedges, up in trees, in cellar stairwells, to name just a few. The captain of your team would accompany the hunting team in order to call out the warning signals.

There was always a "home-base". It could be a rock, or a tin can in the middle of the street, or the trunk of a boulevard tree. When the captain saw that the hunters were farther away from home base than her hidden team, she would yell out, "Run, sheep, run!" and the hiders would bolt from their hiding place and try to tag home base before the hunters could tag them. Those who didn't make it had to join the other team.

A variation of *Run, Sheep, Run,* was my favourite, *Kick the Can*. Everybody hid except whoever was "IT". A tin can, preferably a large crumpled one that would make a lot of noise when it was kicked and skittered along the pavement, was placed in the middle of the street. After counting to fifty, "IT" would begin to search for the hiders. If a hider was found, she would then have to stand patiently by the can waiting to be "freed". Soon there would be quite a few "captives" waiting by the can. Waiting for freedom. Suddenly, a "hider" would bolt out of hiding and race for the tin can. If she got there before "IT", she kicked the can and all captives were free to hide again. If "IT" got there first and tagged the runner, then the runner became "IT" and a whole new game began.

Some street games could get a little rough. In a game called, *Red Rover, Red Rover,* two equal teams would link hands and face each other. First captain would call out, "Red rover, red rover, let Shirley come over" He usually chose the tiniest person on the opposing team. Then Shirley would run at the opposing line as hard as she could. If she broke through, she could return to her team. If she didn't break the chain then she was "captured" and had to join the other team. A smart captain, when choosing his team would pick the biggest, heaviest kids first. We always stood in dread whenever "Fat Albert" (and every neighbourhood had one) assaulted our flimsy chain of hands.

As dusk began to fade into darkness, one by one the players would be called in by mothers whose voices could carry a block or more. "Shirrrrrr-leeeeeeeee!" One by one, the teams would be depleted until the last lucky holdouts knew there was no point in continuing the game – and they would reluctantly head home. By this time, the street lights would be on.

Some readers will recall that while growing up during the Great Depression and World War II, times were lean and mean compared to today. But most of us fondly remember street games in those days before heavy traffic and television helped to put an end to this childhood ritual.

I'm reminded of Francie and Nellie reminiscing in the classic novel, *A Tree Grows In Brooklyn:* "The young kids will never know the terrible times we had."

"No, but they won't know half the fun, either!"

CR

Holiday Turkeys

These days, choosing a Thanksgiving turkey is so impersonal. You peer into a bin of frozen birds and choose one that fits your budget and your roasting pan. Or perhaps you selected your turkey back in the summer when they had that 99 cent special and it's been sitting in your freezer ever since.

Before the advent of the supermarket, shopping had a personal touch. Naomi Sangster shopped at Dearden's Meat Market at 6th and 6th where Westminster Savings now stands. About mid-September, Alex Deardon, the butcher, would ask what size bird she wanted this year. In those days, turkeys were fresh killed and brought into the butcher shops only days before Thanksgiving. There were no freezers. Not even butcher shops had freezers back then, so you picked up your bird the day before Thanksgiving Sunday.

Our bird would be hanging by its feet along with dozens of other turkeys. A manila tag attached to its feet read, SANGSTER. The feathers had been plucked and the head was discretely wrapped in waxed brown paper.

The butcher would then ask, "Would you like your bird 'drawn'?" This meant would you like the butcher to remove the innards and chop off the head and feet before he wrapped it in strong brown butcher's paper. My mother always declined this service because in our family, my father "cleaned" the turkey.

First, he would take a pair of tweezers and carefully remove any pinfeathers the pluckers had missed. Then he would take the bird outside, and grasping it by the head and feet, he would hold the turkey and rotate it over a blazing ball of newspaper to singe off any "hairs".

I remember sitting wide-eyed at the kitchen table as he opened the turkey with the precision of a surgeon and carefully drew out each organ while patiently explaining its inner workings. I watched with fascination as he explained that birds ate gravel because they had no teeth to grind food. When he showed us the egg canal, in a hen turkey, there would sometimes be several eggs in various stages of development. He carefully handled the gall bladder, explaining that if it broke, it could taint the meat with a very bitter taste. He demonstrated how tendons worked the bird's claws by pulling on the tendons and making the bird's feet open and close. Then he would get us to open and close our own hands and pointed out that our own tendons worked the same way.

Finally, when the bird was "clean" and ready to be stuffed, he'd pick up the gizzard. This was the special moment we had been waiting for. He would tell us how turkeys liked to peck at shiny stones, and how sometimes a gizzard might contain a treasure – a lost emerald or diamond from a lady's ring perhaps!

We held our breath as he sliced into the iridescent gizzard and extracted the crop. Then he'd carefully empty its gravely contents onto a piece of paper, and we'd search carefully through the tiny stones for the treasure that would make us rich.

Well, we never found that diamond, or any other treasure. But looking back across the years, I can see that in this very special kind of way, we already were rich.

CR

Radio Days

Many times, my friend Denise and I rushed straight from Spencer School to the Vancouver Sun paper-shack that sat amidst the underbrush and trash of a vacant lot where the Telus microwave tower stands today on Sixth Street. The reason for the rush was to get her paper route delivered in time to listen to the late afternoon radio serials.

Our favourite was *Jack Armstrong, the All-American Boy*, who flew his very own Piper Cub aeroplane and was a teenager for more than twenty years. For Jack, and his pals Billy and Betty, adventure was just around the corner. But Jack had to carry the other two, as Billy was a dumb kid who was always saying things like, "Golly-all-fishhooks, Jack," and Betty was an embarrassment to some of us tomboys because she never waded into risky situations with the boys, but always stood back making distressing little sounds.

I can still hear the melodious voice of the announcer saying, "*Wheaties…breakfast of champions…brings you the thrilling adventures of JACK ARMSTRONG…the Aaaaaaall American Boy!*" I was such a big fan of Jack Armstrong that the first chance I got to eat WHEATIES (my hero's sponsor) was on a visit to my Uncle Philip and his family in Tacoma, Washington. "Do you have Wheaties?" I politely asked my Aunt Janet. She filled a bowl for me and I added the milk. What a disappointment! They weren't even as good as Corn Flakes, and within seconds, the crispy flakes were soggy and mushy! I guess I wasn't cut out to be a champion.

Another one of our after-school radio favourites was *The Adventures of Superman*: "Faster than a speeding bullet…More powerful than a locomotive…Able to leap tall buildings in a single bound! LOOK! Up in the sky!…It's a bird…It's a plane…..IT'S SUPERMAN!!!"

On radio, you couldn't actually SEE him fly, but you were tipped off he was about to when Clark Kent burst from the broom closet as Superman and shouted, "Up! Up! And awaaaay!" At the time, it didn't occur to us that it was a silly thing for a grown man to shout, even if he could fly!

How many of us feel a tug of nostalgia recalling the familiar words from the introduction to the serial, *The Lone Ranger?* "*…return with us now… to those thrilling days of yesteryear…From out of the past…come the thundering-hoofbeats-of-the-great-horse-SILVER!…The L-o-o-o-o-ne Ranger…Riiiides again!*" And how many remember hearing Tonto say to his horse, *"Get-em-up, Scout!"*

How many of us, to this day, when we hear the familiar galloping rhythm of *The William Tell Overture* immediately think of the Lone Ranger? Hi ho Silver! Awaaaaaaaay!

Whenever I was sick and kept home from school, I would get hooked on the daytime radio serials my mother listened to*: Ma Perkins; When A Girl Marries; Portia Faces Life;* and MY favourite*, Our Gal Sunday.* It was the story of an orphan girl from the town of Silver Creek, Colorado, who, in young womanhood, married England's richest, most handsome lord, Lord Henry Brinthrop. Right after lunch each weekday afternoon, to the melancholy banjo background refrain of *Red River Valley*, the announcer asked the question, "*CAN this girl …from a little mining town in the west…find HAPPINESS… as the wife…of a wealthy… and titled…Englishman?*"

Clearly, the answer should have been, "No way!" First of all, Lord Henry was a skirt-chaser who was fiercely jealous without reason, and allowed his arrogant British relatives to insult Sunday in her own home, Black Swan Hall, a "spacious Virginia estate". A better question would have been, "How much longer can Our Gal Sunday put up with this loser?"

No wonder they were called "soap operas". Each fifteen minute episode had two commercials – one at the beginning and one at the end.

Remember? "*Ivory Soap – Ninety-nine and forty-four-one-hundredths percent pure! It floats!*" Or maybe you remember the catchy jingle? *"Rinso white! Rinso bright! Happy little washday song!"* Or maybe *"Halo, everybody, Halo! Halo is the shampoo that glorifies your hair" ?*

You have to admit they were catchy. Otherwise how would we remember them seventy-plus years later?

My ritual preparations for listening to *Little Orphan Annie* in the evening, just before bedtime, included putting on my pajamas, mixing a glass of milk and *Ovaltine* (Annie's sponsor), which I would sip as I sat in front of our big console radio. Sometimes, I would sit **behind** the radio in the little triangle of space formed by the corner of the room. I have no idea why I liked sitting there, hidden in the corner, but I do remember watching the glow of the vacuum tubes that powered the radio. I saved my *Ovaltine* labels and sent them in for a genuine "Secret De-coder Ring" so I could de-code the secret message from Annie at the end of each program and help Annie catch "spies" who were out to play havoc with our "War Effort."

A favourite Sunday evening radio comedy was *The Fred Allen Show*, featuring Fred's weekly stroll down "Allen's Alley" where he chatted with a range of characters who lived in mansions, farm houses and tenement buildings – all apparently next door to each other on the same street.

One character, "Senator Claghorn", who had a southern drawl, would tell Fred Allen at some point each week, "That's a joke, son!" (Loony Toons eventually based a barnyard rooster on this character). And when Farmer Titus Moody greeted Allen with, "Howdy, Bub," it never failed to get a laugh from the studio audience. Another favourite Allen's Alley character was "Mrs. Nussbaum" a long-suffering Yiddisher mama.

One of the longest-running gags on radio was Fred Allen's "feud" with an even bigger radio star, Jack Benny. But it was all in fun, and Benny was his final guest when the popularity of TV finally ended Allen's radio show. The sign-off was always the same. Allen would say to his dumb blond wife, Gracy Allen:

Allen: Say good night, Gracy.

Gracy: Good night, Gracy.

The forerunner of today's TV Program, *America's Most Wanted,* was the crime drama*, Gang Busters,* heard on Saturday nights for years. During one three-year period, the program helped to capture more than 100 real criminals!

Probably the most popular nightly comedy show was *Amos & Andy*. It was so popular at its peak, that movie houses stopped their feature film at 7:00 pm and turned up a radio so patrons could listen. Police departments reported that most car-thefts took place shortly after 7:00 pm because crooks knew that virtually everyone would be glued to their radio set, listening to *Amos 'n Andy!*

In today's "politically correct" times, this radio program would not have been tolerated. It featured the life and times of two slow-talking rather seemingly ignorant Negro buddies. Talk about stereotyping! And to add insult to injury, the two featured actors, Freeman Gosden and Charles Correll who gave voice to Amos and to Andy in a negro dialect - were WHITE!

CR

Untrammeled Snow

All children love the snow. But those of us who were lucky enough to have attended Herbert Spencer School in the early 1940's had a principal who also loved snow. His name was Percy Govier and he perfected the ultimate use of a fresh snowfall in a school yard.

Remember the fun of looking out the window at eight or ten inches of freshly fallen snow? Overnight the world was transformed into a playland. You couldn't wait to get into your snowsuit, extra socks, boots, mittens, scarf and toque (over top of your school clothes, of course) and head for school. Maybe we were tougher in those days, but I rarely remember school being closed just because of a good snowfall.

The first person to arrive at Spencer School on snowy mornings was Mr. Govier, our principal. He'd soon round up a few grade six boys and send them to the four approaches to the 'lower playground' bounded by Sixth Avenue, First Street, Princess Street and the school itself. The boys were honour-bound to protect the lower field from any trespassers. As children arrived for school these boys would direct everyone to other play areas so that the lower playground remained pristine and untrammeled.

Then, after the nine o'clock bell summoned us to our classes where we struggled out of our snow clothes and hung them dripping on the cloakroom hooks, Mr. Govier would go to the grade six classes and choose three or four of his most trusted boy students and after they were all dressed in their snow gear, including the principal, they would head for the smooth and untouched lower playground.

Leading the way, our principal would stomp a HUGE circle on the snowy play yard. Round and round they'd trudge in a line, stomping the fresh snow into a hard-packed circular pathway. Still leading the procession, he'd then head directly ACROSS the circle, cutting it in half. Then quarters. Then eighths. Then sixteenths until our circle looked like a beautiful ready-to-serve meringue pie. Mr. Govier then stepped out of the circle and, at his command, the boys would continue stomping the dissecting paths until those paths too were as hard-packed as the outer circle. When he felt the "pie" was perfect, the boys headed back to class and our Principal got on the PA system.

"Attention all classes! At today's recess we will have a game of Giant Pie Tag on the lower girls' playground. All participants will line up, single file, outside the entrance to the circle. All participants must be dressed for the snow, especially they must have proper snowboots. Twenty-five at a time will participate until everyone gets a turn. And I'm 'IT'!"

A cheer would ring out throughout the school. We would squirm in anticipation, and unbeknownst to us, the teachers had been told to let us go to the cloakroom early and begin the long process of donning our winter gear. Laughter, a bit of rough-housing by the boys, and excited chatter filled the room. We were directed back to our seats to await the recess bell. It seemed an eternity.

Finally the bell! We rushed out the nearest exit and got into line. Such fun! Watching our Principal chase and tag his students was the greatest fun of all.

Those "tagged" were required to step out of the circle until only one was left. Then he or she was now "it". Of course by this time the Principal was exhausted.

Even some of the teachers got into the game. I didn't realize it then because I didn't own a watch, nor did I run my life by the clock as most of us do today, but I'm sure those snow-pie-tag recesses ran a lot longer than the proscribed 15 minutes. Our school bell was rung by hand, not by a computer, so whoever was in charge of the bell that day was probably perched by a window waiting for a signal from – who else? Our wonderful principal, Percy Govier.

CR

Penwipers

Before the invention of the ball-point pen or even the fountain pen, students used to write with a black or red wooden "straight pen" or stylus. (see *The MacLean Method of Writing*)

The pen nibs had to be wiped clean before you put them away or they would rust and cause ink blots on your paper. Therefore, a **penwiper** was a "must". Typically, boys used a piece of old rag, or even their shirt-tails. Some boys even disdained wiping them at all and would "flick" their inky pens at a rival, or a girl whose attention he was determined to get, leaving a long trail of ink drops across the floor or down the sleeve of a blouse.

Penwipers were the one item that couldn't be purchased at *Burr Office Supplies* or *Nixon's Stationery Store*. You had to create one yourself. Girls were very competitive over who had the nicest penwiper. We salvaged scraps of colourful material out of our mother's sewing baskets and then cut the fabric into interesting shapes, such as stars, or circles, or ovals, etc. Some of us were lucky to have a mother who let us use her *pinking shears.* Then to complete the project, we would search our mother's button box for the absolutely perfect button which was sewn onto the middle of the fabric layers to hold them all together and voila! - the perfect penwiper!

My Uncle George Sangster told me about a time **before** inkwells and penwipers, when he started "First Primer" in 1899 at Central School where the Royal Towers Hotel stands today. First Primer was the only grade that mixed boys and girls. From then on they were separated. Not separate rooms – separate schools! In his words:

"We didn't have exercise books. Only a piece of slate in a wooden frame and a piece of felt fabric laced onto the back of the frame so it wouldn't bang on the desk when you set it down. You wrote on it with a pencil made of soapstone. If we wanted to, we could deliberately make the soapstone squeak when we wrote. It really upset the teacher—so we did that a lot.

"During First Primer we sat on benches. Our slate was under the bench on the floor. There were no desks. When we needed to write, we got up from the bench and went behind it and knelt on the floor and placed the slate on the bench. That's how we wrote – using the bench as a table. It was hard on the knees.

"Girls brought a piece of rag to clean their slate. Us boys, why, we'd just spit on it and rub it with our sleeve. Sometimes we'd have contests. We'd get a good, big glob of spit in the middle of our slate. Then we'd tip it first this way, then that way, then from side to side. Then we'd compare to see whose spit went the furthest."

CR

The MacLean Method Of Writing

At Herbert Spencer School we were taught the *MacLean Method of Writing* by Miss McAskill. She was a "purist" and her own beautiful handwriting proved it. Mr. MacLean would have been proud of her.

First, she made us place our writing books at a 45 degree angle on our desks – across the top left corner if you were right-handed and across the top right corner if you were left-handed. She drew lines on the board that were slanted, too.

Feet flat on the floor, back straight, we made a paper ball about the size of a golf ball from scrap paper and placed it in the cup of our writing hand. Without a pen in our hand we would "pretend" write. "Skate on your finger-tips," Miss McAskill would instruct. After a minute or two of pretending, we would insert the wooden pen stylus between our index finger and thumb. Still with the ball of paper in our palm, we would attempt inkless endless circles and straight-line exercises to the count of eight.

The wooden stylus pens were either red or black and gently curved to fit our fingers. We bought little boxes of 12 steel pen nibs which we learned to suck in order to remove any oils before we placed a nib in the stylus. The pen nibs eventually split from use, especially of you were heavy-handed. A split nib caused double lines, blots and low marks from the teacher.

Ink was handy in a little glass container in the top right-hand corner of your desk that fit snugly into a metal inkwell with a flip-up lid. Some boys would annoy their teachers by flicking the inkwell lid. Sometimes in Morse Code.

In severely cold winter weather, the ink would freeze and we had to use pencils.

One of the most sought-after "monitor" jobs in the classroom was filling the inkwells from a large bottle of ink that had a spout. Only the most trusted students were allowed to perform this task. One teacher made the job easier by letting us use a small bulb-

A typical *MacLean Method of Writing* exercise

syringe. It wasn't until I had children of my own that I discovered the ink syringe the teacher supplied was really a baby enema syringe!

Miss McAskill sometimes invited my father to give the class a handwriting demonstration. Dad was naturally left-handed, but in his school days at Central School, anyone caught using his left hand was sharply rapped on the knuckles with a ruler. If the ruler was made of tin, it drew blood! So my father was forced to use his right hand and thus became completely ambidextrous. He could write forward and backward with either hand. He could do it simultaneously! He could write two different sentences at the same time. He could write a sentence forward on one side of a paper and backward on the other side and when held up to the light they were identical!

Dad would also supply the whole class with "blotters" that advertised his insurance business, *The Mutual Life Assurance Company of Canada*. Blotters were an important part of our school supplies. We had to blot the wet ink on a page before we could turn to the next page.

In 1953, when I attended the Provincial Normal School in Vancouver to get my Teaching Certificate, we were required to pass The *MacLean Method of Writing* and the *MacLean Method of Printing* and the compendiums were personally marked by Mr. MacLean himself!

To this day, quite often when I sign a credit card receipt in a store, the clerk invariably says, "My, what a beautiful signature!"

Thank you, Miss McAskill. Thank you, Mr. MacLean

⁂

West Side Story

It seems that each neighbourhood had its own unique ways of having fun. Ralph Bloomquist, a school chum of ours told me about his neighbourhood.

"West End kids played in the old haybarns at Spring Ranch down at the foot of 23rd Street in the 30s and 40s. Sometimes we'd fall asleep in the warm hay for hours. We brought home eggs we'd found in the hay. Who knows how long they'd been there? We'd crack them into a saucer, because some of them were rotten. Mom never asked where we'd got them. Food was food.

"In winter we ice-skated on the frozen flats at the foot of Trapp Road. There was this kid from Saskatoon who had no skates so he wore his gumboots. He was NHL material in our estimation. He could 'outskate' all of us. We never knew his name. We just called him 'Gumboots'.

"We were forbidden to play at the river. So once you're forbidden – that's where you go. We found an old rowboat that we patched up and used boards for paddles. One time we paddled out to Poplar Island. There was this kid who sort of hung around us. He came with us and we got to playing Indians and we elected him the enemy and so we tied him to a tree. After a while we forgot about him and paddled back home. There was hell to pay for that stunt!

"My best friend was Arnie Nelson. We'd hang out down at the CKNW radio station that was upstairs over the Windsor Hotel and Fraser Café. We liked to watch them do the program, '*Bill Rae's Rrrounnnndup, high atop Big Mountain*' Bill Rae would say and then he had this whistle-thing with a slide on it. And he'd slide it so it sounded that we were going up, up, up the mountain.

"Arnie played guitar and sang and he eventually became CKNW's 12-year-old-mascot and he'd sing with the *Rhythm Pals* – Mike, Mark and Jack. As an adult, he made a living with them. They even played New York!

"As kids, Arnie's family had this huge garage where we played 'Radio Station' for hours. We'd clip news stories from the papers to read as the News. We made these little microphones and we'd give newscasts and spin records for hours like real disc jockeys. We even had a little 'On the Air' sign."

Arnold Nelson eventually moved back to Greater Vancouver and was MC at our 50th High School Class Reunion in 2002.

CR

Schoolyard Games

In the 1940s, you could tell what season it was by the games that elementary school kids were playing in the schoolyard during recess.

During the fall, boys would play "Conkers", a sort of chestnut fight. They'd drill a hole through a chestnut, then thread a string through the hole and tie a knot. Then one boy would hold the end of his string and dangle his chestnut while the other boy swung his own chestnut at the end of his string so as to collide with, or "conk" the other chestnut. The object was to shatter the other fellow's chestnut, but never your own.

Apparently, chestnuts harden with age. And if a chestnut survived from one autumn to the next, it was called a "yearsy", and was highly prized. If it survived yet another season, it was called a "twoser", and spoken of with great reverence by small boys.

Boys would also drill holes in two chestnuts and attach one to each end of a length of string, then swing them around and around and then let them go, like a gaucho throwing a *bola*. Sometimes you'd see the same chestnuts hanging from the telephone wires for years, until the string finally rotted.

When spring marble-season was upon us, mothers of young boys began to notice that ONE knee of their son's trousers was wearing through. In the same season, little girls began carrying draw-string bags containing their jacks and ball.

Popularity was assured for the girl with the longest skipping rope. One of my dad's insurance clients owned a cordage factory, so once a year my dad would bring home a nice, long, hemp rope. Friends lined up to "turn" the rope and earn themselves a chance to skip the rope. Remember? *"Down by the ocean, down by the sea, Johnny broke a milk-bottle and blamed it onto me. I told Ma. Ma told Pa. Johnny got a licking, so Ha, ha, ha!"*

Or, *Salt! Vinegar! Mustard! Pepper! Cedar! Cider! RED HOT PEPPER!* At which point the rope-turners turned the rope as fast as they could until the skipper quit or was tripped up.

On the girls' side of Spencer's playground, there were lots of flat, dirt areas. We'd carefully draw the eight squares required in a game of Hop-Scotch. Each girl had her own special "marker" to throw into a square when it was her turn. My favourite was a nice, heavy charm bracelet.

The appearance of yo-yos was another certain sign of spring. You could buy a beginners' yo-yo for 15 cents, or spend three or four times that much for a *Delux Model Cheerio Yo-yo* painted silver or gold that they claimed would "hum" in your hand. New strings came in a crackley paper envelope – two strings for a nickel.

We thought the young men who represented the *Cheerio Yo-yo Company* had the best jobs in the world – getting paid for visiting schoolyards to demonstrate how to "walk-the-dog", "sleep", "rock-the-cradle", or do "around the world." Today, they'd be unceremoniously marched off the property by a security guard!

One spring, my girlfriend Chrissy Georgeson won a yo-yo competition on the stage of the Odeon Theatre on Sixth Street. Boys were supposed to be better yo-yo players than girls, so some of them were pretty upset when our Chrissy showed them up and won a *genuine, golden deluxe Cheerio yo-yo* that really did hummmmmmm.

ରୀ

Halloween

Halloween was quite different in the 1940s. We always felt a shiver of anticipation and adventure when we headed out for "Halloween Handouts"! It was the one night of the year when we were allowed out after dark without adult supervision. Many of us believed that witches and ghosts really did come out that night, and we were wary but excited at the prospect.

Today's kids are faced with real dangers – razor blades or other sharp objects embedded in treats, and poisons or contaminates in homemade goodies. Parents, rightly, insist on accompanying their children because of the very real possibility of danger from those who prey on children.

How joyless Halloween has become compared to that bygone era. We treasured homemade handouts, and even sought them from ladies like the one on Fourth Street who always made sugar cookies with pumpkin faces, or the lady on Second Street who made yummy and sticky popcorn balls, and the one on Durham Street who coated apples in real toffee! During the war years when sugar was rationed, these kindly ladies contributed their precious sugar ration coupons rather than disappoint the neighbourhood kids.

Another special treat we could count on during those lean war years came from local lumber magnate, J. G. Robson. In that era, the Robson home was the beautiful white mansion at the foot of Third Street (now a private school). "JG" himself would open the door holding a shiny silver tray of REAL CHOCOLATE BARS! The kind that we hadn't been able to buy since the war began – *Jersey Milk, Burnt Almond, Malted Milk,* or my favourite, *Crispy Crunch.*

Kids flocked there from every neighbourhood in town to get this special treat. Some boys would try going back for seconds, but old "JG" was too smart for them. He'd always spot the cheaters and say, "Get out of here, you rascals! You've already had yours."

We'd trudge for hours, passing the word to each other about which houses had the best handouts. Then, when our bags became too heavy to carry any farther, we'd reluctantly head home, sure in our minds that it must be at least ten or eleven o'clock. It was always surprising and a little disappointing to find out that it was only about eight-thirty.

The bag of treasures was all ours. Our mothers didn't go through our loot looking for anything harmful. We got to keep it all! In those days, the only real danger on our streets on Halloween night were the ghosts and goblins in our young imaginations.

Times change. And it never crossed our minds to actually play tricks on people. But that wasn't the case when my Dad was a boy.

One year, as teenagers, Dad and a bunch of sturdy friends "liberated" a flatbed dray wagon from Gilley Brothers on the waterfront, hauled the wagon up Eighth Street hill to Royal Avenue, then to the Central School where the Royal Towers Hotel now stands. They completely dismantled the dray, and passed it piece-by-piece through a first floor window they had jimmied open. Then they reassembled the monstrous wagon in the classroom of the most despised teacher in the school – the same teacher who took obvious pleasure in rapping Dad's knuckles with a metal ruler whenever Dad used his left hand to write!

Two great wooden spoked wagon wheels were erected in one classroom aisle, with the other two set up three aisles away. The rear of the wagon touched the back wall, and the great wagon tongue extended up to the blackboard. The next morning the boys in that class got half a day off while the school administration dealt with the situation.

Boys were known to stuff burlap sacks into the chimneys of curmudgeons who didn't like kids. Tipping over outhouses was another traditional Halloween prank. One Halloween, the front gate of 319 Sixth Avenue disappeared off its hinges. Weeks later, while on his way to work, my Grampa Appleton spotted his gate at the top of a big maple tree on Fourth Street.

CR

Woodsman, Spare That Tree

Across the street from our house, at number 314 Sixth Avenue, stood two nice "monkey puzzle" trees. When my dad heard that the owners were planning to have the trees destroyed, he swung into action. Contacting the city arborist for advice, and making a date with the Electric Light Department to borrow their heavy-gang and a truck with a boom arm, he made this proposal to the neighbours: the City of New Westminster would remove the two monkey-puzzle trees at no cost to them and re-plant them elsewhere in the city. It was a deal!

As you can see from the photographs, one of the trees was heavier than the truck. What a sight it was as the tree was slowly lifted from its hole with its huge root-ball swathed in sacking when suddenly, ker-thump - the tree dropped back down into the hole and the truck went up into the air!

I'm not sure how they solved the problem. I was at school when it happened, but they must have found a heavier truck or put more weight on the truck, but eventually both trees were successfully raised and then lowered into awaiting dump trucks.

One of the trees was planted on the lawn of Olivet Baptist Church and the other was planted in Moody Park near the Parks & Recreation office. Both have flourished in their new settings and after more than sixty years they are nearly twice the size they were on transplant day.

Go have a look.

CR

Road Trips

The first road trip I remember? I was two years and six months old. Our family drove to Banff Springs Hotel for a convention. My sister Norma was eight and my brother Ross was sixteen and had just earned a Drivers Licence. He was the reason that this road trip was imprinted on my memory at such a young age, for on the return trip, on the narrow two-lane road through the mountains, we had a car accident.

The road had only two lanes. On one side a sheer mountain cliff and on the other side a sheer drop to a valley below. Ross was driving, when around a sharp curve a nervous driver was clinging to the cliff side which was the wrong side of the road. My brother could not avoid a head-on collision but fortunately, both cars were not travelling very fast. Unfortunately, our car was put out of commission. The guilty driver's car was still drivable. Dad flagged down the next car heading the same direction and was given a ride to Winachi, Washington, where he hired a tow-truck.

My sister Norma and me at Banff Springs Hotel, 1936. Sangster Collection.

Two things I remember vividly: One, being stood on the brick wall at Banff Springs Hotel and gazing down, down, down into the Bow River Valley and two, sharing a lower birth on a train with my mother as we traveled back home while Dad and Ross stayed in Winatchi until the car was repaired. I remember peeking under the window blind and watching street lamps whiz past the train window.

The summer I was six, Mom, Dad, Norma and I drove up the Fraser Canyon to Vernon to visit my brother Ross at the Vernon Army Camp. The very same camp where my dad had endured basic training in WW I.

The drive to Vernon in the Interior of British Columbia was done in two stages. Stage one took us as far as Hope, the gateway to the Fraser Canyon. We stayed at a "motel", a type of accommodation that was a rather new concept invented in California to accommodate the advent of car travel and paved highways. The Hope motel consisted of little log cabins, situated along the very edge of the mighty Fraser. You could hear it roaring past all night long. We got an early start next morning so there would be good light for the treacherous road ahead.

Stage two was the two lane road up the Fraser Canyon, with very little improvement, the same road the Royal Engineers had built to the gold fields in the 1860s. Some stretches were only wide enough for one car and if two cars met, one of them had to drive in reverse to a side-hole gouged out of the rock face where one car could pull in to let another car pass! Worse still, some sections of the road had collapsed and these sections had a wooden trestle-like section which protruded out over the canyon and the Fraser rapids below. Whenever we came to one of these trestles, I remember crouching down on the floor of the car with my eyes shut tight until I sensed we were back on solid ground. The wooden planks of the trestles went thump, thump, thump under our wheels.

My Dad's twin brother, Philip Sangster, lived in Tacoma, Washington, and we drove there once or twice a year. We always made a stop at *Whalley's Gas Station* in, you guessed it – Whalley. Now you know how it got its name. The gas station was the first and, for a long time, the only business in that part of Surrey. Dad would mark down the mileage so he could calculate his gas-mileage for the trip. I usually slept most of the way and would awaken when Dad tooted his horn as we pulled into Uncle Phil and Aunty Janet's driveway nearly four hours later.

On the return trip, we always competed to see who would be the first one to see **the light on Grouse Mountain.** There was no night skiing on the North Shore mountains in those days, but at the Chalet on Grouse Mountain there was one light that could be seen for miles. It wasn't until the 1960s when one summer day we took our young family up the Grouse Mountain chair lift for an adventure, that I got to see the famous light. It wasn't a light at all. It was hundreds of lights! A tall wooden frame supported a huge, round wooden billboard with hundreds of light sockets covering every square inch of it. From the King George Highway in south Surrey it looked like one lone light.

The last stop on our road trip would be at Whalley's Gas Station for a fill-up before we crossed the bridge to home.

CR

Coloured

The first African-Americans I ever remember meeting were *The Mississippians*, a Negro gospel quartet who sang at Olivet Baptist Church one Sunday evening in 1943. Afterwards, the quartet, our minister Reverend J. L. Sloat and all the church choir were invited to our house for tea and coffee and goodies. More singing took place around our piano, accompanied by our church organist, Fred Grocock. But these songs weren't all gospel songs.

Dad asked the *Mississippians* where they were staying that night, and offered to drive them to their hotel. They confessed to not having a reservation yet, so Dad offered to phone ahead and get them rooms in downtown Vancouver. With each phone call he would book rooms for four gentlemen and then he would mention, offhandedly, that, "These gentlemen are coloured." (The polite term of the day.) Suddenly, the hotel was full, the clerk had made a mistake! I stood in the kitchen, a very curious nine-year-old, listening to the phone calls, and realizing that these four nice, talented singers were somehow not acceptable to some people.

Dad apologized to them, but was determined to find them rooms. He finally succeeded by phoning a hotel on Main Street near the CPR station where black porters stayed when their train was there overnight.

The second Negro I met was when I was sixteen, and working weekends in a meat store on Columbia Street called *The Butcher Boy.* The store was owned and operated by Don's uncle, Bert Robinson, and every time this African-American came into the store, Bert would call out, "Hi there, Chicago!" and begin to write up the fellow's meat order for his hamburger stand on the King George Highway.

You've probably guessed by now that our town had no resident black citizens in my growing-up years. We were a WASP community. We had a few Chinese students in our schools, (the Japanese had been shipped inland) and an even fewer number of First Nations students. The only other visible minority I can recall were East Indian.

I recall a visit our family made to Seattle in 1952. We stayed at my brother Ross' house. Directly behind his house was a Negro family who had seven or eight kids. My little seven-year-old nephew, Craig Walton, went outside and soon began to play with the neighbour kids. After a while, we called him in to supper. He was all excited about his new-found friends. And he exclaimed with wonderment on his face, "And ya know what...they're all Chinese!" That was as close as he could come to describing kids who had different skin colour. The terms Negro, Black, African-American just weren't in his seven-year-old Canadian vocabulary.

ෆ

Irving House

The beautiful home of Captain William Irving escaped the Fire of 1898. Then as years passed, most of the other stately homes of that vintage went under the wrecker's ball to make way for smaller lots and houses that didn't require an army of servants for their upkeep.

Luckily, the Irving family home passed to Captain Briggs, Irving's son-in-law. Two of Briggs' daughters remained unmarried, and the beautiful house was bequeathed to them for the remainder of their lives. If my dad's twin, Philip was any example, it's not any wonder the two Briggs girls never married. You see, Philip was "smitten" by Manuella Briggs. Or was it Naomi? Whatever. Captain Briggs caught him hanging around their house one day, and told Philip in no uncertain terms that "his kind", meaning not well enough off (poor in other words), "were not welcome around my daughters," and poor Philip was too intimidated to ever return.

Early one evening, around 1944 when I was ten, my father took me down to visit the Briggs sisters. Dad knew them both well, and he knew they were rattling around in that big house. They used and heated only three or four of the rooms. That evening, we sat around the big dining room table and the sisters served us tea and cookies.

Then Dad got down to business. He said he realized that the house must be quite a job to keep up, and that the day might come when they decided they would like to move to a smaller, more easily managed home.

"And when that day comes", my Dad said, " I would like to have 'First Option' on the purchase of this beautiful, historic house on behalf of the City of New Westminster."

Irving House Museum and Archives, New Westminster, BC.

After some discussion, the two sisters agreed, and Dad produced a legal paper he had already drawn up and Manuella and Naomi Briggs signed their names and so did J. Lewis Sangster. And THEN, on the line marked "witness", ten year old Evelyn Ruth Sangster carefully signed her name, and the deal was sealed. I felt so grown up and important!

Then in 1950, Mayor Sangster received a call from one of the sisters to say that the other sister had to be placed in a nursing home and that she, the remaining occupant of the house, did not wish to remain there alone and was now willing to give Mayor Sangster his "First Option."

The rest is history. Irving House today is the gem of our city thanks to the foresight and love my father felt for the Royal City and its history.

CR

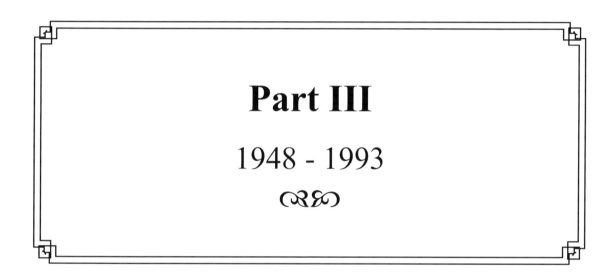

Part III

1948 - 1993

The Great Flood of 1948

As a kid living up on the hill in New Westminster, I wasn't aware of the enormity of the Fraser River flood of 1948 until my father took me down to the waterfront for a local history lesson.

As we stood on the wharf where Dad had played as a boy, the river lapped up between the planks. A farm building and a bloated cow floated past, and I'll always remember the improbable sight of a living room sofa drifting by with three miserable-looking chickens perched on it. Upriver, a fleet of valiant tugs fought an around-the-clock battle to keep uprooted trees and large debris from piling up against the old train trestle.

Dad was a keen student of local history who would be elected mayor of the Royal City later that same year. Turning from the river, he pointed back to the heart of the city and told me that in 1894 the flood waters had reached the doors of the cannery that once stood at Begbie and Front Streets, and that boats were rowed or poled along Columbia Street west of Eighth Street. Within a few days history would repeat itself, as the river continued to rise until a knee-deep lake was again formed at the foot of Eighth Street.

By the end of May the river had flooded sections of both the CPR and the CNR railway tracks and the Trans-Canada Highway up the valley, isolating the Lower Mainland from the rest of Canada. Our family was booked for a train trip to a convention in Toronto early in June, but it seemed obvious to me that the trip would be cancelled. Then we were informed that our CNR tickets would be honored by the newly inaugurated Trans-Canada Airlines (TCA). I was ecstatic, for my girlfriend and I dreamed of becoming airline stewardesses, although neither of us had flown on an airplane. I would be the first.

As soon as our propeller-driven North Star aircraft had taken off from Sea Island Airport and turned east, all 40 passengers pressed against the windows for a bird's-eye view of the flood-swollen Fraser River. It looked like a vast spill of coffee on a huge green carpet. As we gained altitude, the river looked like a long, coffee-colored lake stretching from the Gulf of Georgia to the Fraser Canyon.

It took over two uncomfortable hours to reach Edmonton in that deafening, shuddering aircraft, and to my dismay, the attendants weren't glamorous stewardesses after all, but male stewards, just like on the trains.

We spent a week in Ontario, mostly at the headquarters of Dad's employer, The Mutual Life Assurance Company of Canada in Waterloo, Ontario. While the insurance agents attended seminars and meetings, the wives and families were taken on various tours in the area. One such tour took us to see Mutual Life's "ELECTRONIC BRAIN" (as the guide referred to it). It was a huge machine housed in a building the size of a gymnasium and criss-crossed by catwalks for access by the technicians who looked after this monstrous creation. It whirred, and buzzed, and glowed, and some visible vacuum tubes were as large as small children. We were told it did mathematical calculations and actuary calculations at amazing speeds. The guide told us, with a hint of pride in his voice, that this was one of only two "Electronic Brains" in all of Canada. The Federal Government in Ottawa had the other. At 14, I thought it was particularly boring and didn't come to realize until years later that I had been privileged to witness one of Canada's very first COMPUTERS!

Now back to the story of the Great Flood of 1948. My Fraser River flood history lesson continued two weeks later when we returned on one of the first passenger trains allowed through to the Lower Mainland after the floodwaters had receded and the tracks had been repaired. Our porter woke us near dawn so we could witness the devastation in the Fraser Valley.

As our train wound through the Fraser canyon, someone pointed to a suspension bridge high above and told us it had been skipping on the waters at the height of the flood!

When we reached the farmlands around Chilliwack, it was like traveling through a moonscape. Everything was gray – gray fields, gray stick-like trees, gray farm buildings. Only tall silos were still white above the "bathtub ring" left by the Fraser. Where once stood rows of lush green fruit trees, now stood rows of dead tree skeletons impaled in fields of silt. By this time, the railcar had grown silent as the realities and the immensity of the tragedy hit home.

Dad knew there was more to be learned about this historic event, so the next Sunday he drove our family up the Fraser Valley to observe the flood's aftermath first-hand. Somewhere near Matsqui he turned into the deserted farmyard of an abandoned one-story house. The high-water mark was up near the eves. The door hung open.

The floor of the house was under inches of mud and the bathtub was full to the brim with muddy Fraser River water. A family portrait hanging on the wall had a high-water mark across the dignified face. The family must have left in a hurry, for their clothes were left hanging in the closets. They disintegrated when touched.

Hardly a word was spoken, and I don't think I was the only one with a lump in my throat as we got back into the car and drove away from one family's dream turned into a nightmare by the historic Fraser River flood of 1948.

* * * * *

When I submitted this first-person account to The Record in 1998, they combined my story with an historical overview by Lori Pappajohn and a first-person account by my husband Don. That three-part story won the Neville Shank Award for best historical article in a community newspaper for that year. I thought it appropriate to include Don's memory of the Flood of '48 in this book. Here is his story:

The "Tom Sawyer" Flood Adventure

Don Benson

Growing up in New Westminster's waterfront district, I was captivated by tales about the historic Fraser River flood of 1894. How pioneers had to canoe to church, and how the paddlewheeler *Gladys* went, at will, over river farmlands rescuing stranded livestock. I suppose that's why, when the Fraser rose to 1894 levels by the end of May, 1948, I heard the call of the canyon.

The Fraser River was flowing into and not out of Harrison Lake, the Canadian Navy had launched "Operation Overflow" and someone had seen a cat swimming down the river with a mouse riding on its back! But most compelling for me, the water level at Hell's Gate in the Fraser Canyon had risen more than a hundred feet—higher than the towering Westminster Trust Building, our Columbia Street skyscraper!

On Saturday, May twenty-ninth, my pal Larry "Mousey" Piché and I were supposed to join the Westminster Regiment Army Cadets for a weekend camp-out. But instead, we hitchhiked up the Valley, expecting to make it to Hell's Gate and back by Sunday evening. With portions of the old Trans-Canada Highway under water, we had to hike along back roads for several miles.

Indelible in my memory was coming upon a shaman-like native Indian, chanting, dancing and gleefully proclaiming that white men had stolen the Fraser's gold, chopped down her trees, blasted her canyon walls and gutted her sacred salmon-runs. Now the river was using *Tacouchi,* rampaging floodwaters, to get even.

My highly polished army-issue boots helped us convince an army transport driver to give us a lift through flooded sections of the Trans-Canada to the now isolated town of Hope.

The next day, my fifteenth birthday, we headed up the canyon with a Provincial Police officer, a Province newspaper reporter and cameraman and a Public Health nurse. Later that morning, we reached Hell's Gate and the most magnificent birthday gift I could have wished for was the sight that met us. The Fraser had risen earlier to fill two tunnels sixty feet above its normal level, then continued to rise a further sixty-eight feet, all the way to an old suspension bridge, causing the structure to skip and dance on the river's crest. It was an awesome sight that only a privileged few got to see.

Back at Hope, later that afternoon, Larry and I were in trouble. We couldn't make it back home that day, and with all telephone and telegraph lines washed out there was no way to contact our parents.

What we couldn't have known was that the cadet camp-out had been cancelled and Reservists were sent to man the dikes. We had been listed by flood emergency officials as missing and presumed lost in the flood. But all was forgiven when we reached home late the next day, because our folks were so glad to see us alive.

The City cancelled all adult sporting events, and all Army Cadets were released from local schools to help volunteers handle a million sandbags. I joined my cadet buddies working on the Queensborough dikes which soon became a blur of sandbags and sandy sandwiches. The dikes were so soggy that a fist or a boot print could sprout a leak, and, as the tide crested, whenever a large boat went by, its wash slopped over the top. When the main pump in Queensborough became plugged, the chief City Engineer, Mr. Potter, dived into the cold water to clear the debris. Mr. Spagnol, the grocer, volunteered his horse and stone-boat to haul sandbags, and the poor animal dropped dead in its traces from overwork.

As we labored on the dikes, a steam train hitched to a long line of flatbed cars stood nearby with a constant head of steam, in case the dikes broke. Our instructions were that if the siren sounded the alarm, we were to run to the train and jump onto the flatcars which would already be slowly moving towards the trestle. Citizens of Queensborough who had refused to abandon their homes were given the same instructions.

By June twelfth the crisis was over. Paid workers took over the responsibility for the dikes, and it was time to return to junior high school to write final exams and bask in the notoriety triggered by the "Boys Missing" report that had been published in *The Columbian* newspaper.

CR

Coquitlam, ran into the rear of a BCER bus which had stopped to pick up passengers. The bus was operated by John K. Warfield, 33 Clute street. Considerable damage was done to the front of the auto and Goden received facial lacerations.

Boys Missing — Two city boys have been missing from their homes since 8 a.m. Saturday. They are Donald Benson, 15, 420 Agnes street, 5 feet two inches, 120 pounds, wearing red plaid jacket, blue jeans, and army boots, and Lawrence Peche, 15, 422 Agnes street, five feet one inch, 105 pounds, wearing brown plaid jacket, and dark trousers. Anyone knowing the whereabouts of these boys are asked to phone NW 3331-R.

Furnace Repairs and Installations. Prompt service, moderate prices. Phone Neal & Bolton, Phone 3668. 140 E. Columbia St.

S-E-X Education

It wasn't a topic to be bantered about. In fact, it wasn't bantered at all. In Junior High School, in a girls-only "Health" class we were shown a brief, but strictly biological film on the changes to the female body during adolescence. Notice it was the female body only. I can only assume that the boys' health classes got the male version. I don't recall any instruction following this short film, nor do I remember a question/answer session. My girlfriends and I had all mailed away a coupon to the Modess Company which we had clipped from a woman's magazine for a booklet, "Growing Up And Liking It!" (The exclamation point was theirs.) It was in colour and had nice illustrations, as I recall. But of course, there was no mention of S-E-X.

You can imagine our teenage excitement in 1947 when ads began to appear in the local paper for a one-afternoon-only showing of an educational film entitled "Mom & Dad", to be shown at the Metro Theatre on Twelfth Street on a Saturday. "All children must be accompanied by an adult or show a signed letter from a parent at the box office. Boys and men's viewing is at 1:00 pm. Girls and Women's viewing is at 2:00pm". My mother declined to take me, but a friend's mother (much younger than mine) agreed to take me along with her two girls.

The film included the usual biological story with diagrams of the Female Organs and the process of maturation and menstruation. But it also included the equivalent diagrams and explanation of the Male Organs. This was an eye-opener to the girls in my circle, for such diagrams were not available in any book in our school library and such books at the Public Library were kept in a locked cabinet and only the Head Librarian had the key! We got to see a live birth (Quick! Don't blink or you'll miss it!) as the culmination of a very serious lecture from a white-coated Doctor about the sanctity and commitment of married love between a man and a woman followed by a diagram of how a sperm fertilizes an egg. I can't remember if this was done with animation techniques or if it was done with a diagram and pointer. Either way, the sex act was never discussed.

All this information was leading up to the climax of this educational journey: VENERIAL DISEASE. The same white-coated Doctor began a stern and scary lecture with photo after photo of graphic, horrific examples of the ravages of gonorrhea and syphilis that awaited any person who strayed beyond the safety of the marriage bed! We were horrified. The boys who saw this film must have been really traumatized because the tone of the Doctor's lecture and most of the photos were aimed at the males in the audience.

By today's standards, the film, "Mom & Dad" is laughable. Informative? For its time – yes. But a far cry from the sex education taught today. VD has become STDs and the list is longer and deadlier despite our arsenal of modern-day medications.

But the basic "facts of life" haven't changed since Adam met Eve. I often smile at the memory of one unmarried female P.E. teacher who saved her Sex Education Health classes for me to teach when she took a week off to play in an International Softball

Tournament. She said, "You'll do a better job than I ever could, Evelyn. After all, you've had five kids!"

လ

Inside The B.C. Penitentiary

The B.C. Penitentiary was more than a prison – it was a working farm.

The farmland stretched from the Fraser River up the hill as far as Eighth Avenue, was bisected by Sixth Avenue and was completely fenced and topped with barbed wire. To the citizens of New Westminster, browned and healthy convicts were a familiar sight as inmates laboured on the farmlands.

When the upper fields were to be worked, the armed guards would stop traffic on Sixth Avenue while the gates were opened and the working convicts with shovels, rakes and hoes over their shoulders trudged across the avenue. Then the gates were secured behind them. In harvest time, horse-drawn wagons were part of the parade.

The penitentiary farm supplied the prison with fresh vegetables, mostly potatoes, carrots, turnips, cabbage—vegetables that had a long storage life. If the harvest was over-abundant, the surplus was sent to the Provincial Mental Hospital on the adjoining property.

Children came to know some of the inmates by name and would wave and shout "Hi" as they passed.

The Penitentiary taught many trades. Painting, paperhanging, concrete work and plastering, tin smithing and shoemaking were but a few. Canadian army officers could have dress oxfords and combat boots made-to-measure at the "The Pen". It was one of the big employers in the community and every neighbourhood had their share of "Pen Guard families".

I can claim to have actually been **inside** the prison. Yes, when I was sixteen, our church choir gave a Sunday concert at The Pen. Each car entered the front entrance, one at a time, and a gate was shut in front of and behind each car. The trunk was inspected and mirrors on long handles were passed under the car. The car was then allowed into the prison yard and the next carload of Baptist choirists were waved in and scrutinized. The whole procedure was repeated on the way out.

We were led into the prison library where we hung our coats and donned our choir robes. The inmates were already waiting in the auditorium as we were led through the cell blocks, past the cells. We passed tier after tier of cells that looked just like a James Cagney movie set. Each cell had two bunks, a toilet and a basin.

I have to admit the inmates were a good audience. They applauded loudly and sang along lustily to some of the more familiar anthems. I suppose that was because they were a captive audience.

As we returned to our cars, all the convicts were now in the fenced-in exercise yard which we had to pass on our way to our cars. Suddenly I heard, "PSSSSST, Evelyn! Over here!" I glanced to my left and there, leaning against the fence was a boy who had been in my Grade Eight class. He was older than us in 1948 because he had only recently been released from the infamous Boy's Industrial School of Coquitlam (BISCO). This made him a bit of a celebrity in our Junior High School.

"Hi, Paddy!" I said with a wave, but before I could walk over to say hello, a firm hand gripped my elbow and steered me toward the car. The ladies of the choir were not amused that a member of their group was on speaking terms with an inmate of the B.C. Penitentiary. I raised more than a few eyebrows that day, especially since my father was a deacon of the church!

ஐ

Old Cars and Hot Rods

During most of World War II, no cars were manufactured for the public. Only military vehicles were being produced. Car owners had to make do with the 1920's and 1930's models they had when the war started. Gas and tires were rationed and it was thought unpatriotic to make frivolous use of an automobile. Some put their cars up on blocks for the duration.

When cars started rolling off the assembly line again around 1947, many drivers couldn't get rid of their old jalopy fast enough. They were practically giving them away. Thus the birth of hot rods and street rods in North America because old cars were cheap, and teenagers didn't want to have a car that looked anything like their square old Dad's. So they "customized" old cars by lowering them, removing the chrome, "blanking-in" the holes, painting them in gray primer paint, and modifying the sound by adding special mufflers.

In 1950, the only students to own cars at Duke of Connaught High School were John Rowse in Grade 12 and my Grade 10 boyfriend, Donny Benson. Don had earned money logging up the coast that summer, and after returning to school in the fall he purchased a well-maintained 1929 Model A *4X Bakery* pick-up truck with a wooden bench seat and no doors for $25. My mother thought it was disreputable and unsafe and wouldn't allow Don to drive me to school in it. So I did what any teenage daughter would do. I walked – about a block, and then Don picked me up, out of sight of my house, and dropped me off in the same spot after school. A few months later he fitted it out with a "mint" Ford coupe body for $20 – rumble seat and all! Mother then relented and allowed me to ride in it. After all, it had doors!

His next purchase was a 1930 Hudson eight-cylinder sedan for $50 from Bill Jiry in

Sapperton. A black limousine, it was reputed to have been a rum-running car used very successfully during Prohibition. I remember it had a very long hood, fancy silver flower vases and really hugged the road.

Don and his friend Ian MacFarlane stripped the Hudson down, and Don began racing it at *Digney Speedway* in Burnaby. For awhile the Hudson held speed records there. After two drivers were killed in one night at the track, Don's mother and I both put our foot down. We sighed in relief when Don spent $150 of his racing winnings on a rare, 1936 Nash yellow convertible and his interest turned to sport cars.

Don phoned me shortly after and asked me to pick him up at Horse Shoe Bay. He thought I'd borrow my father's Pontiac, but it wasn't available. So his sister Bonnie Benson and I decided to take the Nash. The reason Don didn't have the Nash in Horseshoe Bay soon became apparent. There was practically no clutch! I'd only just passed my Driver's Test the week before, but, undaunted, Bonnie and I headed through downtown Vancouver traffic, over the Lions Gate Bridge and onto the winding, treacherous original road to

Don tinkering with his $25 Model A Ford Coupe. Bobby Dean looks on - Evelyn Benson

Horseshoe Bay that wound along the sea cliffs.

I soon mastered the technique of "double-clutching" into every gear. It worked! No more grinding sounds! No more derogatory remarks from male drivers, like, "Hey sweetheart, grind a pound for me! Ha ha!" Don was amazed when he saw us drive up in the Nash.

To this day, being adept at "double-clutching" has served me well over the years at our place on Keats Island. Many's the old "beater" I've had to drive with little or no clutch and no car mechanic anywhere on the island.

But my favourite car of all was a 1948 English MG-TC with wire wheels, right-hand drive, and a neat little brass plaque on the dash stating the MG had been officially clocked at 100 mph on the Bonneville Salt Flats in Utah. Sadly, that fire-engine red little sweetie was too small for our growing family. By the time we were expecting our second child we traded it in for a station wagon. The first of many. In those days, no one we knew ever dreamed that a family could have TWO cars. Unheard of!

CR

St. Patrick's Snake Parade

St. Patrick's Day holds a special place in my heart. No, it's not because I'm Irish, although the Magees on my mother's side came from Armaugh, but because it's the day I fell in love with Donny Benson over sixty years ago.

The first "snake parade" I remember was as a child in the 1940s when I watched a chain of high school students wind their way down Sixth Street, led by a leprechaun named Kennedy, wearing paddy green long-johns and a tall silk hat!

What is a "snake parade"? Let me explain. Up until the new Lester Pearson High School was opened up the hill in 1955, each March 17th, St. Patrick's Day, New Westminster high school students would join hands to form a long human chain or "snake", and would wind their way down to our main street, Columbia, where they would enter and exit business establishments. The "snake", which represented the snakes St. Patrick supposedly drove out of Ireland, would criss-cross Columbia Street at several points, bringing traffic to a halt. Teenage leaders at the head of the parade were sure to lead the snake through several beer parlours, where the more unruly high school boys would scoop up and gulp down 10 cent glasses of beer as they wound between the tables.

Two reasons that local kids could hardly wait to be old enough for high school in those days were the intense

Evelyn in the snake parade, followed by Elia Basso

rivalry between the two high schools, Duke of Connaught and Trapp Tech, in team sports, especially basketball and the annual snake parade.

On March 17, 1950, during my first year in high school, for the **very first time** the two high schools, under the leadership of the two school presidents, decided to unite to form a single snake parade. The idea was to forget traditional rivalries for once, and form THE LARGEST SNAKE PARADE IN ROYAL CITY HISTORY!

The gigantic parade started on schedule a few minutes past noon on neutral territory – the playground of the original F.W. Howay Elementary School at Sixth and Royal. There it wound from sidewalk to sidewalk down Sixth Street. The snake was so long that when its "head" reached Columbia Street, the "tail" was still being formed above Royal Avenue, four blocks away.

The boy from the rival high school that I had linked hands with in the chain, had curly hair, a devilish sense of humour and something of the good looks of the actor James Dean of that era. When the snake parade disbanded at the old Carnegie Library grounds on Carnarvon Street more than an hour later, DCHS school president Andy Stocker said in a loud voice as he looked at Don and me, "OK, you two, the parade's over. You can stop holding hands now!" and everyone laughed. That night, Don walked me home from a school dance and the rest is history.

That was over sixty years ago, yet it seems like yesterday. Maybe that's because that curly-headed charmer and I still hold hands. His hair is thinner and we are both gray, but after five children, nine grandchildren and three great grandchildren (and counting) – we go out to dinner every March 17th and hold hands between courses and fondly recall that St. Patrick's Day snake parade long ago.

ᘯ

Ice Cream Parlours

Eating an ice cream cone as we stroll along the Quay often makes me think of *Zeigler's* ice cream parlour that stood on the northeast corner of Columbia and Eighth Streets. Sometimes we kids would hop off the bus from Sapperton where we had been swimming at Hume Park and get one of Zeigler's side-by-side two scoop ice cream cones. You could even ask for two different flavoured scoops, and two scoops were only a nickel.

Kids walking home uphill from Duke of Connaught High School thought of Sixth Street as "Ice cream Row". *Drake's Dairy* at Sixth Street and Fifth Avenue made super-thick milkshakes. *Roxy's* in the next block was famous for their ten cent *Mudbath* – a large scoop of vanilla drowned in a bath of chocolate syrup. Half a block further was the *Windsor Café* where they made very generous twenty-cent sundaes, (as well as the best fish & chips in town). Donny Benson and I used to order ONE bowl of ice cream and fresh strawberries (in season) with TWO spoons. In winter it was hot mince pie with TWO forks.

Kids walking downhill from Connaught headed for either the *Echo Dairy* or *Langley's Confectionary*, both at Agnes Street. Mr. Langley hired the attractive and friendly Piché sisters to mind the soda fountain. Lorraine and Jeannette were favourites with the boys from Connaught and St. Peter's. They claimed THEIR twenty-cent milkshakes were the best in town. They even made twelve-cent milkshakes for kids with not enough money!

Ice cream parlours were an important part of the teenage social scene up until the new high school was opened in 1955. By that time, many families had freezers and ice cream wasn't the "treat" it once had been.

Many's the time I'd finish my dinner first, then jump on my bike and race to the nearest corner store for a "brick" of ice-cream, then race home before it melted. The "bricks" were about the same size as a chimney brick and fed a typical family without having any left overs.

Remember? No freezers.

Cℛ

Jiving At The Bowl

by Don Benson

There has always been a generation gap between parents and kids, but that gap widened to a chasm in the early 1950s when a small army of local teenagers embraced the "hoodlum look" and turned the Hollywood Bowl dance hall on Carnarvon Street into the jumpingest jive joint this side of Seattle.

The two key elements of the hoodlum look, the unofficial dress at the Bowl, were trousers called strides, and a boogie haircut. Strides typically were 24 inches wide at the knee and only 14 inches at the cuff. They couldn't be bought off the rack, but were tailor-made locally at Lee Brothers on Front Street. A boogie hair cut was a crewcut on top and long on the sides so it could be combed into a ducktail in the back with the help of a generous application of *Brylcream*.

Brylcream, a little dab will do ya, Brylcream, you'll look so debonair Brylcream, the gals will all pursue ya, simply rub a little in your hair.

Girls wore ponytails or "poodle cuts" and a few wore strides, but most wore either full-circle skirts with several crinolines or long, pencil slim skirts that nearly touched their bobby socks and saddle shoes. Angora or cashmere twin-set sweaters topped their outfits.

While the Hollywood Bowl of the early '50s belonged to the teenagers, there was an older group in their early twenties who hung around too. One of them, Rusty Clancy, recalled, "Jack Ross, the policeman, used to moonlight as a bouncer at the Bowl. You'd get your hand stamped, so if you were old enough or looked old enough, you could step across the street to the Russell Hotel for a couple of beers at 10 cents a glass."

There were two lines at the Bowl, one sitting and one standing. The girls sat along the wall on one side looking as demure as they could, considering they were being bounced up and down by the spring floor. Alf Toban, the original Bowl owner told me the spring floor cost a lot of money, "They laid two-by-fours on the cement floor then got sacks of horse hair and laid it on the joists. Then the floor boards were laid on top of that thick layer of horse hair right up to the wall which made for a very springy dance floor that didn't tire your legs."

The boys stood across the floor in the stag line trying to look macho and cool. It was quite acceptable for two girls to jive together, which made it easier for the boys to check out their charms and their "dance moves".

The stag line at the Bowl was the epitome of chauvinism and male-bonding. Ed Harrington remembered, "It took some of us all evening to get up the nerve to ask a particular girl to dance. So when you finally did ask, if she turned you down it was devastating. When that happened, to save face we'd have a come-back, like, "Well I really didn't want to dance anyway. I just wanted to find out if you spoke English."

When you did find a dance partner, slow-dancing to moody ballads like *Blueberry Hill* was in vogue. Sometimes they'd dim the lights and call it a "Moonlight Waltz". But when the jazz band struck up the heavy eight-beat rhythm of a jump-tune like *Caravan*, it was the signal for amateurs to clear the floor while the jivers took over.

It was the dawn of the rock 'n roll era. A unique chemistry developed at the Hollywood Bowl when the beat of the Dixieland swing bands and the bounce of the spring floor inspired the jivers, and they in turn inspired bands like Ross Williams' and Nick Simcoe's to new dimensions of musical expression. Word of the phenomenon spread and by the early 50s the Bowl had become a mecca for hundreds of teenagers from across the Lower Mainland who gravitated there every Friday and Saturday night.

Because of its high profile, the Hollywood Bowl soon became a magnet for street gangs like the local Edmonds Street gang and Sapperton gang, Vancouver's tough East Hastings gang and the notorious Alma Dukes.

Many teenagers came to New Westminster by car and it became traditional for street rods and customized cars to cruise up and down Columbia Street on parade before the Bowl opened for the evening.

Hot rods were mostly 30s vintage fenderless Ford coupes that had been chopped in height. Customized cars were lowered in the back, then sprayed with gray primer paint after the chrome had been stripped and fender skirts added. Special mufflers caused them to snarl and rumble when the engine was revved.

Ordinary family cars didn't really qualify to cruise Columbia Street in the 50s, and didn't warrant a second glance unless loaded with girls.

The occasional late-night revelries at closing these days don't compare to the near riots in the 50s when the Hollywood Bowl shut down for the night, particularly after word flashed around that rival street gangs were going to rumble or a couple of renowned street-fighters were going to "duke it out".

Retired Royal City cop Bill Morgan once told me that Alf Toban and his bouncers ran a tight ship. "The real problem was outside on the street when the Bowl emptied at the same time as the Army & Navy Club, the Premier Hotel and the other nearby beer parlours."

Toban recalled Giggy LaBlonde from Royal Avenue. "Giggy was a trouble-maker at first. They called him Mr. Five-by-five because he was five feet tall and five feet wide. Every time he came to the Bowl his gang knew he'd help them out, so they'd start trouble and he was soon in the middle of it. One time he came to the dance and I wouldn't let him in. I told him, this is a dance hall and you don't dance. You only look for trouble. When you learn to dance, come back. He came back about a month later and he'd learned to dance. Suddenly he was a good dancer. Very light on his feet in spite of his girth. When you got to know him, he was a very nice fellow."

Elia Basso Gray told me, "The Hollywood Bowl was well run, but somehow parents thought it had a bad reputation. My girlfriend Lois and I weren't supposed to go there. So of course we went! That's where I met my husband, Wally Gray, from Annieville. When my mother asked how we met I said it was at bowling. Actually, it was 'Hollywood Bowl-ing'".

After the Bowl closed we'd all drift down the hill for fish and chips at the Fraser Café or Chinese food at the Pacific Café, known locally as "Sloppy Joe's", or just to hang out at the BC Electric tram depot at the foot of Eighth Street.

Those were rebellious times and we were part of a social revolution. Before us, teenage role-models dressed pretty much like their parents. But to us, all parents were square, so for the first time in history, teenagers styled their own clothes, haircuts, cars and music. The Hollywood Bowl was "cool" and for a short time it belonged to us.

The Hollywood bowl peaked about 1953 when it was sold out every Friday and Saturday night. By the mid to late 50s Alf Toban was featuring bands with adult appeal and the Bowl began to evolve to a dinner and dance spot, later called Alfie's.

If there was a spirit of the early 1950s in New Westminster, it hung out at the Hollywood Bowl which echoed the music and emotions of our teenage years. At the time, we thought the beat and the bounce at the Bowl would go on forever. But we were young then.

CR

Courtship Of A Beekeeper's Daughter

Do young men today still strive to make a good impression on prospective in-laws when they court a precious daughter? I know they did half a century ago, and few young men overcame greater hardships to make a good impression then my husband, Don, beginning in the spring of 1950. For you see, I was a beekeeper's daughter—and therein lies a tale or two.

Most people won't go near a hive of bees, but Don had absolutely no choice if he was going to impress my father. His first test came the day an anxious citizen phoned my dad to come and remove a swarm of bees from the top of a tall brick chimney on a three-story Victorian house.

"Could you give me a hand to capture a swarm of bees, Don?" asked my dad. "Certainly, sir," answered 17-year-old Don, naively.

My father had arthritis in both hips and could walk only with the aid of crutches, so what he was REALLY saying to Don was, "YOU will capture the swarm of bees while standing at the top of a flimsy 40 foot ladder, and I'LL stand safely below and holler instructions."

By way of explanation, honeybees swarm in the spring to find a roomier new home. Thus, an empty beehive box containing a few frames of comb honey would be an irresistible abode to a football-sized cluster of bees clinging to a chimney.

So, following Dad's instructions, but with growing apprehension, Don climbed to the top of a rickety old ladder, then used a rope to hoist the empty beehive box up to where 10,000 bees were humming menacingly inside a crumbling

A typical swarm of bees hanging in a fruit tree - Sangster Collection

Victorian brick chimney. He balanced the bee-box on the top of the rain-cap, and Dad invited all onlookers to come back at dusk when the bees had settled down some, to see the actual "capture".

Near sunset, Don climbed back up the swaying ladder as chunks of brick and mortar fell ominously from the ancient chimney. Word had spread. Dad now lectured a virtual army of onlookers about honeybees in general, and about how harmless honeybees were. He explained how "we" were going to capture the swarm of bees from the chimney.

Every shift of the rickety ladder caused the bees to buzz ominously as Don began to lower the bee-box which now contained ten pounds of bees. Hand-over-hand he lowered the rope, and to his horror, some of the bees were crawling on the rope and began to sting his hands! His natural instinct was to let go of the rope, but with all those innocent people standing below looking up with rapt attention, he just couldn't. Grimly, he continued lowering away, as the ladder swayed, the chimney continued to crumble, the bees buzzed angrily, and Dad charmed the audience below.

Years later, Don admitted to me that the temptation to let go of the rope was almost overpowering for more than one reason.

Don survived that ordeal and others in the years to come. We've been married sixty years, and one of our keepsakes is a photo taken at our high school grad in 1952. It shows one of Don's ears swollen to twice the normal size from a bee sting, earned, like a badge of honour, in the name of good old-fashioned courtship.

CR

The following reminiscence by my husband, Don Benson was printed in the Royal City Record, and won a BC Award for local history in 1993.

A River Ran By Him

By Don Benson

A half a century ago, New Westminster's downtown district stretched from Chinatown at the foot of Royal Avenue to a little colony of Irish Catholics above Albert Crescent, and from Royal Avenue down to the Fraser River docks. Over the decades since, local writers have reminisced about growing up in historic Sapperton, in Queensborough with its pastures and rich ethnic mix, and in the idyllic and charming Queen's Park area. But almost nothing has been written about growing up under the spell of the river, in our two-fisted downtown district during the 1930s and 1940s.

There can be nothing like it again. I recall opulent mansions like T. J. Trapp's, neglected foundations of buildings gutted in the historic fire of 1898, little cottages with vegetable gardens and chicken runs, the remnants of little creeks trickling through wooded ravines, wood-planked sidewalks, sprawling tenement buildings, a soda fountain and a cigar factory, all jumbled together, sometimes even on the same block.

Other New Westminster neighbourhoods were sometimes visited by hobos who hopped off freight trains from the East and knocked on doors looking for odd jobs or a meal. But in our neighbourhood was a refuge for these forgotten men travelling from nowhere, who stopped at the "jungle"—a clutter of packing crate shacks located between Columbia and Front Street just west of the Patullo Bridge.

Kids in other parts of town built tree forts and shacks for club houses. But they could never match the exclusive meeting place on the second floor of the Masonic Hall where Mousey, Bernie and the rest of our gang held "secret" meetings. We accessed the regalia-filled room through an unlocked window off the back fire-escape, and were able to use it for quite awhile because we were very careful not to disturb anything. We voted to give it up only after Rodney Peters, a new kid on the block, fainted during our secret initiation ritual, and for several horrifying minutes we thought he was dead! In any case, by that time the caretaker, who lived in the basement of the Hall, was beginning to get suspicious.

On Victoria Street, a few doors from the Masonic Hall, was Jim Blair's little cigar factory where Al Miller and his employees hand-rolled tobacco leaves imported from Cuba into *Beaver Brand Cigars*, and debated about sports, politics and womenfolk. Old-time prospectors who rented rooms upstairs in the factory for two or three dollars a month, sat out front on benches on sunny days whittling, spitting tobacco and swapping tales about man's quest for gold. Their theory about Charlie Slumach's famous "lost gold mine" at Pitt Lake, makes more sense than anything I've read on the subject during the half century since.

Like kids growing up in other New Westminster districts in that era, we could make pocket money by delivering newspapers, mowing lawns and hauling and stacking firewood. Downtown we could also set bowling pins as "pin boys", peddle *Liberty* magazines to soldiers on the troop trains for five cents, and sell oolichans we scooped out of the river using cast-off lacrosse sticks.

Typical customers on downtown paper routes during the war years weren't exactly the Brady Bunch. They included prostitutes, bootleggers, bookies and draft-dodgers. One draft-dodger lived virtually imprisoned in a Carnarvon Street housekeeping room, supported by his working girlfriend. He'd peer through the window curtains watching for the paper boy to arrive, then peek into the hallway and scurry out to grab the paper after it was dropped off.

I can't recall a bookie who wasn't a colourful character. One illegal bookie joint operated in the back of a tea shop on Columbia Street. Another, where plainclothes detectives placed bets, was around the corner on Alexander Street. But it was the bookie who took bets at the "insurance office" upstairs in his home on Agnes Street that I remember best of all. I never go to the horse races without recalling the summer day in

1943 when my dad and two of his pals beat the bookie at his own game, and I earned a bicycle for my role in the "sting" that rivaled a Hollywood script for excitement.

Outsiders from Sapperton or Queensborough counted the days until Saturday when they flocked "downtown" to Columbia Street. Kids lined up to see a matinee movie and vaudeville show at the Edison Theatre, while their parents shopped or went for a beer. Old-timers will recall the B. C. ElectricTram Depot, W. S. Collister dry goods store, the old City Market, and David Spencer's department store with its aromas of spices, baking and fresh-made peanut butter. The thing is, I didn't have to wait for Saturday to enjoy the magic of Columbia Street. It was part of my turf.

Growing up downtown in the 1940s, you couldn't escape the river's presence. The sounds of the mills and river traffic were always in the air. Your father headed out each morning to work at a lumber mill, the docks, the cannery, or to handle the produce from the river farms. The docks, the floats, the sandbars were your playground. When you grew up downtown more than half a century ago, the river got into your blood. It became a permanent part of you.

CR

The Weekenders

Most high school part-time jobs were, and still are low-paying jobs.

In the 1950s, the other kids envied us "weekenders". We were the high school kids who had weekend jobs in the lumber industry. We joined the I.W.A. (International Woodworkers of America) and were paid union wages—$10 a day and $15 on weekends: well over $100 a day in today's dollars. We were also assured a summer job as "relief" workers when the regular workers took their vacations. Don and I worked at the Pacific Veneer Plant ("The PV") feeding the "dryers" and sorting the veneer that eventually became plywood.

Dad was on City Council when the two men who started up the P.V. came to see him. According to Dad, the men told him that they had owned a factory of some kind in Europe and they were wise enough to see what Hitler was up to. When told they were free to emigrate but wouldn't be allowed to take any of their assets with them, they decided to outwit the Nazis. They secretly began to convert all their assets to gold. Then, in the midnight hours at their factory, they smelted down their gold and poured it into molds of common tools – hammers, wrenches, etc. then painted them black and threw them casually into the trunks of their cars and drove through customs into Switzerland and hence to Canada. That was the gold that financed the P.V. which became part of the war effort to defeat Hitler by producing all the wing-tips for the famous Mosquito bombers.

One Sunday in 1951, the Foreman on our shift chose his best workers to handle a "very special order" which needed very careful handling. It was hand-fed into the dryers at one end and very carefully handled as it came out of the dryer and placed on pallets. Veneer sheets were normally four feet wide and eight feet long, but this "special order" was TWELVE feet long! It was imported mahogany and there wasn't a single knot hole in any of the sheets. Us weekenders did a good job but we hated it. We were used to the wonderful smell of warm fir and hemlock and spruce. The mahogany smelled like vomit!

Over fifty years later, we were sitting in the City Hall council chambers when a realization came over me. "Don, look at the walls! The walls are beautiful, clear mahogany! And they're TWELVE feet long!" That "Special Order" us teenagers processed must have been destined for the brand new City Hall that was opened in 1952.

CR

Author's note: Staying up all night was nothing new to me. During high school I worked weekends and summers at the Pacific Veneer Plant where I always preferred the Graveyard Shift – 11:45 p.m. to 7:30 a.m. Here's a photo of me all dressed up to go to work in the plywood mill.

Teenage Styles

Members of my generation should be the last to criticize the way teenagers today dress or wear their hair, because looking back I can see that we helped invent the first "teenage tribes" in the early 1950s.

Essentially, until after WWII and the "New Look", teenagers dressed like little adults. Take a look at any of the old "Andy Hardy" re-runs on TV and you'll see what I mean. There were a few innovations like argyle sweaters, Frank Sinatra jackets, saddle shoes and the advent of blue jeans. Then, about 1950, the "hoodlum look" that was introduced by street gangs like Vancouver's notorious Alma Dukes and the East Hasting gang, was also adopted by trendsetters at New Westminster's two high schools, Duke of Connaught and Trapp Tech.

During Easter vacation 1950, a dozen or so boys from Duke of Connaught High School who were staying at a summer house at Crescent Beach got the bright idea to bleach their hair. Within two weeks, almost half the 200 boys at Duke of Connaught High School were blondes! This was before *Miss Clairol,* and some of the dye-jobs done with medicinal peroxide were bordering on orange. Several came out with a faint green tinge.

I remember that in 1952, Connaught girls openly envied two Trapp Tech girls we nick named "Wiffen and Poofen". We thought those two girls were the ultimate fashion plates. Their narrow hobble skirts were longer and tighter than anyone's, which gave them a stylish "mincing" walk. Only one inch of leg showed between the top of their ankle socks and the hem of their skirts. Their sweaters were REAL cashmere or angora. Their earrings were danglier than ours, and their rope-pearls were daringly long. We didn't consider the long narrow skirts confining, even though we had to hike them up so we could run for a bus or try to climb aboard.

My first "New Look" skirt was black gabardine with a "fly front". Mother and I were shopping at *Hudson's Bay* in Vancouver and after much pleading and begging on my part, Mother gave in and let me take my choice into a dressing room for a try-on. I looked in the mirror at my 15-year-old image and thought I looked at least seventeen.

Don in strides with me in plaid skirt

I turned, and pulling aside the curtain I strode confidently towards my mother – and fell flat on my face! The length of the skirt, (past my calves) and the narrow confines of the pencil-slim hemline wouldn't allow me to stride anymore. I too had to learn to take "mincing" steps.

Fashionable Connaught girls began wearing identical navy blue Burberry raincoats in rain or shine, identical saddle shoes with bobby socks, and identical little kerchiefs knotted jauntily under one ear. Virtually every girl in school carried an identical purple and gold (our school colours) Seagrams Crown Royal rye whiskey bag as a purse which caused some confusion in the dressing-room after gym class.

And to think WE felt sorry for the girls from Saint Ann's Academy a few blocks away because **they were compelled to dress alike!**

ନ୍ଧ

Note: Kim Benson wrote the following for her fellow students in the Class of '76 at New Westminster Secondary School.

Grad '52 – The Way It Was

My parents, Don and Evelyn Sangster Benson graduated from New Westminster's old Duke of Connaught High School in the Class of 1952. Many of you will remember my mom as Mrs. Benson the Substitute Teacher at NWSS. In that very same grad class were some of your parents too: Bob Dragvik, Cal Thompson, Gwen Edwards Gertsch and Ron Lord. I thought it might be interesting to compare THEIR Grad to OURS.

To help provide us with perspective for Grad '52, I asked my dad about The Fifties. What was it like?

"Looking back, I can see it was a time of massive change. It was the era that gave us television, freeways and shopping malls (then called Plazas). Everything was suddenly bigger. Especially the new cars. The Fifties were boom times.

"In a way, it was the era of the teenager and the car.

"We had teenage 'gangs' then…but it was a cultural thing, really. We wore pants that were wide at the knees and narrow at the ankles, called 'strides' or 'drapes'. Some of us wore 'boogie-cuts' … a crewcut on top and long on the sides combed into a ducktail. Adults called it the 'hoodlum look', but we weren't really hoodlums.

"Mostly the 'gangs' provided a way of belonging and conforming. No one wanted to be different…an oddball. If you didn't go along with the gang you would be left out. And that would hurt.

"Our parents didn't understand our clothing or our slang. They didn't approve of our dancing, called 'jiving', or our music, which gave birth to rock 'n roll. Has anything really changed?"

My mother recalls that, by popular consensus, the girls of 1952 wore white dresses and shoes to the Grad Ceremony and the boys wore suits and ties. Caps and gowns were never worn at high school ceremonies. Gwen Edwards Gertsch recalls that caps and gowns were reserved for graduation from University. Although a group picture was taken of the seventy-five graduates of the year, there were no "Grad Portraits" taken of individuals.

For the '52 Grad Dinner and Dance held at The Gai Paree on Kingsway (later Severin's, then Diego's, now a high-rise), most guys wore their first suit, styled with narrow lapels, a one-button single breasted long jacket, high-waisted "strides" and a narrow, square ended knit tie. His one "formal" concession to the evening was a boutonniere, provided by his date. The only time a guy rented a tux in those days was to get married, and the choices were black or white only.

The girls of Grad '52 went all out in floor-length gowns of net over silk or taffeta and lace. Short little gloves were a "must", and if the gown was bare-shouldered, a matching stole of net or lace was mandatory.

Girls, or their mothers made most Grad dresses. My mom tells how she and several close girl friends made the rounds of exclusive Vancouver dress shops pretending they were rich debutantes from a Vancouver private girls' school. Whenever one of her friends found her "dream dress", Mom would make a sketch, and later create an identical dress for her friend at a cost of $12 or $15 for fabric, instead of the outrageous $45 to $75 the dress shops would have charged. (Note: I.W.A. wages were $1.25 per hour in 1952!)

Corsages were worn on the shoulder, never on the wrist or in the hair. Gwen Gertsch remembers getting a gardenia, and my Dad bought my Mom her very first orchid…a white one.

Transportation arrangements for getting to Grad and Aftergrad events were very different from our day. Almost no students, and very few teachers, had cars. Dad had a "blanked and lowered" 1936 Ford but drove my mother's family 1949 Pontiac for that very special occasion. Apparently, his hot rod made his future mother-in-law "nervous". Many kids were delivered, and then picked up later by their parents or a relative. For some, the only option was bus transportation as there simply wasn't a family car, and taxis "cost too much".

For those kids who did own a car, it may have been too under-powered for our New Westminster hills. With some models, you would take a run at a hill, then, near the top a couple of passengers might have to hop out to lighten the load and help the car over the crest. Bob Dragvik drove around in an "Austin" like that. Ron Lord and his brother shared a tiny "Morris Minor". It only held one couple. Fortunately, the Lord twins went to different schools and didn't graduate on the same night.

In the early Fifties, the only stimulant used by high school students was alcohol, and then, almost exclusively by the boys. The legal drinking age was twenty-one then, but both my dad and his pal Bob Dragvick had "grad night drinking stories" to tell. Ron Lord was suspiciously evasive on the subject.

Dad recalled that the exit from the banquet hall out to the parking lot was guarded by a teacher. To get past him required a subtle plan. So, one of the girls charmed and kidded the teacher into dancing with her. During this diversion, one of the guys slipped out to the car and brought back a "mickey" of gin in a corsage box. By the time the teacher had returned to his post, the 12 oz. mickey had been disbursed among the six boys at the table.

Bob Dragvik recently reminded my dad that he (Bob) didn't go to the Grad Dinner and Dance because he didn't have a date. Actually, he had made a date with a girl from another school, but later cancelled. He confessed that the girl seemed charming after he had had a couple of beers one night, but then turned out to be "a real dog" in the sober light of day.

Because Bob wasn't going to Grad, he and his friend John Swanston volunteered to deliver a trunk-load of beer to Crescent Beach, and to get the bonfire started for an aftergrad beach party. And that led to an encounter with the law.

It turned out that there had been a jailbreak at the B. C. Penitentiary that evening, so there was a road-block on the Patullo Bridge. When a Pen Guard at the roadblock asked them to open their trunk, the boys refused. They quickly whispered to the Guard (so the Mounties wouldn't hear) that it was their Grad night, and the trunk was full of beer! The Guard was a good sport and settled for a quick peek into the trunk before sending the boys on their way.

A popular destination immediately after the Grad was Vancouver's Chinatown. The favourite restaurants were the "WK" and the "Mandarin Gardens". Gwen Gertsch recalls feeling very grown up, going out on the town in an evening dress. Some of the grads ended up at breakfast parties where obliging parents got out of bed at 4 a.m. to cook bacon and eggs for eight or ten happy teenagers. Other kids, after changing from their finery into jeans and t-shirts, joined Bob and John at Crescent Beach where they watched the sunrise.

Mom and Dad and their group of friends drove to Blaine and then finally all the way to Bellingham looking for a place to get breakfast. In those days, not one single eatery was open! They ended up at the Fraser Café on Columbia Street.

Almost everyone showed up for 9 a.m. classes. Some after only 2 or 3 hours sleep, and others after staying up all night for the first time in their lives.

- Kim Benson 1976

CR

Panorama Roof

Whenever I hear the words Dal Richards and Panorama Roof, I remember an evening at the Vancouver Hotel when Don and I were naive teenagers in a more innocent era.

It was the early 1950s and we were just out of high school. Four of us, to celebrate a birthday, dressed "formal"—the girls in our grad dresses complete with frilly crinolines and the boys in suits and narrow ties. The girl was my life-long friend Shirley Steeves Hardwick and her escort's name I can't recall. Shirley and I were students of Teacher Training at the Provincial Normal School at Twelfth and Cambie, and Don and I were newly engaged. We went to the Panorama Roof nightclub "high atop the Vancouver Hotel" for an evening of dinner and dancing. We danced to many "Big Band" tunes and *Blueberry Hill*, *Sentimental Me* and, of course, *The Hour of Parting*, Dal Richards' theme song. It was an older crowd and they sometimes moved back on the dance floor to stand and watch us teenagers do the graceful "slow jive" of that decade.

Like teenagers of all eras, we were part of two worlds. We were almost overwhelmed by the formalities and the silverware at dinner, yet felt very grown up and sophisticated at the same time to be part of that opulent setting. It was common knowledge at that time that grown-ups brought their own liquor and kept it "under the table" as no liquor was available in restaurants or night clubs. It was the law! We teens, trying so hard to appear older than our years, had brought a "mickey of gin". There was no mixer, so we surreptitiously laced our fruit cocktail with good old Gilby's.

Later in the evening when it was getting close to closing time, Don excused himself from the table and headed to the Men's Room down the hall. It seemed to us that he was taking an inordinately long time when he suddenly slipped back into his seat looking pale and shaken.

"If anyone asks," he whispered, "Say I haven't left your sight all evening!"

When he regained his composure, he quietly described his visit to the washroom. Apparently, while he was attending to business and had his back turned to the rest of the room, he heard a man "propositioning" another man, using such words as "good-looking" and "sweetie". He was dying to get a look at these men so when he casually turned around and walked to the sinks, he could only see ONE man. And that man was talking to the only other person in the room – Don!

Don pretended not to notice him, but when the older and much larger man tried to block the doorway to prevent Don from leaving, Don decked him with a right to the jaw. He told us he heard an unmistakable "CRACK!" (Don's many years in competitive boxing came in handy.)

The rest of the evening was spoiled. We nervously kept one eye on the door expecting the police to arrive at any moment. We stayed to the bitter end and planned to leave the nightclub with the other exiting patrons. Dal Richards and his wonderful orchestra were playing *Auld Lang Syne* as we moved towards the exit. We strained to glimpse the lobby, expecting to see the police.

As we nervously passed the dignified maitre d' who was stationed at the door, he caught Don's eye and formed a circle with the thumb and index finger of his right hand to form the international sign for "Good! Well done!" and gave Don an unmistakable wink of approval.

In hind sight, we realized Don had done the Vancouver Hotel a favour by ridding them of an "undesirable" who must have caused the hotel considerable embarrassment over time. It's just too bad they didn't tell us sooner so that four teenagers could have better enjoyed their first visit to the fabulous Panorama Roof.

That November evening wasn't over yet. Driving my Dad's forty-nine Pontiac which was plastered with "Vote SANGSTER for Mayor" signs,

Don drove us to Kitsilano to show us where he grew up and later spent his summers with his grandparents just three doors up Creelman Avenue from the beach. We mistook a service road for a beach-side drive and when it came to a dead end, Don made a u-turn onto the sandy beach.

Soon we were hub-cap deep in sand and unable to move! The other boy in the group volunteered to find a phone booth and summon a tow truck. No cell-phones in those days.

As we waited for Shirley's escort to return we relived the excitement of our evening at "'The Roof". Our sides were sore from laughing when suddenly we realized that the tide was coming in! It was no longer a laughing matter.

Unbeknownst to us, our friend had somehow phoned "Buster" of *Buster's Towing* at one a.m. and woke him up. He assumed it was a prank and called the police. Yep. The police.

Next thing we knew a spot light was shining on our car. Two officers approached us and Don rolled down his window. They check his license and then looked at the registration of the car which belonged to James Lewis Sangster, the Mayor of New Westminster. I think the policeman's first thought was that we had stolen the car, but the Constable had the good sense to question the rest of us first before he arrested us. When he heard our story and realized I was a Sangster and we had permission to use my father's car, he radioed for a tow-truck.

The police stayed until we were safely towed back onto the street. One officer was kind enough to inquire if we had enough money to pay for the tow truck. He actually took out his wallet and offered us a personal loan! We thanked him profusely for his kind offer but we had enough cash amongst us.

The irony of the evening was that we went from fearing and dreading the arrival of the police to being grateful to them for rescuing us.

Times have certainly changed. The "cover-up" at the swanky Panorama Roof and the understanding and helpfulness of the cops at the beach is certainly a different kind of policework than we are used to today.

CR

Television in the Fifties

Several of my high school girl friends baby-sat for doctors or lawyers in the Queen's Park area who had TELEVISION SETS. How we envied them! We'd offer to take their place, **for free,** anytime they weren't available to baby-sit.

Then Don's Aunt Ruth and Uncle Bert in Malliardville got a TV and Don and I would volunteer to baby-sit for them. Other times we visited them on a Saturday night to watch a movie on KVOS Bellingham, which was the only channel available. At least twice during an evening, the *Please Stand By* sign would appear on the screen and we would wait, sometimes for half an hour or more. Years later, I read an article about the three veterans who started up KVOS, and how sometimes one of them would have to drive out to the transmitter and make a repair, while their audience was "standing by".

Of course the programs were black and white and some of the screens weren't much larger than a dinner plate. Colour TV was rumored, but still a few years in the future. But we used our imaginations. I remember one of our little boys saying, "What's that guy's name?" pointing to the screen. "Which guy?" I asked. "The one in the red plaid shirt," he said, pointing to the black and white picture.

Kids who lived in the West End, out near Twentieth Street, could get two channels from Seattle and sometimes one from Tacoma with only a simple pair of "rabbit ear antennae". How jealous we were. My daughter's husband, Dave Stewart, grew up in the West End near the escarpment and he thought everyone could get all those channels. Rabbit ears were touchy. You had to turn them this way, then that way in various positions to finally get a picture. Sometimes, when the best picture was fuzzy, we took turns standing beside the TV set holding onto one of the "ears". Humans made great receptors!

Soon, houses all over town began to sprout antennae from their roofs. You could tell at a glance which families now had TV.

As newlyweds, we lived in Sapperton at the foot of Simpson Street, just around the corner from the dispatching office of Sapperton Taxi. Many times, during an evening of watching *The Jackie Gleason Show*, or *Your Hit Parade,* the screen would go fuzzy, and a voice would come out of the TV set - "Joe, pick up three at the King Ed." "Roger". Then the screen would clear and the show would continue.

Repairs to those early TV sets were frequent and costly. Pretty soon every pharmacy in town carried a wide range of TV vacuum tubes. When the set was on the fritz, you'd take the back cover off the TV and expose a wide array of glowing tubes in all shapes and sizes. Some of the tubes were as small as your thumb and others were as big as a fat ear of corn. Sometimes you could spot the dead tube right away and you would remove it and take it to the nearest pharmacy and buy a new, matching tube. Other times, you weren't sure which tube was the culprit, so you took several tubes with you and the clerk would "test" them for you.

Every time your TV set conked out, you prayed it wasn't the PICTURE TUBE which meant hiring a bonafide TV repairman. The service charge and the cost of a new picture tube could ruin your family budget for months. Today, we'd toss the old set and buy a new set. In those early days of the Fifties, a new set (black & white with a 12 inch screen) cost between $100 and $200, depending on how fancy the wooden cabinet was. In today's dollars that would be between $1000 and $2000. So, TV Repair was a booming business in those early days of television in the Fifties, and like today's plumbers, if you could find an honest and reliable TV repairman, you hung onto him and treated him well.

Because KVOS TV in Bellingham was the only reliable channel we could get, our youngsters became very familiar with their station identification. One late December evening as five-year-old Scott and I walked west on Sixth Avenue, the planet Venus hung low on the horizon, shining like a 2 carat diamond. Mindful that Christmas was only a few days away, little Scott pointed excitedly at the bright star and exclaimed, "Look, Mommy – There's Jesus' star of Bellingham!"

Never underestimate the power of advertising.

CR

Queensborough Swing Bridge

Someday we may have a foot-traffic bridge from the new Port Royal end of Queensborough to the Westminster Quay. What a delight that will be! But many people remember when that old swing bridge was the only bridge to LuLu Island between New Westminster and Marpole in South Vancouver. It carried vehicles, pedestrians and trains, and often swung open for boat traffic at the most inopportune moments.

In the early 1950s, when my brother-in-law Bobby Benson was only 19, he nearly played stork because of that old swing bridge. He was driving cab for Royal City Taxi and was on his way to St. Mary's Hospital with a woman passenger from Queensborough who had told him, "Don't spare the horses!" Suddenly, the gate on the old bridge dropped right in front of his cab!

"My passenger was in labour and moaning in the back seat," Bob told me. "And this very slow sawdust-barge was inching its way slowly through the bridge opening. I radioed my dispatcher yelling, 'Help!' He told me to hang in there and he'd send an ambulance. It got there in minutes – but on the other side of the bridge. I could see the flasher, and see the attendants but it didn't do me much good. Nor my passenger, neither. She was making really strange sounds by this time!

"Slowly, the span began to swing closed. As soon as I could, I booted it across and the attendants unloaded my passenger, just in the nick of time. After that, I avoided Queensborough fares whenever I could."

But Lulu Island teenagers really appreciated the old bridge. What a perfect excuse it provided for being late for curfew. The tugs preferred to work the slack tide. So when that happened around eight in the morning, tug after tug kept the bridge open, giving the kids a perfect excuse to be late for school.

Queensborough mothers would have shuddered had they known that their kids, mostly boys, used to have contests to see how many times they could jump across the gap between the opening span and the solid bridge deck before it got too wide!

I often wondered how many kids got out of doing their chores, or how many guys stayed late in town visiting a sweetheart, only to say, with a straight face, "Gee, Mom, sorry I'm late, but the bridge was open. Again."

When they opened a new high level Queensborough Bridge in 1960, they destroyed a perfect alibi.

CR

Spinster School Marms

Until the late Fifties, the term *Spinster School Marm* could be used to describe almost every female teacher in School District #40, with a few rare exceptions. In addition to spinsters, if a woman was widowed, or had an invalid husband, or was divorced, she could be hired. Such was the case for my friend Margaret Andrusiak. As Mrs. Greenall, Margaret was the sole support of three young children and therefore employable. She taught at Lord Tweedsmuir Elementary School.

Margaret began to "keep company" with Peter Andrusiak and one Easter Break, Peter proposed and Margaret accepted. The first Monday back to her classroom, there was a knock at the door. In walked the Superintendent of Schools. The students quickly stood up, and in unison said, "GOOD MORNING MR. SHIELDS!" Roy Shields acknowledged the greeting then asked their teacher to please step outside into the hall. Margaret told me word-for-word what he had to say: "Congratulations Margaret! I hear you are engaged to be married. You must be pleased. Now, I would like your resignation on my desk by tomorrow morning."

Where was the B. C. Teachers Federation? Or the B.C. Civil Liberties Association?

In 1953, I had a similar experience. It was the last week of my teacher training at the Provincial Normal School. I had an appointment with the Superintendent of Schools for the City of Vancouver. One of my professors took me aside and said, "I see you're wearing an engagement ring, Evelyn. I strongly advise you to take it off when you go for your interview. They aren't interested in married women." So I hung my ring on a chain around my neck for my interview and was hired as a Grade 3 teacher at General Gordon School. Thus, newly-hired MISS Sangster showed up on Opening Day as MRS. Benson.

Where did this prejudicial practice come from? I believe it was a Depression Era hold-over. During the Depression 1929 to 1939, jobs were so scarce that only teachers with families to support were hired or kept on. If a young man was living with his parents and being supported by his father, he too was let go. It made sense for the times and the policy continued long after the Depression was over.

I personally believe that this policy also precluded the necessity to deal with the possibility of shhhhhh- p-r-e-g-n-a-n-c-y! My first day at General Gordon, I discovered an old Keats Island Baptist Camp chum who was teaching the Grade One class. Edna Mae Slade wore a roomy smock over her good clothes because six-year-olds had grimy hands. At least that was her excuse. But she swore me to secrecy that she was pregnant and if the School District knew about it they would not have renewed her contract. She and her husband needed the money and she hoped her disguise would allow her to teach until the Christmas break! She managed to get away with it.

It's sad to realize that many of the wonderful school teachers I had in twelve years of schooling were MISS by choice. It was EITHER / OR. They could have a career or they could have marriage but they couldn't have BOTH. I wonder how many turned down proposals or left the choice until it was too late?

This attitude pervaded the nursing profession too. Girls who entered a nursing school knew they might as well be entering a convent. They lived, ate and slept at the hospital. They got very little time off. Weekends had a very strict ten o'clock curfew and very thorough bed-checks.

When I was in hospital having my first baby, one of my nurses was a chum from my high school days. She was only weeks from her graduation and a hard-earned R.N. degree. She slipped into my room early one morning grinning like a Cheshire cat. She reached under her stiffly-starched uniform bib and showed me a diamond ring on a long chain. She, too, swore me to secrecy. "If they found out I was engaged before the end of my three year training contract, I would be turfed out and wouldn't graduate!"

We've come a long way, baby!

CR

From Here To Maternity

How things have changed is probably more apparent in Maternity Wards than in any other experience in life. Today, barring any complications, an expectant mother is admitted, gives birth and is discharged within as little as twenty-four hours. She is accompanied by her husband or a trusted "birth companion" (mother, sister, girl-friend) who has been well-trained in a pre-natal class and who plays a helpful role in the birthing process. It is now legal to have a home-birth attended by a certified mid-wife.

Some hospitals provide, on request, a "Birthing Suite" where any or all family members can attend the birth. This includes children!

In my day, fathers were NOT allowed in the Delivery Room. They were relegated to the Fathers Waiting Room where they paced and smoked. Doctors of that day couldn't be bothered with a nervous, untrained male in the room who might faint at the sight of blood.

Beginning in 1955, I made five trips to the maternity ward. I can assure you, that except for the first baby (which I could hardly wait to get home to his lovely antique bassinet, a brand new Gendron baby buggy and boxes and boxes of baby clothes, equipment and toys, the result of a well-attended Baby Shower), I was never in a hurry to be discharged.

In the Fifties, the usual stay for a new mother was five days. A mother who had one or more small children at home would sometimes hide out in the washroom or a phone booth when that fifth day arrived and the grapevine said her doctor was on the ward and might discharge her.

I was one of those mothers. I used to pray, "Maybe he'll forget I'm here!" Where else could a young woman get a week's rest – breakfast, lunch, and supper in bed? No cooking or laundry chores. Someone else made your bed daily with fresh linens. At bedtime they brought you hot chocolate and cookies. Six times a day they brought you your new Bundle of Joy to be fed, then whisked it away. You had no crying baby to disturb your sleep, no mucky diapers to change, no formula to mix or bottles to sterilize or heat. These chores were all done in the nursery by very competent hands.

Where else could a young mother spend time on herself doing her hair, manicuring her nails and looking beautiful when her husband came to visit? Where else could she read to her heart's content and catch up on her "Soaps"? And once a day a fresh-faced student nurse would ask, "Would you like an alcohol back-rub?" Would I? You bet I would!

The four-bed wards were like a college dorm. You got to know the other women on a very intimate level and missed them when they were discharged. By my third trip to maternity, the "teacher" in me was put to good use advising and reassuring first-baby moms on the care and feeding of a newborn. I knew considerably more on that subject than any of the ward nurses, most of whom were young and unmarried.

I remember little Mrs. Nishi who told us of her trip from Japan as a bride for a man she had never met. She brought a sizeable dowry with her – beautiful china dishes and finely embroidered linens as well as many beautiful kimono outfits. Not long after, she and her family were "relocated" to the Interior and she had to leave all her beautiful things behind. Worse still, they lost their home and her husband's state-of-the-art fishing boat. He was one of the top independent fishers on the B.C. coast.

On the day she was discharged, we were privileged to observe the traditional dressing of a new-born Japanese baby. Wearing only a diaper, the tiny baby girl was first wrapped in a plain white cotton kimono. Then a plain pastel kimono. Next a more colourful kimono. I forget how many layers in total, but the final kimono was an extravagantly embroidered silk kimono with tiny matching silk booties. The darling little girl now looked like an exquisite oriental doll but both arms extended like a crucifixion and she couldn't move.

In the Sixties, the maternity ward was all agog over a couple of new parents who were "Hippies". Most of us, including the nurses, thought that Hippies were only found in San Francisco, although there were stories of a growing hippy community at Jericho Beach in Vancouver. As the young couple prepared for discharge, we each found some excuse or other to be in the hallway as the bearded, beaded husband wheeled his long-haired, beaded wife to the elevator. The baby was wrapped in a large red and white engineer's kerchief – and all three were barefoot!

In 1919, when my brother Ross was born, the maternity ward was a separate building called the Royal Columbian Maternity Pavilion.

It was located back of the main building quite close to Brunette Street. After giving birth under anesthesia, new mothers were kept IN BED for at least a week or even more. They weren't allowed out of bed and had to rely on nurses for bedpan service.

Mother was uncomfortably balanced on one of those cold, metal conveniences when all the young nurses were suddenly all a-twitter. Word swept through the building that the handsome young Prince of Wales, the World's Most Eligible Bachelor, would be driving along Brunette Street at any moment! All the young nurses raced out the back door to the street to wave and cheer their future King Edward VIII, leaving only the Matron and a couple of older women on duty.

Mother loved to laughingly boast that, "The Prince of Wales once kept me sitting on a bed-pan for nearly half an hour! I guess it's my only claim to fame."

Now you know from whom I get my quirky sense of humour.

CR

Laundry – 1950s Style

Five kids, and there was no such thing as "disposables". For over ten years it seemed I had at least two in diapers, so every day was laundry-day for me. Here's a typical morning at the Bensons:

Seven a.m. alarm. Downstairs, switch on the coffee and head down the basement. Put the hot water hose into the wringer washer and turn on the tap. Back to the kitchen, make Don's lunch. Down the basement and switch the hot water hose into the left hand laundry tub. Fill the washing machine with the "Whites" (laundry had been sorted the night before). Take a cup of coffee upstairs to Don and wake the school-age kids. Back to the kitchen and set out milk and cereal and run upstairs to get youngest out of her crib and bring her down to change and dress her and put her in a highchair with a cookie.

Down to the basement and put the hose in the OTHER sink with a dash of "Bluing" (Makes the whites whiter, didn't you know?) Put the whites through the wringer from the machine to the first rinse-tub. Fill the machine with the "coloureds". Back to the kitchen to supervise breakfast and dressing of school-age kids. Send Don off to work.

Feed pre-schoolers, then back down to the basement, swing the washing-machine's wringer out over the rinse-tubs and put the "whites" through the wringer into the "bluing rinse'". Swing the wringer back over the machine and put the coloureds through the wringer into the first rinse tub. Fill the machine with the "darks" then back upstairs I go.

Help the school-age kids find their homework, boots, coats, mittens, whatever, and shove them out the door. (Thank heavens they came home for lunch) Oops! Don't forget to give them a recess snack!

Feed the baby. Put her in playpen then down to the basement again.

This time, the "whites" get put through the wringer directly into a laundry basket. The "coloureds" go into the blue rinse and the "Darks" go from the machine to the first rinse. Carry the laundry basket upstairs to the back window from which I can reach the clothesline. Begin hanging the "whites" on the line while keeping an eye on the pre-schoolers.

Back to the basement. Wringer the "coloureds" into the laundry basket, the "darks" into the final rinse, pull the plug on the first rinse-tub and hook the drain-hose from the machine into the emptying rinse tub and switch on the washing-machine pump. Upstairs with the basketful of "coloureds" to hang on the clothesline.

One last trip (for now) to the basement to wring the "darks" into the laundry basket, shut off the washer and wipe it dry. Drain the last rinse-tub and carry the "darks" upstairs to hang them on the clothesline. Whew!

Everyone had clotheslines in those days. You could pay a telephone gang or the City Electric gang to sell you an old telephone pole for a case of beer. And they'd deliver it to your yard! My husband was very popular in the neighbourhood because, as a telephone lineman, he could be cajoled (or bribed with a beer) to climb a neighbour's clothesline pole to re-string a new wire or replace an old pulley wheel. And clothesline pulley wheels ALL screeched and complained with each heavy load. You could even tell which neighbour lady was putting out her wash by the distinctive sound of HER pulley!

But laundry day wasn't over yet. On a nice sunny day, or better yet, a nice windy day, every piece of clothing or linens on the line had to be pulled in, folded, sorted, put away in dresser drawers or closets or assigned to the dreaded IRONING BASKET.

Before permanent press, most of the laundry had to be ironed. God bless steam-irons! Before they were invented, my mother had to "sprinkle" each item. Then she rolled the damp garment up tight and placed it in a basket with all the other roll-ups for a day or two until they were all "damp". THEN they were ironed. If left damp too long, everything went moldy!!

So although I was blessed by having a steam-iron, I HATED ironing. Only what was **absolutely necessary** for work or school got ironed by yours truly until the ironing-basket-overflow reached epidemic proportions. Then I would grit my teeth, set up the ironing board in front of the TV and stay at it until the Late, Late Show was over and there was nothing else on TV but the station logo. I admit that when I got to the bottom of the basket, some of my girls' frilly dresses and petticoats that we insisted our little girls wear to Sunday School and parties had lain in the bottom of my ironing basket for so long that they were too small for either girl, and I had to give them away. Un-ironed, of course!

What did I do if it rained? Our basement had row after row of narrow rope strung from one end of the basement to the other. I didn't have to carry that heavy laundry basket up the stairs, which was OK by me, but laundry hung in a basement just doesn't SMELL as good. Ask anyone of the pre-automatic-dryer era about that wonderful smell of fresh air and sunshine that clung to clothes dried on a clothesline. They haven't yet invented a dryer-sheet or a fabric softener that can duplicate that wonderful smell.

But would I give up my automatic dryer for a clothesline? GET REAL! Clotheslines are strictly for the birds!

☙

Typhoon Frieda

On a night in October, 1962, we hired a baby-sitter and, along with our good friends Denise and Bob Gray, we drove to Armstrong Avenue School to hear the great Tommy Douglas speak. Although none of us was a member of the New Democratic Party, we felt it was an historic privilege to listen to this great statesman. At the turn of the new millennium, Tommy Douglas was named *Canadian of the Century.*

Unfortunately, that night he had to cut his speech short when his assistant crossed the stage and whispered something in his ear. Mr. Douglas then announced that we had better all head straight home as a "typhoon warning" had just been issued.

I recalled that twice in my twelve years of New Westminster schooling we had been dismissed early and told to go directly home because a big storm called a typhoon was heading our way. A typhoon is a hurricane that is born in the Pacific. Fortunately, both times the storm veered off back into the Pacific Ocean, and we were spared.

Not so this time. As we exited the school gymnasium we were met by strong gusts of wind and driving rain. Garbage cans, pieces of cardboard and other debris flew down the street. Denise went straight home, and Bob reported to the New Westminster Police Auxiliary to patrol Columbia Street the rest of the night.

Don walked our baby-sitter safely to her home, while I moved our two girls out of their back bedroom which faced the storm, into our bedroom at the opposite side of the house where the baby slept. The powerful, howling gusts were hitting the back of our house, and we feared the windows might blow in from the force, so we closed all the blinds and curtains. Two of our boys were secure in their basement bedroom. We were too unnerved to sleep. About three in the morning a fireman pounded on our door. "There's a power line down in your back lane. Don't let anyone to go out that way tomorrow until it's been dealt with."

We peeked out a back window and saw a long electrical cable arcing and spewing blue flames like the neck of a mythical dragon over the neighbourhood. At one point, it struck our phone line and steel clothesline. The phone jangled and then went dead.

The next day we found our clothesline – a tangled ball of fused metal!

The morning dawned clear and sunny. We were in the "eye" of the storm. Our electricity was quickly restored because our neighbour, three doors down, was foreman of the Hydro crew that serviced our area.

What a mess! Twenty-foot limbs from Douglas fir trees across our lane were piled four feet deep in our backyard. It looked like a logging site. Oddly enough, neighbours on either side of us had hardly a branch. But both neighbours had lost their TV antennas and many of their duroid shingles were missing. Our antenna was fine, and we weren't missing any shingles.

One of those twenty-foot limbs, six inches at the butt, had imprinted itself, vertically, on the stucco of our house a mere three inches from our large dining-room picture window!

The rest of the Lower Mainland didn't fair as well as our neighbourhood. Many areas were without electricity and would remain so for a week or more. Frozen food seemed to be the biggest concern at first. People lined up at commercial frozen food lockers that had auxiliary generators. Soon they were full up and turning folks away. Hardware stores sold out their barbecues and hibachis and bags of charcoal. It was October, and most furnaces had stopped working. Fireplaces were put to double use – for heat and for cooking. People slept on their living room floors in front of their fireplaces just like the pioneers of old.

A lot of trees came down. Some trees blocked roadways and some damaged buildings. And many trees brought down power lines. In New Westminster, the beautiful stand of stately evergreens in Tipperary Park was decimated. One tree fell against the next tree which hit the next tree and the domino effect flattened the park.

What a beautiful day that was in the "eye" of the storm. But as night again settled in, the winds returned and we were struck by the outer ring of the storm for a second night of howling winds. More damage to more roofs, but again, we were lucky and didn't lose a shingle.

In the days that followed, people were desperate for duroid shingles to patch their roofs before the winter rains, so they bought whatever they could lay their hands on. Red roofs had black shingle patches, and green roofs had red shingle patches, and black roofs had brown shingle patches, and brown roofs had green shingle patches. Roofs stayed that way for decades. And if you looked over the city rooftops from, say, the Top of the Royal Towers Restaurant, you couldn't help but smile at seeing every TV antenna in town leaning drunkenly at the same forty-five degree angle as far as the eye could see!

The storm caused a lot of inconvenience but no loss of life. The people of Yamaguchi, Japan, our Sister City, sent over a team of landscape artists, who made order out of chaos in Tipperary Park. Today, our beautiful Japanese Friendship Garden is a tranquil oasis in the heart of our city, thanks to Typhoon Frieda.

☙

Author's Note: Because so many of the memories in this book were my father's, and because he featured in many of my own remembrances, I wanted to pay tribute to his life and his passing. What better way than in the words of his first granddaughter, Kim, who adored her Grampa, and in her early years was his "shadow". They were both "lefties" and they shared an unspoken camaraderie. Here is the essay she wrote at age 15.

My Grampa - J. Lewis Sangster

It was the morning of Sunday, May 12, 1968; Mothers' Day. We five children arose to find Dad already up. After making us a breakfast, he suggested we go for a drive so as not to disturb Mom. He took us to the park where my younger brother, sister and I went immediately to the swings, not realizing what was in store for us. My two older brothers and Dad remained at a picnic table by the car.

Finally, after some minutes, Dad called us back and solemnly said that he had something to tell us. I sensed the foreboding in his voice and hurried the other two children over. He stood there for a moment, looking at his family. Mark was 13, Scott 11, Janet 8, Jay 5 and I had just turned 10 a couple of weeks before.

At last he said, "Last night, ...Grampa passed away." I immediately started crying. Janet followed. Scott had tears in his eyes and Jay who wasn't yet old enough to understand just stood there. Mark and Dad, who had known last night, acted as the "men". Later, I found out Mom had been the first of anyone to receive the news that her father had died.

My Grandfather was 76 years old. He had been in the hospital ten days and had died because of congestive heart failure, a result of 20 years of leg paralysis. Grampa was too stubborn to use a wheelchair and had hauled himself around on crutches since 1947.

I had four grandfathers at that time (two being great-grandfathers) but to us he was "Grampa". The others we had called by two names, such as "Grandpa Gus", but to us he was THE Grampa. I especially, had become very close to him and his death had hit me hard. But pride was soon to overcome grief.

You see, my Grampa, J. L. Sangster was considered important in New Westminster. He had served 30 years on city council as both alderman and mayor. He was responsible for getting Irving House and for the city being put on an "improvement tax" system instead of "property tax". That didn't really mean too much to me at age 10, though.

What made Grampa's death so memorable was the next few days. His passing on received front page coverage on both Columbian and Sun newspapers. The Obituary had asked that no flowers be sent, yet 160 bouquets arrived from different people and organizations. The flag on City Hall was lowered to half mast.

We three older children were permitted to attend the funeral. We sat in the balcony of the family church, Olivet Baptist. The church was filled to capacity and over a hundred people remained patiently outside. I couldn't cry. I just couldn't. I felt proud.

Later, the procession was led by police escort, and traffic police-men were stationed at the major intersections along the route. And these stationary officers saluted the hearse and first limousine.

I still miss him, even after nearly six years that have passed. I am still, however, filled with pride knowing how much he was loved by the city he had loved so dearly.

Nothing stands out so clearly in my memory as that of my Grampa.

-Kim Benson, Grade 9 (1974)

Note: By 2008, Kim Benson had served for fifteen years as the elected Trustee of the Howe Sound islands for the British Columbia Islands Trust. She proved to be a caring and dedicated politician, and her Grampa would have been very proud of her. She was his special buddy.

CR

Moonwalk

At the turn of the century when my father was growing up in New Westminster, a big question of the day was, *"Do you think Man will ever fly?"* A big question in my generation, the "Buck Rogers" generation was, *"Do you think Man will ever get to the moon?"*

Like everyone else in the civilized world, our family was glued to our television set when Neil Armstrong and his crew prepared to make the first lunar landing. The date was July 20, 1969.

Just as the Apollo II Command Module was approaching its moon landing-site and all eyes were riveted on the screen – the phone rang! When I answered it, the distressed voice of my widowed mother cried, "My TV just died. I don't want to miss the moon landing!"

I said, "Mother, grab your coat and go stand outside and I'll pick you up in two minutes!"

I jumped into our car and sped the three blocks to her apartment building. With an agility that contradicted her years, Mother hopped into the car and we raced back towards my house.

As we drove through the usually busy intersection of Sixth and Sixth, an eerie realization came over me: **we had not encountered a living soul**! Nothing was moving. Not a car. Not a bus. Not a living human being. No one mowing a lawn. No one standing at a bus stop. No children riding their bikes. Come to think of it, I don't even remember seeing a dog or a cat.

It was as if the world had come to an end and Mother and I were the only survivors. The whole city was silent as we hurried into the house, praying that we hadn't missed the big moment.

We were just in time. The lunar module was just setting onto the surface of the moon and a voice said, "The Eagle has landed!" Pandemonium broke out at NASA.

All of us there in our living room – my husband, our five children, my mother and I – all applauded and cheered. Then we all grew silent as the module's door slowly opened and Neil Armstrong stepped onto the moon's surface. He planted the flag – wired to stand stiffly out because there is no wind on the moon – and spoke the immortal words, *That's one small step for Man; one giant leap for Mankind.*

It has been estimated that 94 percent of the world's television viewing audience watched that lunar landing decades ago. I believe that statistic. The silent and deserted streets of our city confirmed it.

CR

The Irish Sweepstakes

Before the advent of the *B. C. Lottery Corporation*, and similar corporations in other provinces, lotteries were against the law in Canada.

This did not hold true for Ireland. There, once a year, a horse race in Dublin was the focus of lottery ticket holders in many countries of the world. Now it wasn't against the law to BUY an Irish Sweepstake Ticket in Canada. It was only against the law to SELL Irish Sweepstake Tickets. So venders of these illegal tickets were very careful not to get caught and buyers of these illegal tickets were very closed-mouth about their source and only told trusted friends where they could be purchased.

During the Depression of the 1930s, C. J. Pineo who owned a shoe store on Columbia Street was informed that his ticket on the horse race was one of the lucky ones and his allotted horse was one of the favourites. Mr. Pineo hedged his bet by selling "shares" in his ticket to professional gamblers. His horse won!

With his share of the winnings, and remember, this was at the height of the Depression, Mr. Pineo built a mansion for his wife with professional landscaping and a beautifully crafted granite retaining wall across the front of the property on St. George Street. Some locals referred to it as "Pineo's Folly" because it appeared to be far too large for the average family unless they could afford servants.

In later years, the mansion was sold and turned into a Rest Home for the Elderly and named *Blue Spruce Cottage* because of the towering blue spruce in the front yard. Today, the mansion has been restored and artfully expanded to become the *B.C. Home for First-Responders* and their families when police, fire fighters and rescuers are injured on the job and require medical treatment in the Lower Mainland for their rehabilitation. It is now called **Honour House** and this beautiful old mansion serves a humanitarian purpose in British Columbia, thanks, in part to illegal gambling known as "The Irish Sweepstake".

In the nineteen sixties, my brother-in-law Bob Benson, unbeknownst to the rest of the family, became an importer, distributor and seller of Irish Sweepstake Tickets. Don had just flown back east to Montreal for a three-day meeting of the Canadian Lacrosse Association when I got word that his younger brother had been arrested and that Bob's young wife was very upset at the way the Mounties has searched their home and left it in shambles. She was an immaculate housekeeper.

When I drove to the Vancouver Airport to pick up Don from his return flight, and before I could blurt out the astounding news that his brother had been arrested, Don accused me of hiring private detectives to follow him to Montreal and stalk him wherever he went! Didn't I trust him?

It seems that from the moment he boarded his plane to fly East, he became aware that he was being "tailed". He and his lacrosse friends led the RCMP detectives a merry chase all over Montreal!

When Don finally absorbed the news of Bobby's arrest, we put two and two together and figured out it was the Mounties following him, expecting Don to lead them to the source of the Irish Sweepstake imports. They obviously thought it was not a coincidence that Bob Benson's older brother was suddenly booked to fly to Montreal, the entry-port for illegal tickets from Ireland. We both had a good laugh over that, and brother Bob got off with a fine and swore he would "go straight".

He did.

૱

Christmas 1961

The first time I, as a mother, faced the *Is-there-a-Santa-Claus* question was in 1961. By that time, my husband and I had four children. Our oldest child was six and, for the first time, expressed doubt at the existence of Santa Claus.

This is what I told him: "Yes, Mark, there IS a Santa Claus. You see, whenever someone gives 'in secret' to someone else, **without expecting any thanks or praise** except for the look of happiness on the other person's face – then the 'giver' **IS** Santa Claus. You see, Mark, Santa Claus represents the SPIRIT OF GIVING." Little Mark looked puzzled, so I continued.

"So, starting THIS Christmas, YOU can be Santa Claus too!"

My six-year-old son's eyes grew wide. "I will give you some money, and you and I will go shopping and YOU will pick out something to put in each stocking – something for Scott and Kim and Janet and Daddy and me. Then on Christmas Eve, Daddy and I will wake you up, and you will tip-toe to the Christmas tree and, in secret, put your presents into each stocking! Won't it be fun on Christmas morning when your brother and sisters open their stockings and you see the look of happiness on their faces when they open up what **you** gave them?

"But Mark, you must always remember, that being Santa Claus is a very, very grown-up job! And you must never tell any child who still believes in the jolly old fat man in the red suit what YOU know about Santa Claus. It is your job to help keep the magic alive!

"Any questions?"

My little boy looked at me, his eyes wide with wonderment, and said, "Do you mean you and Daddy BUY all that stuff? Wow!"

Son Mark kept the secret. And so did all his siblings as they each grew old enough to play Santa. And in our house, every single present under the tree said, "From Santa", so no one ever knew the giver of any present. We continued this tradition through the years until our grown-up kids brought their mates for Christmas-stocking morning, and eventually their children - our grandchildren.

The day finally came when our large fireplace mantel held TWENTY stockings, and it became a bit much! At that point, we declared that each family should now start their own family Christmas traditions and take turns inviting US to their homes for Christmas.

So, (regardless of the season) Merry Christmas, everyone!

ℭℜ

Mark (9), Jay (1), Santa, Janet (3), Scott (7) and Kim (5).
This was Christmas 1963.

Earthquake!

My first earthquake experience was on a Sunday morning in either 1942 or 1943. I was in Sunday School at Olivet Baptist Church in the Primary Department (Grades 1, 2 & 3). Suddenly, all the little chairs skittered to one side of the room as if we were on a ship that had tipped to one side. The hanging light fixtures began to sway erratically. Then once again, all the little chairs skittered across the room to the opposite side. By the time our teachers realized what was happening, it stopped. I have since learned that the **AVERAGE earthquake lasts only 20 seconds**.

My father, who was Superintendent of the Sunday School, had stepped outside to retrieve something from his car when the earthquake struck. He said he clung to the side of the church building because the walkway that ran beside the church was rippling and he couldn't maintain a footing.

That earthquake was nothing compared with the one Don and I experienced in Puerta Vallarta in 1995. We were staying on the second floor of a three-storey condo complex. We had just finished breakfast when we felt the quake. "Earthquake!" we both yelled and bolted for the archway that led to our outdoor lanai. Don grabbed the post and I grabbed Don and we both held on for dear life.

The noise was deafening! We hadn't realized earthquakes are noisy, but when a wooden building twists like that, every nail in the place squeals. We looked out over the gardens and lawns of the resort next door. Several gardeners were huddled together clinging to a small tool shed. The lawns were undulating in huge waves, not unlike when you whip the end of a garden hose and the hump travels the length of the hose.

There were two definite movements during the quake – we felt like we were on a roller coaster climbing then

Don stands by a pool in the foreground. Note behind him the earthquake-damaged hotel. Royal City Record, Nov 1, 1995. Photo by Evelyn Benson

falling over hump after hump while at the same time it was like riding a rickety old train that rattled your teeth and shook your head back and forth. Remember I said the average quake lasts 20 seconds? This quake lasted 110 seconds – **nearly two minutes**!

We could hear people screaming. I couldn't see anything worth screaming about until we went outside when the quake was over and saw the highrise hotel on the other side of our complex. Balconies had fallen off! Whole slabs of wall were missing! For the next week whenever the electricity came back on you could see into the hotel rooms where bedside lamps shone. Apparently one man had jumped from the second storey when he thought the whole building was coming down. He broke both legs.

A man from our complex had been in the swimming pool when it struck. He told us that at one instant when he was standing in the centre of the pool, he looked down and his feet were standing on bare concrete! He was eventually thrown out onto the lawn.

Of course there was no electricity. Water was sporadic, and often muddy. Fortunately for us we had bottled water and beer on hand and the makings of sandwiches so we were ok until things got back to normal. No restaurants were open because the gas was shut off. All the grocery and corner stores were a mess. Everything had flown off the shelves and the floors were ankle deep in broken glass, liquor, mayonnaise, mustard, syrup, squashed fruit, you name it. You couldn't buy bottled water or flashlights anywhere.

We always travel with flashlights and candles. We made up an emergency escape satchel with Passports, money, change of clothes, etc. and kept it by the door in case there was a bad aftershock. There wasn't.

The people from the highrise either caught a plane and left Mexico or were aided in finding accommodations at other resorts. One Irish family opted to return home to winter. The mother said to me, "I'd rather be cold than dead!"

The epicenter was 50 miles away off the coast of Manzanilla and registered at 7.2. They tell us we're due for a Big One here on the west coast so I always keep bottled water and extra food on hand just in case.

And all our bedroom slippers now have hard soles. They say broken glass is the biggest hazard. I hope we never have to find out.

CR

Two Scotsmen – Or Was It Three?

Massey Theatre was born on our kitchen table.

Sandy Christie was Chairman of the School Board and his lilting Scottish burr pleased the ear. Mayor Lewie Sangster's mother was a Christie so, even though there was no genealogical proof, Dad and Sandy felt they were kinsmen. And they both appreciated a wee nip, especially if it was Johnnie Walker Red Label.

The Second World War was over, and the wartime ban on construction had been lifted. The government in Victoria decreed that any educational construction would get a 50% boost in construction dollars from the provincial government. In other words, until further notice, schools could be built for fifty cents on the dollar!

As plans began to take shape to build a new junior high school to replace the aging Lord Lister Junior High and the F. W. Howay Junior High with a state-of-the-art Vincent Massey Junior High at Eighth Street and Eighth Avenue, these two New Westminster men realized that when Duke of Connaught High School was demolished to make way for the new City Hall, New Westminster would lose its only auditorium/theatre.

The three Scots sat around our kitchen table – Lewie, Sandy, and Johnnie Walker. And here they cooked up a scheme.

Why not incorporate a new, state-of-the-art theatre in the new junior high school? The School Board would have full use of the facility during the day, and the community could use it in the evening hours. And the price was right – fifty-cents on the dollar. Half price!

Now it just so happened that the Premier of British Columbia at that time was another New Westminster boy, one Byron "Boss" Johnson. A phone call from Lewie to Byron, and a couple of well-placed phone calls from Byron to those in charge of building allotments, and the deal was sealed.

I was a teenager when the opening ceremony of the brand new Massey Theatre was held. There was no Queen Elizabeth Theatre yet in Vancouver. The Orpheum was a movie theatre. So when Broadway shows came to Greater Vancouver, they booked into the new professional-sized theatre in New Westminster. One of the first shows was *The Man Who Came To Dinner* starring none other than Monty Wooley! I attended Opening Night with my father, the Mayor, and afterwards we went backstage to meet the stars. Monty Wooley asked my father the population of New Westminster and my dad said approximately 32,000. Mr. Wooley shook his head in amazement and said, "Do you realize that having a theatre of this size and quality in a small city is unbelievable! Do you realize what a gem you have?"

Dad beamed and his eyes twinkled, and as everyone knows, nothing could please a Scotsman more than to know he and Sandy had pulled a fast one, and saved the City a lot of money. So if you take a good look at the label on any bottle of Johnnie Walker, you'll notice he is tipping his hat.

Now you know why!

CR

Duke Of Connaught High School

In September of 2005, former classmates gathered to remember their old high school, Duke of Connaught (DCHS), which stood on the City Hall site from 1912 until 1955 at which time it was demolished. The Lester Pearson High School at Eighth Street and Tenth Avenue then became New Westminster's only high school.

To commemorate the fiftieth anniversary of the demise of DCHS, alumni raised funds to place an engraved bronze commemorative plaque with a two-dimensional replica of the Duke of Connaught High School, designed by Weldon Haley (Class of 1948) a well-known B. C. architect. Located just east of City Hall on the former school site, the memorial sits on a small plaza amongst the trees, flanked by benches and shrubs.

Former students, the youngest of which was 66 years of age and the oldest well into their nineties, left behind a very different city than the one they returned to in 2005. Gone are the *Columbian Newspaper*, *Drake's Dairy*, *King Neptune Restaurant*, *Hollywood Bowl*, *BCE Tram Depot*, *Pacific Coast Terminals*, *Eaton's*, *Sapperton Metro Theatre*, *Columbian*, *Edison*, *Fox* and *Odeon Theatres*, *W. S. Collister*, *Farmers' Market*, *Trapp Motors*, *Baxter Motors*, *John Bones Pool Hall*, *Lou's Barber Shop*, *The Pastime Club*, *Piggley Wiggley*, *Pacific Café*, *Roxy's*, *Langley's Confectionery*, *Windsor Café*, *Fraser Café*, *Premier Hotel*, *Spots Café*, *Sally Shops*, *Pineo Shoes*, *Rollerdrome*, *Royal City Cannery*, the "old" YMCA and more.

The three-storey brick YMCA building which stood across Royal Avenue from Connaught, was an important extension of the school itself. Because the school had no gymnasium of its own, generations of DCHS students casually jay-walked across Royal Avenue (no traffic problems then) in all weather for Physical Education classes in the Y's two gymnasiums. Joe Francis, a future city alderman, worked the front desk. He pushed a button that unlocked a door to "buzz" students into the locker rooms and gym areas.

The Y had a cafeteria with a nickel juke box featuring the latest tunes from the weekly radio hit show, *Your Hit Parade*. The chefs, Joe Francis's twin brothers Bob and Bill, served up milkshakes and hamburgers to hungry students during lunch hour. But their real claim to fame was their cream pies and legendary butter tarts.

In the 1940s and 50s, black entertainers like the *Ink Spots* and the *Mills Brothers* booked to play Vancouver nightclubs, weren't allowed to stay at Vancouver hotels but could rent rooms upstairs at the New Westminster YMCA. They always had a great rapport with neighbourhood kids and DCHS students.

DCHS had a 600 seat auditorium with a stage, balcony, lighting and sound. Evening and Sunday concerts and plays were held there, with the only rent paid by performing arts groups like the Vagabonds coming from donations at the door to help pay the janitor. It doubled as our civic theatre for decades, and inspired the concept of attaching Massey Theatre to the New Vincent Massey Junior High when it was built in 1950.

There was something "British" about Connaught that went beyond the name and its school colours of royal purple and gold. Its athletic teams were called the "Dukes" and all its teachers had Anglo-Saxon names. Some even had British accents and wore tweed jackets, spats and smoked pipes.

The school stood on "Royal" Avenue and sat up on a knoll, like a castle. It was subliminal, but somehow we all knew the school had been named for Queen Victoria's youngest son, HRH Prince Arthur, Duke of Connaught. All these things, taken together, gave our school a touch of class.

T. J. Trapp Technical, the rival school down Royal Avenue, produced Victoria Cross medal winner Pte. "Smokey" Smith of the Seaforth Highlanders. Not to be outdone, Duke of Connaught High School produced Major John Keefer Mahoney (Class of 1929) of the Westminster Regiment, who also won the VC.

The fierce rivalry between the two schools, particularly on the basketball court for the Sangster Cup, emblematic of the City Championship, is the stuff of legends. Seldom spoken of was one of the overriding reasons for the intensity of the rivalry, which was socio-economic. Of course there were many exceptions but, for the most part, DCHS students aspired to post-secondary education and the family business or profession, while Tech students planned to enter commerce, the trades or industry. It was the "Dukes" vs. the "Engineers", to some degree a white-color versus blue-collar rivalry.

Track and field practices and local track meets were held at Queen's Park Stadium which had a cinder track. But big track meets were held at Brockton Oval in Stanley Park, reached by B.C. Electric tram.

New Westminster has always had close ties to Crescent Beach and parents of several DCHS students had large summer homes there. At some point early in the school's history, a tradition developed that saw DCHS sororities, fraternities and clubs "camp" in the summer homes during Easter holidays. Mostly, the guys would hang out, play cards, stroll the beach, sip a Lucky Lager beer or two and strategize ways to get girls to visit their temporary frat house.

When Don started Grade 10 at DCHS in 1949, new boys to the school were initiated by having their trousers removed by senior students, who ran them up the flagpole while teachers looked the other way and girls pretended to. This tradition was called "de-panting". One former student put up such a fight that his trousers were taken across the street to the bus depot and thrown on top of a bus headed for Prince George!

Initiation into the DCHS Girl's Hi-Y Sorority required that initiates wear pajamas, bathrobe and slippers to school, with curlers in their hair and absolutely no makeup. That "reality check" cooled at least a few budding romances, as all the girls were shapeless and even some of the prettiest girls looked ghastly.

Where Don grew up on Agnes Street, a block from Duke of Connaught, a traditional harbinger of spring was the sound of the DCHS girls' bugle band practicing its repertoire of marching tunes after school. In June of 1955, when DCHS closed it doors for the last time, a "wake" was held by a crowd of 1,000 "mourners" on the old school ground, today's City Hall parking lot. The girls' bugle band played The Funeral March and hundreds of former students wore black arm bands.

In 2005, when a troupe of young NWSS girl cheerleaders bounded onto the stage at the Reunion, dressed in traditional purple and gold outfits and led the crowd in a few of the old DCHS pep rally cheers, for many of the old-timers it was their last hurrah.

> **PURPLE and GOLD; Never say die!**
> **V-I-C-T-O-R-Y!**
> **Are we with it? Well, I guess!**
> **D-C-H-S YES! YES! YES!**
>
> **YAAAAAAAAE! CONNAUGHT!**

ଓ

Royal City Musicals - in the Beginning

The Royal City Musical Theatre Society was also born on our kitchen table. It was 1989, and Don listened as I expressed my disappointment at the high school's drama department's refusal to stage any more community musical productions. I'd had key roles in community shows like *Showboat* and the *Fiddler On The Roof* and really missed them. I expressed to him my determination to bring musical theatre back to the beautiful Massey which was under-used and, in my opinion, under-appreciated. Don agreed to back me all the way.

First, I went to Linda Barron, newly elected School Trustee with my plan. She called in Russ Pacey, Director of Curriculum for School District 40 and we came to the conclusion that we should bypass the school system altogether and form a community-based non-profit society I called a meeting of interested friends including Belle Puri and Bernie Legge who suggested the name *Royal City Musical Theatre Society*.

When I think back to that day in 1989 when I told Ed Harrington I was going to bring musical theatre back to the Massey and I'd like him be our director, he wasn't too enthusiastic. But I cajoled and pressured him to join us until he agreed. Ed was quick to recruit old friends Dolores Kirkwood as choreographer and Jim Bryson as musical director. Ed told me later that he only intended to give us his help for the first year – just to help get us on our feet.

Every year, when Royal City Musical Theatre Company's production, bursts onto the stage at Massey Theatre, a few of us old-timers will be spirited back to the company's opening night in 1990 when we wondered – *WILL ANYONE COME?*

On Ed's advice, our first production was *Joseph And The Amazing Technicolor Dreamcoat,* a little gem not yet discovered by Broadway and Donny Osmond. Part of the show's appeal was that it required only a single borrowed set, minimal royalties paid to New York and very few costume changes. The City gave us a small grant and I borrowed money, interest-free for six months, from close friends. We would need 636 paying customers at each performance to meet our expenses of $32,000. At every performance, as I took my place with the pit choir that stood facing the audience on the side steps of the stage, I silently counted heads until I reached the magic number of 636 to break even, and sighed with relief.

Today, hundreds of talented performers flock to auditions, but in 1989 we practically had to Shanghai a cast for *Joseph*. Scant weeks before opening, we only had SEVEN of the required TWELVE brothers! So we beat the bushes. Husbands, brothers, neighbours, sons and nephews were badgered and bribed until we had our dozen.

Over six thousand patrons applauded *Joseph. BUT WOULD THEY COME BACK NEXT YEAR?*

We were constantly looking for promotion ideas for our next production, *The Wizard of Oz*. Publicist Vic Leach came up with a "Search for Toto Contest". On a warm and sunny Sunday, folks from all over the Lower Mainland brought their dogs to Westminster Quay to be judged by a respected adjudicator from the Canadian Kennel Club. Dog food companies provided dozens of prizes for the canine contestants. The winning pooch, in the arms of our "Dorothy", Dana Cole, hit the front page of both local papers AND the Province, in full colour, no less!

Today RCMT has a full-time office manager and an army of enthusiastic volunteers and is reasonably solvent. In the early years Royal City Musical was run from our kitchen table. Yes, the same kitchen table on which it was born. I was founding president, and husband Don was treasurer and initially we carried the costume budget on our personal Visa. A few faithful friends gave us interest-free loans each season. A lot of quick decisions were made at that kitchen table.

One snap decision was made right in the middle of a performance of *Wizard.* When Dorothy's house lands in Oz, the trembling Munchkins warily approach. Suddenly, a cuckoo clock in the house frightens them into scattering. But at one performance, the cuckoo clock sound-effect failed. The children got right up onto the porch. From my vantage point in the pit choir I could see they were confused and on the verge of panic so I leaned into the nearest mike and sang out, "CUCKOO!" Later, Don said to me, "Now THAT'S what I call an Executive Decision!"

At the 1991 auditions for *Oklahoma!*, Ed chose Robert Firmston and Kristina Baron as the romantic leads. We later found out that they were engaged to be married! It was a promotional dream. Don hired a pinto pony and photographed our "Laurie" on the horse in her gown and veil while "Curley" held the reins dressed in western finery. The media loved it. And it gave Vic the idea to later hold a very successful garden manure sale.

To help promote our 1993 production *42nd Street,* we advertised for tap dancers of all ages to come to Royal City Centre in an attempt to get into the record books for having the most tappers on a stage. CBC covered the event. Even our Board of Directors joined the tappers, which provided comic relief for the audience.

In *42nd Street* there's a show-stopping number featuring a line of leggy New York showgirls. We hired a Vancouver designer who had costumed Las Vegas showgirls and he produced flesh-coloured body-suits with a few strategically placed posies. At the first dress rehearsal, our teen-aged chorus of dancers in these scanty costumes had to be coaxed out of their dressing room. By the end of the production our shy teenagers were strutting their stuff on stage and off with all the confidence of seasoned chorines. Their number, "Dames" drew enthusiastic applause and whistles night after night.

That fall, our variety fund-raiser, *September Showcase,* included a Ukrainian dance number featuring colourful costumes, voluminous petticoats and expensive high-cut red leather boots. Two days before the show, a car containing the costumes and boots was broken into while parked in Vancouver's seedy Downtown Eastside, and the costumes were stolen.

September Showcase co-producers Bob Sibson and Don Benson (after tipping off the media) headed for Skid Row and began searching through back alley dumpsters. There were several altercations when street people accused our two of invading THEIR dumpster! Our men witnessed local-types dealing drugs, drinking rice wine, shooting-up or making-out in doorways. But none of these miscreants were wearing petticoats or red leather boots. Just in time, someone gave CKNW a tip and the costumes and boots were recovered. The media coverage helped sell a lot of tickets, but no, it wasn't a publicity stunt. Truth IS stranger than fiction.

Those early years were fun. But it took three years of borrowing, and penny-pinching before Royal City Musical Theatre was able to stand on its own two feet. Now, twenty-odd years later, the enthusiasm has not faded and the quality of the shows get better and better. After all, they have a Canada-wide reputation to uphold!

CR

Don and Evelyn Benson discuss Royal City Musical Theatre plans with Ed Harrington in Mazatlan, Mexico - 1992
Photo by Denise Gray.

Herbert Spencer School Opening

When I addressed the students of Herbert Spencer School on the occasion of the opening of the new Spencer in 1993, the talk must have struck a chord, because their drama club wanted to incorporate some of my stories into an historical play. In part, the talk went something like this:

"Fifty years ago I was in Miss McAskill's grade three class in the old Herbert Spencer. Boys and girls had separate playgrounds and separate entrances in those days and were strictly forbidden to play together.

"During freezing weather, even when the classrooms were cold enough to freeze the ink in the inkwells, the girls were not allowed to wear slacks. We had to leave them in the cloakroom and wear dresses in class".

(At this point in my speech, I heard a Grade 7 girl in the back row groan, "Oh brother!") When the laughter subsided, I continued:

"Ten years later, I returned to Spencer as a Student Teacher for Miss McAskill. It was really fun to eat lunch in the Staff Room with all my ex-teachers and call them by their first names. Imagine looking your Principal, Mr. Griffith, in the eye and saying, "Brian, please pass the salt".

"Then, over the decades I returned to Spencer, first as a parent of five students, then as a substitute teacher, and now as the grandparent of five students and as a writer of local history.

"How many think that History is something that happened a long, long time ago?" I waited until most of the hands were raised. "Well, you are partly right. History is also what's happening RIGHT THIS MINUTE! So tonight, when you get home and tell your parents about the events here today, you will be telling them brand new history!

"And someday, boys and girls, you will tell your own children and even your grandchildren, that you saw the bulldozer take down the old Spencer, and that you were there the day they opened the new Spencer. Perhaps your children and grandchildren will go to Spencer too!

"So remember this day – April 15, 1993. This is an important day in the history of our community – and YOU are an important part of that history."

CR

Appendix

This Old House

Five generations of the continuing Appleton/Sangster/Benson family (see Family Tree) have lived in the house at 319 Sixth Avenue in New Westminster for well over a century, and many of the stories in this book are about the residents of that venerable old home.

The original house, built in 1890, is still intact. It forms the eastern one-half of the existing house. The property was originally a Crown Grant issued to John Robson, the famous Premier, Mayor and newspaperman in 1864 as part of a subdivision "in the suburbs of New Westminster". In 1868, Robson sold the 36-lot subdivision for $2,500, about $70 a lot. At that time, today's nearby Fourth Street was called Clement Street.

The property changed hands several times during an 1888-89 land-boom soon after the Canadian Pacific Railway was completed in 1886, and was finally sold, along with the lot next door on the corner, to Alexander Gunn, a Scotsman, in 1889. The "Gunn Cottage" at 319 Sixth Avenue was completed in March, 1890, in time to become a honeymoon cottage for Alexander Gunn's brother Hugh Gunn, and his new wife Maggie.

The original house had four rooms and a front porch. The cottage was constructed from first-growth fir and hand-forged nails. Around 1900, a lean-to kitchen and porch were added at the rear. A number of Gunn children were born in the house, and the Gunn family eventually built a larger house next door at 315 Sixth Avenue.

In 1905 the home at 319 was purchased for $740 from Hugh and Maggie Gunn by George Moffat Appleton, the mechanical engineer who laid out the original machinery at Fraser Mills, known in its day as the largest lumber mill in the British Empire. The property had a small barn and seventeen fruit trees and two more lots. Moffat Appleton and his brother Jack dug out a basement for the house by hand, and the concrete floor they laid is still in perfect condition.

In the 1920s, the Appletons sold the house to their son-in-law James Lewis Sangster and their daughter Naomi who raised three children there – Ross, Norma and Evelyn. The house was extensively renovated in 1942, with an addition on the west side.

The Victorian windows were replaced with leaded-glass windows, giving it the appearance of a 1940s house, and a "modern" oil heating system was installed.

In 1965, the Sangsters sold the house at 319 Sixth Avenue to their son-in-law Don Benson and their daughter Evelyn, and they raised five children there – Mark, Scott, Kim, Janet and Jay. They added a second addition of two bedrooms, laundry room, a second staircase, kitchen and bathroom on the west side to create a townhouse for their daughter. The whole house got electrical and plumbing upgrades.

In 2009, Don and Evelyn Benson sold the house at 319 to their youngest son, Jay Lewis Benson, who has completed extensive renovations, bringing the house into the twenty-first century. He maximized insulation, added new flooring, thermal windows, a high efficiency heat pump and extensive landscaping. His sons Jayson and Michael, who live with him, represent the fifth consecutive generation to reside in the house.

Although the old house at 319 Sixth Avenue has been in the continuing Appleton/ Sangster/Benson family for well over a century, and in the Benson family alone for nearly half a century, by family agreement, the house is catalogued by the City of New Westminster as "The Gunn Cottage" after the original owners.

CR

A postcard showing the house in four generations of evolution.
Sangster Collection

Genealogy of "This Old House"

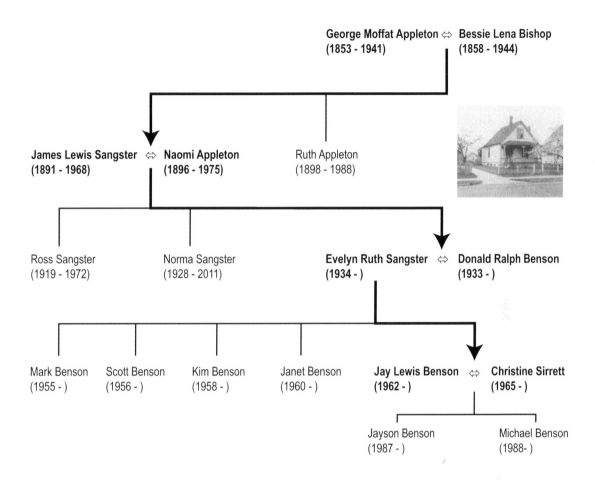

George Moffat Appleton ⇔ Bessie Lena Bishop
(1853 - 1941) (1858 - 1944)

James Lewis Sangster ⇔ Naomi Appleton
(1891 - 1968) (1896 - 1975)

Ruth Appleton
(1898 - 1988)

Ross Sangster
(1919 - 1972)

Norma Sangster
(1928 - 2011)

Evelyn Ruth Sangster ⇔ Donald Ralph Benson
(1934 -) (1933 -)

Mark Benson
(1955 -)

Scott Benson
(1956 -)

Kim Benson
(1958 -)

Janet Benson
(1960 -)

Jay Lewis Benson ⇔ Christine Sirrett
(1962 -) (1965 -)

Jayson Benson
(1987 -)

Michael Benson
(1988-)

A Hippy Benediction

One day in the 1960s, two hippies appeared at the door — barefeet, love-beads, long hair. She wore a colourful blouse and ankle-length skirt and he had the typical scraggly beard and a beaded pouch at his waist. Andrea was Don's cousin, so we made them welcome. I managed to find enough "vegan" food for them while we cooked hamburgers in the back yard.

As they were leaving, the bearded hippy paused on the front porch, and gazing at our house he slowly shook his head and said, "**Man, this house has good vibes!**"

I've always thought that would make a great plaque for the front door of this old house.

About the Author

Evelyn Sangster Benson

Born at New Westminster near Vancouver, B.C. in 1934, Evelyn Benson is a member of the pioneer Sangster and Appleton families. Five generations of the continuing Appleton-Sangster-Benson family have lived in the same heritage house for more than a century, a rarity on the West Coast. Her father was New Westminster Mayor J. Lewis Sangster.

In 1953, Evelyn married her high school sweetheart, Don Benson, who is today City Poet Laureate Emeritus and an accomplished Masters Pentathlete. Both Bensons are regular history contributors to local media and devoted community activists. The Bensons have five children, nine grandchildren and three great-grandchildren.

A trained vocalist and actress, Evelyn conceived and co-founded the highly successful *Royal City Musical Theatre Company.* She is a former Citizen of the Year and the only New Westminster recipient thus far of the coveted national *Lescarbot Award* for outstanding contributions to Canadian culture.

An award-winning journalist and former high school teacher, Evelyn recognized over half a century ago that when pioneers passed on, their stories would be lost forever if they weren't recorded for posterity, so she began interviewing old-timers to make sure that didn't happen. She continues to preserve precious oral history.

CR

Index of Surnames

Dear Readers

You, too, have stories to tell, so tell them to someone before it is too late! Better still, write them down or tape-record them. Future generations will appreciate your efforts. And let's not forget about photographs—ATTACH NAME STICKERS to the back of all your photos, especially ones that were left to you by previous generations. Start today!

Sincerely

Evelyn Sangster Benson

www.westminsterpublishing.ca

8282036R00113